# BECOMING BRUTAL

Overcoming fear, pain, failure and addiction to become one of the world's toughest ultra-endurance athletes

**CLAIRE SMITH**

**To Jess and Jake**

My biggest achievements and
what I am most proud of.

First published 2021 by Brutal Books - www.brutalbooks.co.uk

ISBN: 9798861994705

Copyright © Claire Smith 2021 - www.brutalclaire.co.uk

The right of Claire Smith to be identified as the author of this work has been asserted by her in accordance with the Copyright, Designs and Patents Act 1988. All rights reserved.

A CIP catalogue record for this book is available from the British Library.

Designed and typeset by Claire Smith

# CONTENTS

| | |
|---|---|
| 6 | Introduction |
| 9 | **Chapter 1:** Hard from the Start |
| 24 | **Chapter 2:** Running Away |
| *35* | *Life Lesson: Finding positive habits...* |
| 38 | **Chapter 3:** Ironman is a Triathlon? |
| *56* | *Life Lesson: If you're going through hell, keep going* |
| 58 | **Chapter 4:** Double Trouble |
| *66* | *Life Lesson: Taking on massive challenges* |
| 73 | **Chapter 5:** Ultra Crazy |
| *93* | *Life Lesson: Listen to the voices in your head* |
| 97 | **Chapter 6:** I Become a Tramp |
| *112* | *Life Lesson: How to stay stopped* |
| 114 | **Chapter 7:** A Brutal Business |
| *140* | *Life Lesson: Getting shit done* |
| 143 | **Chapter 8:** Suffering for Others |
| *174* | *Life Lesson: Staying motivated* |
| 176 | **Chapter 9:** Ten Days of Hell |
| 197 | **Chapter 10:** A Wild Pig Chase |
| *216* | *Life Lesson: Face your fears* |
| 223 | **Chapter 11:** Nutella Pancakes |
| *246* | *Life Lesson: Ultra Faffing* |
| 253 | **Chapter 12:** Mexico Mini-break |
| 276 | **Chapter 13:** Double Deca Diaries |
| *299* | *Life Lesson: Fuck It* |

'If your dreams do not scare you,
they are not big enough.'

— Ellen Johnson Sirleaf

*October 2019*

*Despite it being the middle of the night, I was boiling.*

*The Mexican air was still humid, even though we had experienced so many storms in the last few days that I had lost count. I took my jacket off and tied it round my waist. I was in the middle of a triathlon, but this was no ordinary triathlon. This was a Double Deca. I was over halfway through the 2,240-mile bike section, but right at that moment, I was definitely not racing.*

*I just needed to stop. I pulled at the brakes on my bike and unclipped my shoe from my pedal.*

*This event had come at the perfect time. Back home, my life lay in tatters. My relationship was over, my business was crumbling, and my future felt so uncertain. Many people close to me had questioned my sanity for travelling so far, to do such an incredibly hard event, when back in the UK I'd been struggling just to get through the day.*

*But I had known that it was exactly what I needed. I moved off the seat, carefully, the pain from my saddle sores making me catch my breath. Then I just stood and stared across the lake at the lights of León reflected in the water. I suddenly felt really happy. I wasn't worrying about what was happening at home or what was waiting for me after the race.*

*I just felt free.*

# INTRODUCTION

I'm known as Brutal Claire.

The name derives from my event company, Brutal Events, not because I'm particularly brutal. However, over the last ten years or so, I have taken on some pretty tough challenges, and sometimes I've even managed to finish them. They include Half, Full, Double, Triple, Deca (10 times the Iron distance) and Double Deca (20 times the Iron distance) triathlons, a Lanzarote Ultra Triathlon and the World's First GymQuin, which was 5 Iron distances in a gym – and one of my most stupid ideas to date.

I live in Dorset with my two children (who somehow are now adults) and three cats. I'm a graphic designer by trade, but started my business in 2010. Brutal Events specialises in holding tough swimming, running and triathlon races in amazing locations like Snowdonia and along the Dorset Coast Path. It has been incredibly hard work, but I've truly loved it, as I have been lucky enough to meet the most amazing people and work in awesome places, like Llanberis in North Wales.

For much of my adult life, I have struggled with addiction issues and an eating disorder, both of which I have now managed to successfully overcome (although these things never entirely disappear and still require work).

Starting in my late teenage years, I also fell into a pattern of abusive relationships which, although they were incredibly difficult at the time, made me much stronger, more independent and capable. And because of these problems I faced, I feel extremely passionate about helping others with similar issues and showing them how you can break free and live a healthier, happier life.

So over the next 300 or so pages, I will share with you my mistakes (there have been a few...), the struggles I faced with open-water swimming, the pain and suffering of ultra events, and how I manage my time between running a business, looking after my kids, training, three cats (seriously, you have no idea how demanding they are) and all the nasty details that you probably don't need to read.

But it's my book, so I get to make the rules. My hope is that I can help and inspire more 'normal' people (particularly women) like myself to take on life-changing challenges. And if I don't, I hope you can have a laugh at me attempting stupidly hard events and trying not to screw them up.

Oh, and by the way, you won't find any 'How to Train for a Double Deca' training plans in this book, as I'm not a coach or a nutritional specialist. But I do have a decent amount of long-distance training and race experience under my belt, some of it personal and some from organising Brutal Events. My brilliant team and I have helped athletes of all shapes, sizes and abilities finish some really tough races, and I get a huge amount of pleasure from it. So if any of my advice does help you complete a long-distance triathlon – great. But don't email me complaining that eating pork pies during a Double Ironman made you feel sick.

The final point I need to make is that I am not very good at sport. Now, I've read books before where the author has said something similar, but then as you read on, you discover that they won their age group in a local triathlon, or ran a sub 3-hour marathon in the past. Have no fear, dear reader, there will never be any parts in this book where I casually throw in that I ran a 10k in a blisteringly fast time or used to swim for my county.

Although I must confess that I did come second in the UK's first Double Ironman triathlon. But that was mainly due to the fact that there were only four women competing, one pulled out and the other put her hip out during the run. Still, second is second…

But if you have any preconceived ideas that I have any natural athletic ability, I must ask you to lower your expectations before reading on.

# CHAPTER 1
# HARD FROM THE START

My early childhood was fairly normal.

I was born in Bournemouth and lived there for a while. We then moved to Hereford for a few years, until my parents split up and I had to return to Dorset. I wasn't very happy about this, but when you are only eight years old, you don't have much of a say in any family decisions.

The separation forced me to grow up quickly. I have a strong memory of standing in front of the mirror at a motorway service station, just after my mum had pulled me from the family home, and reprimanding myself for crying. I told myself to stop, to pull myself together, although the tears continued to roll down my face.

Life from then on became a little harder. I was used to running free in the fields which surrounded the tiny village I had lived in on the Welsh border. Now I lived in a small flat on a street where all the houses looked the same. People seemed less friendly too and I found it hard to make new friends. I hated my new school and didn't settle there at all.

We later moved to a larger, three-bed semi-detached house, but that wasn't much different. On a positive note, it did have a railway track at the bottom of the road, and I loved the sound of the trains rushing past. Sometimes they would even make my mum's decorative plates rattle on the dresser, which I thought was pretty cool. But I still longed for my old bedroom, friends and life. I missed my dad very much too.

## HARD FROM THE START

My older brother Nick had chosen to stay in Hereford, because he was at that age where he was taking exams and a new school would have been too disruptive for him. Although I loved my mum very much, I remember wishing that I could have had that same choice. I saw my dad every six weeks or so, but that was very traumatic; I used to both look forward to it and dread it in equal measure.

My parents would meet halfway, in a grey, depressing car park in Bath. The dreaded 'swap' would then take place, when I would move from one car to the other. My parents wouldn't really speak to each other, and in the early days, my dad would even cry when I left him. Seeing this would break my heart.

Life continued in this way until my dad met someone else and his life started to improve. Unfortunately for me, his new partner had her own children, and I seemed to be far less important in his life. The visits became less frequent, they moved in together, and when I was at their new home, I felt like I was not particularly wanted. Although I tried to tell myself that this wasn't the case and that my dad still loved me, I could never quite shake the feeling that my new stepmother (whom I thought was awesome, as she raced on hand-built rafts over 100 miles on the River Wye) just didn't like me. For a twelve-year-old, this was devastating.

At one point, my step-mum made a comment about my thighs looking big on a photo of me coming down a water-slide during the only holiday they ever took me on. I was mortified and remember my face becoming flushed with shame. To be fair, they did look big, but I think up to that point in my live, I had been unaware of the fact. I knew I wasn't as skinny as my cousin, Emma, but until then, it just hadn't been a problem.

## HARD FROM THE START

After that though, I became obsessed with trying to reduce the size of my thighs and bum, and it became something that followed me for years to come. I would try to survive on ridiculously low amounts of calories and do intense, high-impact aerobics to burn fat. By my mid-teens, my eating problems were just a normal part of my life. Sometimes they would become more manageable, but other times, especially during periods of high stress, they would take over and I would focus intently on remaining as skinny as possible.

I experienced yet more family issues during through my teenage years and these left me feeling like I didn't fit in anywhere. I was angry and became very self-destructive. The decisions I made were now based on how much damage I could cause myself – mainly, I think, because I couldn't make sense of my emotions.

I became completely disinterested in school and apart from in my beloved art class – the only time where I could truly lose myself and be happy – I stopped working in all my subjects (especially PE, which I detested. I would pretend that my asthma was too bad to be able take part in lessons).

At this time I also started shoplifting, smoking cigarettes and weed, and drinking a lot of alcohol, to the point of regularly blacking out. I don't remember when I first got high, or even had my first taste of alcohol, but I do know how I loved the feeling of the drugs hitting my bloodstream. I loved how they took the constant feeling of self-hatred away and gave me relief. I loved the recklessness which followed and the confidence that I felt. From around thirteen, getting high or drunk simply became the thing me and my friends did, as often as we could.

## HARD FROM THE START

My relationship with cannabis only lasted a few years, as a direct result of what happened to me while I was hanging out with a small-time drug dealer called Skinny. One night he introduced me to the bong; up until this point, I had only ever smoked joints. This was also the night when we smoked what I later discovered to be a very strong resin, cut with something else... What it was exactly, I never found out.

I remember feeling very nervous and intimidated, but I was also aware that I was in a crowd of much older kids and did not want to look like an idiot. So I took a deep breath and inhaled...

The drug hit me immediately and my head started spinning, scarily fast. This was not the nice, mellow high and happy feeling I was used to getting from the familiar joints me and my friends smoked. This was a horrible, frightening head-rush, and adrenaline flooded my body, making me feel shaky and sick. I tried to hide it, but panic overcame me. I made some excuse and escaped into the night, but the fresh air only seemed to increase the unpleasant effects. Somehow I made it home, but that night I had terrible anxiety and experienced horrible hallucinations.

After that, every time I tried to smoke even a simple joint, I would have flashbacks, panic would once again engulf me and I would have to stop. I realised from then on that my relationship with cannabis was well and truly over. But have no fear, because alcohol stepped in to fill the void.

In fact, alcohol become my new best friend.

When I was growing up, buying drink was not hard. It certainly

## HARD FROM THE START

wasn't like now. There were particular off-licences and corner shops which had very relaxed views on selling to their underaged customers. It was also extremely cheap, and two litres of cider was a very affordable night out.

More often than not, we would make our way to an area of beach which nobody really knew about, down the foul-tasting drink and enjoy (or not, sometimes) the results. This would mainly involve laughing a lot, falling over, arguing about nothing, getting off with someone nearby and ending with throwing up and becoming unconscious.

For a few years I absolutely loved drinking. It made me happy, helped me relax, made me feel better when I was down and most importantly of all, helped me to like myself. For a little while at least. However, I would soon find out that alcohol was not my friend at all but, quite literally, the worst enemy you could ever have.

Around this time, I also started to have sex, losing my virginity at just thirteen to a man who was ten years older than me. I was entering a world that I was simply not emotionally ready for in any way, especially with someone so much older than myself.

Looking back, this period was just a classic case of trying to get someone's attention. I desperately needed somebody to notice that I was struggling and to help me. But I was viewed as a stereotypical teenager, being a pain and causing trouble. Which, at the time, was fine by me.

Even my first job, which I also got at thirteen, was hard. I started working in a nursing home, close to where I lived, as a care

## HARD FROM THE START

assistant. This would obviously be illegal these days, but at the time, the owners of the business had no qualms about employing someone so young.

The work involved washing, dressing and feeding patients who had dementia and other illnesses. I remember coming in one Sunday morning to start my shift and walking in on a resident who was in the final stages of dying. That was my first experience of actually seeing what death looked like (it was nothing like the films, I noticed) and the experience never really left me. It didn't put me off though, and I continued working in nursing homes for years after.

At seventeen, I left home. My mum and step-dad Alan, were also looking after my younger brother Philip, who was a bit of a handful too, and my destructive behaviour wasn't exactly making their lives easy. So when I told them of my plans, I think they welcomed it.

I moved with a friend from school into a two-bedroom flat in the most undesirable (and cheapest) part of Bournemouth. What I didn't know was that the property was owned by one of the biggest criminals around. Not ideal. Even the couple who lived upstairs were a drug dealer and prostitute, so I shouldn't have been that surprised really.

The problem with living in this rather dark and shady world was that it spilled over into my own. And while I wasn't exactly sweet and innocent, I wasn't super thrilled to wake up and find the stolen contents of a record shop being stored in our living room; even at one point, a load of brand-new sofas and armchairs which had been nicked overnight. Although we did get to choose a new three-piece suite for the flat...

## HARD FROM THE START

One day, we came home to find we had a new house-mate, who was to live in an extension which had miraculously appeared at the rear of the property. His name was Jez and he had just been released from prison, where he was serving time for assault. In fairness, he was quite a nice chap, but still!

The last straw for me though was when I came home from work to find yet another criminal showing a housing officer from the council 'his room' so he could claim benefits. They were actually in my room and he had removed all of my possessions and replaced them with his. As I entered, he shot me a look that made me retreat to the living room until they had gone. But I was furious and started making plans to find a new flat as soon as possible.

Despite leaving school with only an A in Art and a C in Drama, I managed to land an apprenticeship with a local graphic design firm. It was a small business, with only two other employees and the boss, Howard. Starting here was a real turning point in my life. Up until then, I had no real direction or support regarding my future. I had obviously been working, but only at jobs that required staying power, mainly because they were so grim, like those nursing homes. I tried to be a chambermaid at one point, but fell out with the hotel's manager because he didn't agree with my method of getting rid of some of the unwanted guests (FYI, spraying furniture polish on cockroaches does *not* kill them).

I also tried the local convenience store and was placed in charge of the bakery section. I was quite proud of this, initially. But after a while the novelty of 5am starts, burning my arms on the large oven and being constantly unable to produce French sticks that weren't floppy (pro tip: lean the sticks against the wall and nobody will

## HARD FROM THE START

know), got the better of me and I left that job too.

Working at the local dairy seemed a better option: I could work nights and that would leave my days free. Perfect! I lasted just one shift, as the smell of gone-off milk was absolutely foul and stayed with me for weeks after.

The last place I tried was working at a bar in town. I was sure that this would be the job for me, as music and booze were two of my favourite things. This particular venue got extremely busy on a Friday and Saturday night, which in itself wasn't a problem, but unfortunately the owner didn't own a till that added the drink orders for you. This meant you were left having to do sums in your head. For some of the staff, this wasn't a problem, but for me (I still can't add up) it was my worst nightmare. On that first evening, I took a large drink order, and as I started to lose track and the numbers began to jumble in my head, I literally had to make up a random figure for the customer. He looked puzzled as I thrust a load of coins into his hand for his change, and after that night, I never dared to return.

Office work was very different from my other jobs and it took me a while to get used to it. The graphic design apprenticeship came with a day release from the local college, which I absolutely hated. I found the environment too similar to school and soon realised the course work we were doing there had nothing to do with graphic design in the real world. This made me despise it even more, and I managed to convince my boss that I could leave the college but remain employed. As the company was very busy, and with only four of us there, it made sense.

## HARD FROM THE START

My boss, Howard, was a well-liked and respected man. He knew his stuff and worked hard. A little too hard, maybe… Howard was a true workaholic and was always in the office early and left very late. He was patient and kind, taking the time to explain everything I needed to know about the world of printing and design. He never once made me feel stupid, or criticised me when I made mistakes, and I thought a lot of him. And in a world where I was struggling to trust men, always finding they had hidden agendas, my new boss showed me that they weren't all the same.

Our work included designing logos, brochures and other promotional materials. One client we had was involved in producing the sex phone-line adverts you could find at the back of certain newspapers. These basically consisted of a large image of a topless woman with words and phone numbers scattered around her. I spent many an afternoon clipping paths around women's breasts and other parts of their anatomy, or typing out cheesy one-liners designed to entice desperate men to call. We had to have a special protocol for when other (more normal) clients would enter the office, when we would have to shrink the window down and replace it with another, less dodgy image, as quickly as possible.

During my time at the design firm, I found my first real boyfriend, Sean. We met one Friday night in my local pub and got on instantly. The relationship was fiery, passionate and it moved fast. Due to my dubious living situation at the time (prostitutes, drug dealers…), we decided to move in together. In hindsight, this was much too early, and I would live to regret it.

Sean was a jealous bloke, which initially I found flattering, but after a while I began to find his controlling ways troublesome. He liked

## HARD FROM THE START

a drink and used to smoke weed regularly too. He also had mood swings which left me feeling confused. I never really knew when I had done or said something wrong until it was too late and he was angry with me. One evening, he got cross with me over something I can't even remember. The next thing I knew was that he had hit me, hard across the face. I was stunned. Once I had shaken off the shock, I told him to leave and not come back. But later that night, he returned, full of apologies and promises of never doing it again.

That was the start of a very difficult twelve months. Abusive relationships are never simple. People who have not experienced one can be quick to judge and ask incredulously, 'why would you put up with that?'. The problem with these types of relationships – be it physical, mental or both – is that the person who is being abused always feels that they are to blame in some way. And it's very hard to separate yourself from the situation you are in and see the damage that is being done to you.

I remember, towards the end of my relationship, standing in the kitchen of a good friend. I was very low, drinking too much and constantly either breaking up or making up with Sean. I was exhausted and confused. As I stood there, tears rolling down my face, I looked at my arms. They had bruises on them from the pushing and falling over during the fights we had. I suddenly realised that my arms were now *always* bruised. That was the moment I knew that it was over, and that what was happening to me was not my fault.

Leaving him was so hard, but I finally managed to do it, escaping from the flat we shared and moving to another part of town where he would not find me. I did see him again, years later, in the bread

## HARD FROM THE START

aisle of Asda. I was horrified and tried to avoid him, but he came over to me and apologised for how he had treated me during our relationship. That was brave, and from that gesture I was able to forgive him, but unfortunately the damage had already been done.

The next few months were tricky, but I started to get back to living a life in which I didn't worry about being out with a friend for a drink or coming home late from work. I was free and I began to feel like myself again. I threw myself into my job, working long into the night, learning everything I could. I was like a sponge, soaking up all I could about design and printing. In short, my work became my life. I guess it was how I coped with things after Sean. I never really talked to anyone about it properly and I didn't deal with the emotional fall-out. I just worked, and when I wasn't working, I drank and partied.

I stayed with the design company for a couple of years until I decided to leave and set up on my own. Starting my little business was the most exciting thing I had done at that point in my life, and I loved coming up with the company name and designing my very own logo and letterhead. Once I had everything printed, I set about walking round the local industrial estates, seeing if anyone needed work doing and handing out my cards. I was just nineteen, but I was ready to take on the world! Unfortunately, I discovered that setting out on my own was actually a lot harder than I thought and soon had to subsidise my little company with freelancing for other designers and printers. It was not quite the vision I had for my business, but it was a start.

After a few months, a printer I was working for put me in touch with a friend of his who needed a designer to work on some magazines.

## HARD FROM THE START

Initially, I was excited to see what publications I would be working on. I had already worked on *CD ROM User* (yes, I'm *that* old) and I went along to the meeting with my portfolio and high hopes. It turned out that the 'magazine' (I use that term loosely) was actually an in-house, almost comic-style monthly publication that was basically just adverts. Nothing else. No articles, no information, just adverts for computer parts.

I obviously got the job and started what soon became full-time, soul-destroying work, designing and amending the most boring adverts ever. Initially, I tried to make hard drives and RAM upgrades exciting, but there is only so much anyone can do. The owner of the company was a guy called Nick; he was in his mid-thirties and we got on pretty well. After each magazine had gone to print, we would go to the local pub, where the other printers hung out, drinking, day after day.

I would be the only girl at the pub, but that never bothered me. I enjoyed being 'one of the boys' and would down my pints of lager as quickly as the men around me. I was proud that, at nineteen, I could hold my own. In hindsight, this was not a good sign regarding my relationship with alcohol. After a while, the guys around us decided that Nick and me were having an affair. We actually weren't, but the power of suggestion is a dangerous thing (mixed with six pints of Heineken) and one night we ended up having a clumsy, drunken kiss.

Nick was living with another woman at the time, although he was constantly moaning that he wasn't happy with her and wanted the relationship to end. We spent a few weeks trying to pretend that it wasn't happening between us, but I knew what we were doing

## HARD FROM THE START

was very wrong and I had no intention of being the 'other woman'. So I decided enough was enough, and gave him an ultimatum. Leave her or end it with me.

I honestly thought he would finish things between us and I had already started looking for somewhere else to work, but the next day he came into the office and announced he and his girlfriend had split up. My first and unchecked thought was, 'oh fuck'. Not the best sign. But as with previous situations I had found myself in, I pushed away the nagging feeling I had that this was a very bad idea and we started a proper relationship.

At the time I was paying a lot of money to rent a flat that I now barely lived in, so it seemed sensible to move in with Nick soon after his ex had moved out. It did feel wrong, but I thought I was in love and this seemed the 'thing people did'. Around this time, I also began to feel like I wanted a baby. This was a very strange feeling for me, as I had never really seen myself as a mother; I was more interested in business and boozing. But here I was with these powerful, overwhelming emotions and I felt almost desperate to start a family with Nick.

Those feelings didn't last very long though. One day I was driving down the road near our house. There were cars parked on both sides of the road, and I wasn't going more than 30mph, but somebody suddenly opened their car door and I smashed into it. The accident wasn't really a big deal, but what it highlighted was. I called Nick, who was in the pub, as it was a Sunday, and he was already quite drunk. I told him what happened and asked if he would come home, as I was pretty shaken up and didn't want to leave the house. He told me in no uncertain terms that he was most definitely not leaving

## HARD FROM THE START

the pub and to pull myself together and come and have a drink. I refused and hung up. That was the moment when I knew I needed to leave this man.

But as I already suspected, karma was a bitch. I was soon to get what I probably deserved by getting involved with man who was as good as married to another woman. A few days after the prang and pub incident, I discovered I was pregnant. It had only taken two weeks of my coming off the pill (and quickly going back on it, after I came to my senses). I couldn't believe it. I was twenty years old and living with a man sixteen years older than me who I had decided to leave only days before. What was I going to do?

I decided to try and make it work. We had the business, the house and now a baby on the way. I felt it was for the best, but our relationship began to deteriorate fast and we started to argue a lot. Nick was still drinking heavily, I was feeling constantly sick from the pregnancy, and I was resentful of him being in the pub while I sat alone at home. I began to feel like his ex-girlfriend and wondered when he would find another woman and cheat on me too. When he came home, swaying and slurring his words, I would be furious and shout at him. Pretty soon our rows turned physical. I slapped Nick and he hit me back, and that was the start of my second abusive relationship.

The worst thing was that I blamed myself for this one, as I had hit him first and also felt that I had 'brought the violence with me' from my first abusive relationship. Many have since pointed out that a decent man would not have hit me back, especially as I was pregnant with his child. The violence escalated from then on, and there was one occasion when I was truly scared for my unborn baby.

## HARD FROM THE START

I was no longer hitting Nick when we argued, as I was heavily pregnant by then and really trying to make the best of the situation I had got myself in. One night he came back, very drunk, and I remember lying on our bed, curled up in the foetal position, begging him not to hurt the baby. He didn't, he just made threats, but that was enough to terrify me. But when he pushed or hit me, even in his inebriated state, he was careful to ensure he didn't mark my face.

By August 1996, I was two weeks overdue and had to go into hospital to be induced. My mum had never been able to give birth naturally, due to the shape of her pelvis, and I was concerned I might have the same problem, as my baby had not dropped down in preparation for labour. I had also experienced sharp pains in my pelvic area, almost as if the baby's head was trying to engage but couldn't. Being induced was not a pleasant experience, as the labour went from 0 to 100 in just 15 minutes, and I found it hard to deal with the pain coming on so fast. It was suggested that I had an epidural and I agreed. During the procedure, the heart monitor around my belly went quiet. The midwives tried adjusting it, but it quickly became evident that my baby's heart was stopping and I was rushed into theatre for an emergency Caesarian.

My daughter was born and thankfully survived. Jessica was a beautiful baby and I was over the moon with her. I had to go on an IV and have a blood transfusion straight after the birth, but none of that mattered; my baby was healthy. From that moment on, everything changed. It was me and Jessica against the world. I left Nick when Jess was less than six months old, moving into a small flat just down the road from him, stupidly close to the pub he frequented. Naively, I thought that we could remain friendly and co-parent together.

## CHAPTER 2
# RUNNING AWAY

The next few years were a blur of bringing up my baby, working part-time, and trying to cope with my drunken, spiteful ex-boyfriend. No matter what he did, I always found myself forgiving him and his disgusting behaviour. He demanded a DNA test, sent me letters from his solicitor threatening to take Jess from me, and came round, late at night, always drunk, banging on my door.

When Jessica was two and a half, I was living on my own with her in a town about twenty miles away from Nick, trying to make a break. I found myself becoming more and more isolated and getting very depressed. I was drinking regularly again, after being able to moderate and almost stop my alcohol intake when I was pregnant and breast-feeding. And it was then that I found myself back with him, sat in a pub one Saturday so he could see Jess. We started talking about trying again, and I think the thought of not being alone any more, living above a dental surgery in a town I hated, sold it to me and I agreed to come back and try and make it work.

I had some conditions though. One was that he did not get drunk every night. Although he could have a few beers at home, he was not to go to the pub. I would, however, allow one night a week when he could get hammered. The other condition was that there was to be no violence from either one of us. It seems bizarre to me now, reading these rules back, that this was how we started our volatile, broken relationship for the last time, but he agreed and we also decided that if everything was good twelve months later, we would get married. We must have been drunk that afternoon.

## RUNNING AWAY

To my surprise, and not without some hard work, our relationship began to improve. Of course, there was some resentment on both sides; it was hard to forget some of the things that had happened while we were apart. But on the whole, it was working. Nick stuck to his drinking deal and I threw myself into trying to improve the business, as he had lost a lot of work recently, as well as running the home. And as things were on the up, when the twelve months came and went, we decided to get married. I didn't want a big event; it's not my style and we didn't have the money for it anyway. So we chose a registry office nearby and then went to a restaurant for the reception.

It was three months after the wedding when the trouble started again. Nick went out on a 'planned bender' with a business associate. When he came home, I knew something was wrong. He was angry and resentful, shouting at me about totally random things. I tried to ignore him the best I could, knowing that anything I said would make it worse. He would settle down soon enough and fall asleep, I hoped. What happened next, I did not expect. He lunged at me, punching me in the side of the head. I was stunned for a moment; where had this come from? He hit me again and I fell to the floor, mostly to protect myself I think. He then kicked me hard in the stomach, which was even worse as we had been trying for another baby. While this was going on, all I could think about was that our daughter (who could sleep through actual earthquakes) was in the room opposite ours.

I got to my feet and made it to Jessica's bedroom and locked the door behind me. Not that it would stop him, as he had broken our bedroom door down in the past, but I hoped he wouldn't try that this time. I curled up around my little girl, already knowing that this

## RUNNING AWAY

was it. No more. The next day I woke up, clear-headed, and made a plan. Nick rose a few hours later, looking the worse for wear, but he never acknowledged what he had done or apologised. I lost all my feelings for him that night and over the next few weeks, planned me and my Jess's escape. He had another 'business trip' with his colleague coming up (in reality these were just excuses for them both to get fucked up), but for me, it was the day I was leaving him for good.

That morning, after he had gone to the station to take the train to Southampton, I pulled out the bags that I had packed and hidden under the stairs and put them into the boot of my car. I got Jess ready and we drove the five miles or so to my mum's house. She was away in Scotland at the time, so I had the place to myself. I made sure that my car was hidden, parking it in the estate opposite where Nick wouldn't find it, and I never once put the lights on at the front of the house. As far as my husband was concerned, we had disappeared.

---

During my entire childhood, teens and first few years of being an adult, sport had played very little part in my life. When I was about fourteen, I briefly rowed in a four-person crew for my local club, which I absolutely loved doing. But due to teenage girl stuff and the inevitable distractions, my crew drifted apart and I stopped rowing. It wasn't until I found myself as a single mum, sitting in a damp flat, with a dull part-time job and no other friends with babies, that I started looking for something to fill the gap that had appeared in my life. I remember feeling guilty about this, as I adored my little girl, but I was finding motherhood a little boring after working in the busy printing industry.

## RUNNING AWAY

It was then that I discovered marathons…

Now, when I say I discovered them, what I mean is, I bought a book about running one. I didn't actually enter one for about ten years, but that was when the seed was planted. I did, however, run a half-marathon not long after buying that book. Being a single mum, my training consisted of waking up early, before most people were up, popping Jess into her zip-up snow-suit then into her pushchair, and hitting the pavements for a run. Jessica never seemed to mind bouncing around and fell asleep within minutes, leaving me to enjoy my early-morning endorphins. I would return feeling clear-headed and happy. It took me a long time to make running a regular part of my life, but this was when I started to make the connection between exercise and enjoying a more balanced life.

A year or so after I left my husband, I started working for a local printing company in the repro department. This was where we took a file from the designer and prepared it for the printing presses. It may sound a little dull, but most jobs that came in would have technical issues, so a big part of the role was trouble-shooting, something that I was good at and enjoyed. The company was a reasonably sized firm, with fifty or so employees from accounts to machinists, print finishers and salespeople. Most were men, which was not a problem and something I was used to from my previous jobs.

After a few weeks of working there, I realised that once a month there was a 'boys night out' organised by one of the top salesmen, Mark. I did not like Mark. I found him loud and cocky, like a lot of sales types. I confronted him in the kitchen one morning, demanding to know why girls couldn't join his nights out. He

## RUNNING AWAY

looked a little shocked, and then shrugged his shoulders, saying 'come if you want'.

So, the following Friday, I got ready to go out with 'the boys'. I felt nervous; I hadn't been out properly for a long time and I had a few pre-drinks to settle my nerves. Big mistake... I remember getting to the bar and meeting everyone, but not a lot after that. I think I tried to keep up with the other guys, but I hadn't been a hardcore drinker for a while and was seriously out of practice. The following Monday when I arrived at work, the receptionist smiled at me. It was the sort of smile that makes you nervous. I paused for a moment, wondering what had I done. 'Everything OK?', I asked her. 'Oh yes', she said, smiling that smile again. I went upstairs to our office and, as none of the repro guys had joined us that Friday night, everything felt normal.

Until Mark the salesman came up. That morning he was not so cocky though; in fact he was weirdly subdued. He then announced that he had broken up with his girlfriend over the weekend. He didn't say much else, but later the helpful receptionist filled me in. They had been on the rocks anyway, but apparently they had split up because of some drunken blonde that had thrown herself at him, literally and physically. It took me a moment to realise that it had been me and all the memories flooded back. I was mortified, my face flushed, and I just wished the floor would open up and swallow me whole.

Mark obviously liked a challenge though, and we became a couple soon after that. My daughter and I were still living with my mum, and she was helping with childcare after school and when I went out with Mark. This situation worked well on paper, but the reality

## **RUNNING AWAY**

was that I was struggling with it. I had left home at seventeen and here I was in my late twenties, back home. It wasn't long before I found a one-bedroom flat in town and we moved out. This gave us back our independence and also allowed Mark and me to spend some real time together. He and Jessica got on really well, and it made me feel good seeing them together. At that time, Jessica was seeing her real dad once every two weeks for an afternoon, while I kept a close eye on his behaviour.

Sometimes I think this period in my life was when I was at my most normal. I had a steady job, decent boyfriend and lived in a nice flat. We would go out when we could, but we were just as happy staying in together, with Jess. I was also, by this point, going to the gym regularly too. My drinking was still a little heavy, and I was always trying to control my calories, but to be honest, I figured I always would be, as I had been doing it so long. But all in all, I felt happy and a year or so later, we started talking about getting a place together.

At first we rented a cool, three-storey house. It actually wasn't the most practical of places, but I loved the quirkiness of it. Around this time, I also became self-employed again. I felt happiest when I was my own boss and I could fit my work around looking after Jessica. Some months later, we began to think seriously about buying our first house and also talked about having a baby together. I was so happy and Mark was a good man. He was strong, stable and was able to deal with me and my demons, which unfortunately continued to rear their head every so often, mainly when I drank. I often tested him, tried to get him to hit me or pushed him away, seeing if he would leave me. He never did either. He would just ride the storm and wait for me to become

## RUNNING AWAY

calm again. In time, I relaxed and started to trust him.

I became pregnant with my second child almost as fast as my first. The morning sickness, which for me was *all-day* sickness, kicked in early. I had hoped that it wouldn't be so bad this time around, but it was. I consoled myself with the old adage that the sicker you feel, the stronger the pregnancy, but it was hard on me. And Mark too. I had promised that it would be 'fun' trying for a baby, but the reality was that he now had a grumpy, nauseous girlfriend to live with for nine months. It wasn't all bad though, as we had found a house we wanted to buy and entered the exciting and stressful world of chains and mortgages. A few months later, we moved in.

The next few years consisted of having Jacob, our awesome new baby (who refused to sleep, but we loved him anyway), Jessica starting 'big school', buying another, bigger house, and generally being a 'normal' family. We got married, got a dog and I even bought a Volvo. I was a proper housewife. I used to iron my husband's shirts and our house was always spotless. I also took great pride in being in shape, despite having had two children. The reality was though that I was still massively restricting my calories. And my drinking, which I thought I was moderating, was still definitely an issue, albeit a controlled one.

After a while, I began to feel like I was missing something. I was still working part-time from home as a graphic designer, and looking after the kids and house more than filled the rest of the time. But there was something not quite right. Running had become a regular thing for me by then, but more of a weight-controlling hobby than a life-consuming one. Whilst out one day, on the hill behind our house, those thoughts of running a marathon came back

## RUNNING AWAY

to me. More specifically, the London Marathon. I had been inspired (like everybody else) watching it on the TV and wondered if I could actually do it?

I entered the ballot (like everyone else) and was surprised and more than a little scared when I got a place (I have never been successful since then!). I started training, or should I say, over-training, from then on. I devised a plan based on some ridiculous idea that I could finish the marathon in under four hours. This naïve plan was based on running six days a week and sometimes twice a day.

It wasn't long before I became injured, but being the determined (stubborn) person I am, I ignored it for as long as possible. But it got to the point where I could barely run to the end of the road without being in a lot of pain. The injury, I eventually found out, was a tight IT Band (the tissue which runs all the way down your leg from the hip to the shin-bone). But because I had let the problem go on for so long, it had become very inflamed and sore.

It was around February at that time, and I had to finally face up to fact that I simply would not be able to continue training for the London Marathon. I had to let my dream go. I stopped running and tried to put it to the back of my mind. Life went on as normal for another few months, but then towards the end of March, the hype for the marathon began to step up. I remember receiving an email asking if I was ready. And I sat back in my office and wondered if I could still do this. I hadn't run for weeks and had no idea if my injury was still there or not. I changed into my kit, laced up my trainers and went outside. I tentatively began to run, slowly at first, but then the further I went without pain, the more excited I got. It was gone! The knee pain had disappeared.

## RUNNING AWAY

So, with two weeks to go until the London Marathon, I decided that, despite not training since February, I would do it. Mark looked a little confused later that night when I told him, but it was obvious that I was very keen to take part, so he got caught up in making plans with me. My best friend from school lived in London, so I called her and asked if I could stay with her the night before. Mark agreed that he and the kids would come up and meet us at the finish. Before that though, I had to go and register at the Expo in London. This meant travelling up the week before the race to pick up my number and timing chip. Walking around with all the other runners and looking at all the stalls selling expensive kit that I really shouldn't buy made me feel like a 'proper runner' and I found that I rather liked that feeling.

I distinctly remember the train journey the day before the race. I was so nervous. My stomach flipped every time I thought of the following day. What had I been thinking? I wasn't ready for this! I hadn't trained properly; it had been two months since I had even run more than five miles... Why was I so impulsive, I wondered. Still, here I was with a small bag of basic kit and nutrition for the 26.2 miles I would hopefully run with thousands of others in less than 24 hours' time.

The next day came all too soon and I fought through the crowds on the Underground to make it to my designated start area. I was completely overwhelmed with the amount of people on the trains and then walking to the start. I had never seen anything like it before, but I couldn't help but get caught up with the excitement that surrounded everyone. It was tangible – you could literally feel the nervous energy like a vibration in the air. I found the numbered area where I was due to start and looked around for the toilets.

## RUNNING AWAY

When I found them, the queue snaked for what looked like about half a mile down the road. I decided that I would find one on the course once we had begun.

The start of the London Marathon 2005 was a strange experience, as after the initial rush of adrenaline when the gun went off, we all had to shuffle to a halt and then walk painfully slowly for a good few hundred yards because of the sheer amount of people on the course; there just wasn't room for us all to run off the line. After a little while, the crowds thinned out and I was able to start plodding. I definitely wasn't going to be one of these runners who got carried away. I knew I hadn't trained properly and all I wanted to do was finish. I was also really nervous about my knee pain returning. So an easy, steady pace it was.

The event was a bit of a blur, if I'm honest. All I remember was feeling good from all the support on the route. There wasn't any point where there didn't seem to be a crowd. One of my running buddies from home had told me to wear my name on the front of my T-shirt, and now I understood why she said this was so important. Random strangers would call out 'Go Claire!' and 'Keep running, Claire!' It was so much more motivating when they said your name.

Towards the last five or six miles, I was running under a bridge when I saw a woman crouched down, crying. I think she had hit the well-known 'wall' that many people seem to encounter around that time in the race. I debated whether to stop or not. I decided against it, as I was really concerned that I wouldn't be able to get going again. This was my first marathon, after all. But for the next few miles, I really regretted not stopping to just give her a hug or drag her along with me to the end. I promised myself that in the future,

## RUNNING AWAY

if that ever happened again, I would stop and ask.

The long run down the Mall is as good as everyone says it is. And it's also a bloody long way! Eventually I crossed the line, grinning from ear to ear. I had done it! My time was 5 hours and 44 minutes, so no records broken by me that day (a bloke from my running club actually asked me if I had stopped for a cup of tea on the route!). But I didn't care; I had got my medal and I was a marathon runner. After a little while of looking around, I found Mark and the kids. They were thrilled I had finished and there were tearful hugs all round. We wandered back to where he had parked and finally I was able to sit down. It felt amazing. What wasn't so good was getting up again once we got back home. I literally couldn't walk, I was so stiff. Still, it amused the children.

But that was nothing compared to the next day. Simple things like going down the stairs or trying to sit on the loo became mammoth tasks involving searing pain which made me cry out loud. Jesus, what had I done to myself?

It was worth it though. That week I floated around in a cloud of happiness and revelled in feelings of achievement. Everyone was so proud of me too. It became a turning point in my life. I felt good about myself in a way that I hadn't felt before. Normally I used alcohol to numb my negative emotions, but it was a short-term fix that invariably ended badly. But this long-distance running thing… It gave me the same positive feelings, but without the self-loathing that followed the bottles of wine I consumed. It lasted longer as well.

From that moment on, I became a long-distance runner. I had a new identity and I liked it.

## LIFE LESSON
# FINDING POSITIVE HABITS TO REPLACE NEGATIVE ONES

People often say to me, 'you must be crazy to do this stuff', and I often reply 'yes, I am'.

And I'm not being sarcastic (well, maybe sometimes…), I really am a bit unhinged. And I'm not the only one either. Many people in the ultra endurance world are the same.

I used to really struggle with my craziness. My drinking was a part of my trying to manage it, I think. But the reality was that it only made it worse. When I started running, however, it improved. And when I entered the ultra endurance world, things *really* improved. I finally felt like I had a place in the world and that I had found my tribe.

Not only that, but running and triathlon training stabilised my moods and lifted my cripplingly low self-esteem. It also helped with my eating disorder, as I felt like I was able to eat more to fuel my training sessions. Putting on a few pounds now didn't seem like such a big deal, as I would undoubtedly lose them on the next long run or bike.

I also felt like I no longer needed to punish myself. In fact, that actually seemed kind of dumb. Why would anyone want to deliberately starve themselves and feel so weak and ill for the sake of being a size 6 or 8? My body wants to sit at a certain weight, and these days I just let it do just that. Have my issues with body image and eating completely gone? No. I had a moderate form of anorexia for over twenty years, and as anyone with an eating disorder will tell you, it doesn't just go away. But I understand it now, and when I have problems in my life and feel the need to start restricting my calories, I stop and remind myself how far I've come. And that nothing is solved by losing 3 or 4lbs; if anything, I will end up tired, grumpy and binging on Maltesers later that night.

Recognising your negative habits and replacing them with positive ones is a great way to successfully make changes in your life. And they don't have to be huge problems or disorders like alcohol addiction or anorexia; this method works just as well on issues like spending too much time on your phone or in front of the TV. The first step in making changes is to understand why you are doing what you are doing. Once you understand this, it's easier to stop or reduce the negative habits.

To a large degree, everything you do which impacts your life negatively is a distraction. You are trying to avoid feeling something painful or stressful in your life. Think of a smoker, having an argument or after a bad day, then reaching for a cigarette and inhaling deeply. They think they are relaxing, and that the cigarette is helping them do this, but the reality is that they are taking a drug (nicotine) which is creating a chemical reaction in their body and that, quite simply, the high is distracting them from being pissed off with their boss.

It's the same with alcohol, sugar, caffeine and anything else that creates a high or a buzz. And certain personality types are more susceptible or sensitive to addiction, which is something I wish I had known from an earlier age, as I just thought I was weak and had no self-control when I couldn't just have one glass of wine or eat one packet of crisps. If you have an addictive personality, do not beat yourself up about it; understand it and then find something healthier to replace it.

And it's not just chemical substances, it can be the sense of achievement that you get from anorexia or bulimia. With these disorders, you are creating strict rules around food which you have to adhere to. It's incredibly hard, so when you get to the end of the day and you have managed to stick to the ridiculously low amount of calories or burned off everything you have eaten though hours of cardio, you feel in control, and this, in turn, creates a sense of achievement and the high/buzz follows. It is the same with anything excessive – workaholics, shopaholics and even people who create drama in their lives for no good reason are trying to distract themselves from the real issues.

In my opinion, there is little point in pretending that you aren't the way you are. I have an extreme and addictive personality. I know this and understand that I need to find a healthy way to still be me, but without the alcohol, drugs and the drama that comes with all of that. Ultra running and triathlon are what I use, but you need to find your own healthy replacement to improve your life.

## CHAPTER 3
# IRONMAN IS A TRIATHLON?

So life, after my London Marathon, began to revolve around running. I trained around four times a week, met other runners and finished a few more marathons. At that time I was a member of the New Forest Running Club and one day overheard a conversation between a couple of the fast guys (whom I never saw much of). The super-tall one said, 'I'm training for an Ironman this year, it's really bloody hard and I'm shattered.' The small skinny one replied, 'Bloody hell mate, rather you than me'.

That was the moment when I decided that I was going to do an Ironman. Whatever that was...

In my head, I was pretty sure that it involved running through fire and over big walls. 'I can do that', I thought. It wasn't until the following week, when I was chatting over coffee to a friend, that I found out that an Ironman was, in fact, a triathlon. No fire and no walls.

Shit.

At that point, I could only swim two lengths of very bad breaststroke (head firmly out of the water, legs everywhere) and I hadn't been on a bike since I was at school. I then discovered that an Ironman was, in fact, a stupidly long triathlon, with even really good athletes taking ten hours to compete one. 'Ok... I can still do this', I said to myself (I hadn't told anyone yet). I just need to learn to swim and get one of those expensive bikes, with the weird pedals. I also needed to tell my husband.

## IRONMAN IS A TRIATHLON?

So, after an awkward conversation with Mark, which involved him asking 'why?' a lot, it was decided that I would try a Half Ironman first. Sensible idea, I thought. I found a good one, near my in-laws, and entered that day. It was called the Wimbleball 70.3. Bit of a funny name, I thought, but still, it's only a 'half', so a nice easy way to prepare for the proper one.

The following weekend my father-in-law, Des, drove me round the bike course. And I cried.

Before I could even get on the bike though, I needed to learn to swim properly. This in itself was a massive task. I had never even attempted to do the front crawl and I had huge panic attacks when I swam towards the deep end of the pool. So I signed up for lessons and, along with a few others, stood in the shallow end learning how to put my face in the water without freaking out. A few weeks later, I was able to swim a couple of strokes of crawl and get to the other side of the pool with slightly less anxiety.

After the set of lessons I had booked were over, I joined a gym with a 25-metre pool and set about mastering front crawl. I used a pull buoy to keep my legs from sinking and swam lap after lap, focusing on trying to take a breath at the right time so I wouldn't get a mouthful of water. I would watch endless videos on YouTube about technique, and I would even practice standing in my kitchen while I cooked the kids' tea. After about three months, I was finally able to say that I could swim thirty lengths of front crawl. All I had to do now was up that to eighty…

I quickly learnt with triathlon that you couldn't focus all your energy on one leg of the event (like the swimming), as there were two other

## IRONMAN IS A TRIATHLON?

sports to obsess over. The bike needed as much attention as the swim, and as I said, the last time I had been on a bike was when I was a teenager. Up to that moment, my husband had been going along with 'all this mad stuff' relatively well, as it was keeping me happy and the distances weren't too crazy. But when I mentioned that I needed a new bike, and not just any old bike, a proper one for triathlons, he put his foot down. 'My dad can give you one of his old ones', he said. I tried to protest, but the conversation was over.

I loved my father in-law. Sure, we had clashed a few times, as he was as stubborn and strong-minded as I am. But we had a mutual respect for each other and shared a love of decorating houses and generally getting shit done. Des also knew his stuff when it came to bikes. He was a member of a serious road cycling club and was very capable on the mechanical side too. But as I stood in his (immaculate) garage, I looked around at the selection of bikes he had and realised that they did not look like the ones in the triathlon magazine I had recently subscribed to.

Des lifted one down from the rack and said, 'this is yours'. I tried very hard to look excited, but I had pictured myself on something a little different during my many daydreams of completing the Half Ironman. My 'new' bike was a metallic blue with a worn brown seat (which looked ridiculously painful) and pedals with leather straps hanging from them. But the worst thing of all was that the gear changer was on the crossbar. I looked in horror at this and Des caught me and said, 'you'll be fine, it takes a little practice, that's all'. I wasn't convinced.

The bike and me travelled back to Bournemouth and I set about 'practicing', but boy, did I struggle. It didn't help that the frame was

## IRONMAN IS A TRIATHLON?

too big for me and I kept getting my feet stuck in the straps on the pedals. But I never got used to the gears. One day they got jammed and the bike and me came to a sudden and startling halt. I almost flew over the handlebars and at that moment I thought, 'fuck this'. That weekend, while my husband was having fun on a stag do in Dublin, I went to the local bike shop and bought my first bike.

This one was more like my dreams, although it was still fairly basic, or 'entry level' as the bike guy explained. It also wasn't cheap! And by the time you had added pedals, shoes and all the other bits of necessary kit, the monthly payment was not as low as I had worked out the night before. The shop offered a basic fitting service, and when I explained what race I was doing, the bike guy suggested a triple chain ring for my gears. 'It will help with the hills in Exmoor', he explained. I needed all the help I could get, so I agreed on his making the set-up change. I later found out that serious cyclists called these 'granny gears'. Once again, my image of becoming a sleek triathlete crumbled slightly. But I hadn't forgotten what those hills looked like on the drive around with my father-in-law.

After a few short training rides close to home, I decided to make the drive to the venue of the Half Ironman in Wimbleball to cycle a lap of the course. I still had a few months till the event, but I couldn't find any hills close to home which replicated what I had seen (and now featured regularly in my nightmares) and I didn't want any surprises on race day. When I got there, I drove the course again, just to familiarise myself with it. 'Fuck', I thought, it really was as bad as I remembered. The course was undulating, but there were also two big climbs on it, *and* we had to do two laps. The thing I dreaded most was getting to a point on the hill where I was riding so slowly that I would fall off. The problem with having pedals that

## IRONMAN IS A TRIATHLON?

you clipped into, I had discovered, was that you can't unclip once you are on a steep hill. Well, I couldn't anyway.

I drove back to the car park, unloaded my bike from the back of my Volvo, pulled my bike kit on and then my helmet and shoes. I couldn't put it off any longer. I stuffed a few cereal bars in my jersey pockets, pushed a bottle of sports drink into the cage on my bike and set off. I hadn't realised when I was in the car, but there was a hill to climb just to get out of the lane where the race began. 'At least I would warm up after the swim', I thought. Once on the actual bike lap, I settled into a steady pace and waited to hit the first big hill.

During my previous rides near home, I had begun to feel some twinges in my lower back, but just put them down to my body getting used to cycling on such a different kind of bike. I had only ever ridden a 'shopper' (a bike with a basket on the front) for getting to and from school and later a heavy mountain bike, when I refused to ride the other one any more (because it was definitely not cool). But as I rode along the lanes of Exmoor, the back pain returned. This time it was a bit sharper, making me move around to try and find a position that eased it a little. I didn't know it then, but this was the start of what would become a long, hard journey to try and find the cause of my back pain. It was something that I wouldn't resolve until almost ten years later with the help of an MRI scan.

After a little while, the back pain paled into insignificance as I rounded a corner to find the first big hill looming. I took a deep breath and began to climb. As the road got steeper, my breathing became more laboured, not helped by the anxiety I was feeling. Was I actually going to make it to the top? I was so relieved (and a

## IRONMAN IS A TRIATHLON?

little surprised) when I finally saw the end of the climb. I had done it! Or at least I thought I had, until I realised that it was a 'false summit' and the hill continued up round the bend. 'Holy shit', I muttered, between pants.

I managed to make it to the top of that hill, but it was exactly as bad as I thought it would be. The second hill was just as steep and there were definitely moments when I really worried about falling off. Once I returned to the car park, the sense of relief that I had managed to complete a whole lap was overshadowed by the small fact that I would have to do two of those laps on race day. And that was *after* a 1.2 mile swim…

Ah, the swim. Now that was a whole other problem I needed to deal with.

I loaded the bike into the car, changed my shoes and wandered down to the lake to look across at the vast expanse of water. It was a beautiful lake, no doubt about that, but all I felt was fear. I had never swum in open water. As a child, my first memory of being in the sea was with my dad when I was about six or seven. He was holding me tightly as we jumped the waves, laughing. But the next moment, I felt his grip tighten around me, and then his fear as a large wave headed our way. I don't remember what happened next, obviously nothing too serious, but his terror of the waves was instilled in me from then on.

Another memory I have from a similar age is from a different day out on the beach with my family. I had wanted to go exploring, but my older brother Nick had better things to do then hang around with his annoying little sister. So, being a fairly determined child,

## IRONMAN IS A TRIATHLON?

I decided to head off on my own. My memory of what happened next is pretty hazy, but I found myself in sinking sand and I was, well, sinking!

I remember the sense of panic from not being able to move my legs. I was up to my waist by then. The next thing that happened was feeling strong arms reach down and pull me free from the strong grip of the sand. Two men had come to my rescue. Did I thank them? I don't think so. I was absolutely distraught because my Mr Man swimsuit was covered in dark brown mud. I ran back, crying, to my parents (who had no idea what had happened to me), and my next memory is of them each holding an arm and washing me in the sea.

So it's hardly surprising that during my first time in a lake, on a triathlon training camp, I started to hyperventilate. I had never experienced this before and wondered what the fuck had happened to my breathing. The coach, who was behind me, knew exactly what was going on and told the rest of the group to start swimming while he stayed with the muppet making stupid noises. It took a little while of my putting my face in the water, then immediately pulling it out again, gasping, but I eventually managed to swim a little way. And although I was pleased, I was also shocked at how uncomfortable I was in the water.

From then on, my open-water swimming phobia became something that I had to deal with every single time I got into the water. Even the smell of my wetsuit became something I associated with panic. I wondered if I would even make it out of the swim at Wimbleball. The thought of having to be rescued by the water safety boat filled me with dread. During the lead-up to the race, I tried to get in the

## IRONMAN IS A TRIATHLON?

sea or local lake as often as I could to try and prepare myself. I hated every moment, but refused to give up.

Another part of open-water swimming which I was finding challenging was having to wee whilst in the water. In your wetsuit. Other swimmers laughed and told me it was one of the best things about it. I thought it was weird and a bit disgusting to be honest. But after a while, I too discovered that filling your wetsuit full of hot piss while swimming in chilly water was in fact highly pleasurable.

What a world I had entered…

Race day weekend arrived and Mark, me and the kids drove to my in-laws, which was about thirty minutes away from the event venue. The car was absolutely rammed. The amount of kit you need for triathlon is staggering. I had spent the week leading up to the race making lists and piling clothes, shoes and items of nutrition around the house. How do people do this long-term, I wondered? I was going to get this Ironman completed and that would be me and triathlon finished for good. As much as I was getting some kind of satisfaction from learning new skills and facing my fears, I can't say that I was exactly loving triathlon and had no plans to have it as part of my life.

The night before the race, we said goodbye to the kids and went and stayed closer to the event HQ. I was utterly paranoid that I would somehow miss the start. So it was almost funny when I woke the next morning to find that the alarm hadn't gone off and I was already thirty minutes behind schedule. 'Fuuuuuuuuuck!, get up, get up', I screamed to Mark. 'We're late!'. He rolled his eyes and sighed. 'Claire, it's half past four, we've still got time'. But I was rigid with

## IRONMAN IS A TRIATHLON?

terror. I had never experienced this before a normal running race. It was dark, chilly, and in a few hours, I would be getting into a lake with a thousand other people. Why the fuck was I doing this to myself? Why had running marathons become not enough?

But before we could leave the B&B, I had to eat my breakfast. The night before I had laid out my porridge, jam sandwiches and some kind of meal replacement milkshake. I had worked out that this added up to around 500 calories, which would set me in good stead for the swim. I looked at it all and my stomach lurched. I gingerly put a spoonful of porridge into my mouth and gagged. My husband sniggered. I threw him an evil look and took a deep breath. I can do this. Once the porridge was done, I grabbed the rest of the food and we got in the car. Trying to eat a sandwich when you are incredibly nervous is almost impossible. I had virtually no saliva in my mouth and bread was not the best choice.

We arrived at Wimbleball along with hundreds of other cars, found a parking space on the field and began unloading my kit. When we had registered the day before, we had seen the vast marquee that housed rows and rows of numbered pegs. This morning we walked around trying to find my number, along with hundreds of other half-dressed people doing the same thing. All I kept thinking was 'why, why, why, am I doing this?' I was as far out of my comfort zone as I had ever been and it was not a pleasant feeling.

Once I was sorted, I pulled on my wetsuit and tried to drink my milkshake. I felt sick to my stomach and all I wanted to do was go home. But how could I? I had already spent thousands on a new bike, kit, my race entry and the training camp. I glanced at my husband. This was not where he wanted to be either and I knew

## IRONMAN IS A TRIATHLON?

that. Yes, he was being supportive, but this wasn't something he had signed up for. Recently we had started to have some issues in our relationship, and although I thought that Ironman would be good for me, I had the sneaking suspicion that it wasn't so good for our marriage. I pushed these feelings to the back of my mind and told myself to focus on the race.

6am was fast approaching and we all made our way down to the lake. I said goodbye to my husband, a little dramatically, as if I might never return. I think he was wondering where he could get a coffee. The start itself remains something of a blur. The mist just lifting off the water as the sun rose; a mass of neoprene bodies pushing into the water. Nervous people fiddling with hats and goggles; me, standing there, trying to calm my breathing and not turn and run back to the car.

Once the starting horn had sounded, I waited in the shallows for the main bulk of the athletes to clear. This was hard enough without being booted in the face by some idiot trying to take two minutes off his swim time. I then swam for a few minutes, letting the cold water fill my suit, trying not to react too much to this. I knew it would warm up soon; just try and relax, I told myself. After a while, I stopped and looked up. I was confused. Where was everybody else? I spun around and realised with horror that I had swum in the wrong direction. Sighting was something I had yet to learn, and it looked like I was going to have to do it today.

The rest of the time spent in the water was split between looking up in panic, adjusting my course accordingly, and trying to have a wee. I was still struggling to relax enough to just go in my wetsuit, but I also didn't want to have to waste time in transition using the

## IRONMAN IS A TRIATHLON?

Portaloos. So between this and swimming in zig-zags, my mind was occupied enough not to induce any major panic attacks. This was a bonus, and I hauled myself from the lake feeling like I had just swum the English Channel! I was thrilled that the scariest part of the race was over and I had survived.

All I had to do now was cycle 56 miles over a particularly hilly route and run a half marathon.

Climbing the hill that took us out of Wimbleball and onto the main lap was harder than I remember. Probably because of the swim had taken it out of me and I was also pretty cold. After getting to the top though, I was definitely not cold anymore. The bike section passed without too many issues; the hills hurt as much as before and the second lap was harder still. At one point my chain came off. But after a minute or two of panic, I took a deep breath and pulled it back on the chainrings, covering myself in oil in the process.

After over 4 hours of cycling, I free-wheeled down the hill I had started up what seemed like days ago and rode into transition. I couldn't believe it – I had survived the swim and made the bike cut-off. Now just that half marathon. I was actually going to do this!

Well, that's what I thought, until I got off the bike and realised that my legs had broken somehow. I tried to run and quickly realised that was not going to happen. During my training, I had read about 'brick runs', where you get off the bike and go straight into a run session, but thought that was just for proper athletes, not for the likes of novices like me. I was more than a little worried, but just kept walking it out and hoping that at some point my legs would feel less like an eighty-year-old's. After about fifteen minutes, I was

## IRONMAN IS A TRIATHLON?

able to start jogging, slowly, then gradually picked up my pace. As I began to feel a little better, I managed to eat a few Jelly Babies and half a banana from the aid station, then checked my time. I was good – I had plenty of time to finish within the 8-hour cut-off.

Part of the run went over a huge dam with awesome views on either side. The rest of it was along country lanes and through the main park. The sun came out and for the first time that day, I felt relaxed. After all the training, stress and panic, I was going to finish my first triathlon. On my last lap, I felt a little overwhelmed. I could hear other people finishing and I could also see the gantry that you ran under. Spectators lined the edges of the route, cheering and clapping, and apart from the London Marathon, I had never experienced this before. My normal running races had been quiet affairs, and by the time I finished there were never that many people left. Which was how I liked it.

Crossing this finish line was truly special though. I had visualised it during my training, even when I had worried about whether I would make the swim and bike cut-off times. But here I was, having a medal placed round my neck, being congratulated, and Mark was hugging me and saying well done. He looked genuinely proud of me too, which gave me hope that maybe we would be OK.

After the Half Ironman, I began training hard for my next goal, Ironman UK. But despite the positivity I had felt after completing my first triathlon, my marriage really wasn't doing well. It had been limping along for a while, but now started to properly fall apart, and as hard as I tried to ignore it, the cracks were more like massive, gaping landslides. I think one day we just realised that, other than the children, we really had nothing in common any more, and the

## IRONMAN IS A TRIATHLON?

more I immersed myself in the world of long-distance triathlon, the further apart we grew.

Now there is never a good time to blow up your life, but three months before your first Ironman is certainly not ideal. Most people would probably have postponed the race (or splitting up) until the following year, but I've always been the type of person to just get on with things.

What happened in those twelve weeks was, looking back, really fucked up. I left our home, taking Jess, Jake and the dog, and moved into a rented house. I found a new job that would enable me to bring in some regular money but also allow me to pick up the kids from school and have Fridays off so I could continue my long training rides.

I was naturally struggling to deal with it all, but I had also massively underestimated how heartbroken I felt. The marriage was over, but I didn't expect to feel so utterly desolate and raw. I felt as if I was inside out, with all my nerve endings exposed. I would start crying in random places, like Sainsbury's. And I didn't seem to care that I would be standing in the chilled goods aisle, holding some chicken breasts, with tears rolling down my face...

To top it all off, my addictions kicked back into overdrive. Despite not having smoked for years, I started again; I was also drinking way too much and eating less and less. Not ideal prep for Ironman training, but at this point that was the only thing I was holding on to. It was my lifeline, but it was also the very reason why my marriage had failed. Giving up on Ironman meant (in my head) that all this pain would have been for nothing.

## IRONMAN IS A TRIATHLON?

So on Fridays I would drive to Sherborne, where Ironman UK was held then, pull my bike out of the boot and head off to ride laps. Sometimes, in an effort to distract myself from my back pain (which had become almost unbearable now I was riding serious miles), I would listen to music, but this only made me more sad. And there were many times I cried, cycling on those lonely roads, wondering what the hell I had done to my life.

But doing an Ironman isn't supposed to be easy (at least that's what the adverts said). So I somehow managed to balance my Jekyll and Hyde lifestyle, and on Sunday 19 August 2007 stood in transition with a thousand other triathletes, feeling the most alone I have ever been in my life. To top it all, I was still having huge panic attacks about swimming, and this morning was as bad as it had ever been. It was so bad in fact that I started to devise a plan to leave my bike and make a run for it. I figured I could drive back later and pick it up.

In the weeks leading up to the race, I had developed a sneaky suspicion that this panic attack was going to happen, so a few days before I'd got a tattoo, an African symbol of endurance. As I looked towards the transition exit, I glanced down at the tattoo on my wrist and swore under my breath, 'Fuck's sake'. I had to do it now.

The lake was covered in a thick blanket of morning mist, and the race director announced that the start would be delayed until it cleared. My initial feeling of relief was short-lived. It was only putting off the inevitable, after all. After about forty-five minutes, it had cleared enough to allow the safety kayakers to paddle out and the swim could start. The only way I could get myself into the lake that day was inch by inch. Literally. 'Just go in up to your ankles,'

## IRONMAN IS A TRIATHLON?

I said to myself. 'Now to your knees...' 'OK, up to your waist, you can still get out if you need to.' And that is how I started my first Ironman.

The swim was the normal blur of dark, slippery, wet-suited bodies kicking and bumping into me. I didn't enjoy it at all. When I got out of the water though, I felt elated, because in my head I had completed my first Ironman. Not just the swim, but all of it. I had worked myself up so much that the relief of actually getting out of the lake was incredible. The bike and run sections were easy. A little naive maybe, but that's how I felt.

I tripped and scrambled my way into transition, a big grin on my face, not caring how I looked. I tried to take my wetsuit off and was a little confused by the fact that my hands didn't seem to work. 'That's odd', I thought. I had started shivering by then and one of the marshals came over, took one look at me and called for another member of staff to assist. They removed my wetsuit with lightning speed and helped me with my bike kit. They then wrapped a silver blanket around me and told me to sit down as 'I wasn't going anywhere until I had warmed up'.

This was the first of many post-swim experiences with mild hypothermia that I would have in the years to come. I wasn't too badly affected this time though, and after I had eaten a cheese and Marmite sandwich and convinced the marshals that I wasn't about to fall over and die, I was allowed to get my bike from transition. I had been really stressed about trying to find it in amongst the thousands of other bikes, but I needn't have worried, as mine was pretty much the only one left. Another thing I would experience more of in the years to come!

## IRONMAN IS A TRIATHLON?

In the briefing the day before, the organisers had warned us that race day was going to be unusually cold for August and advised us to wrap up. In a panic, I took the opportunity to get some new kit at the TriUK stand, buying a new jacket and some leg-warmers. I knew how long the bike section was going to take me and didn't need to be freezing out on the laps by myself. Once I was on my bike, in my many, many layers, I felt like a 'proper' triathlete. That was until the amazing Bella Comerford (now Bayliss) flew past me, IN HER PANTS! Well, that's what it looked like. I was stunned and a little embarrassed. That was the moment I really understood the difference between professional athletes and mere mortals like me.

The bike was a long, slow drag. With my back pain really pulling me down, I had to stop and stretch, which would give me some relief for ten minutes or so. But as I would find out in the years that followed, nothing would really help apart from getting off the bloody bike. I was so relieved to finally get into transition and have the intense pain disappear almost immediately once I had racked my bike. I was also thrilled to see some of my friends had made the hour's drive to cheer me on. This really picked me up. And now all I had left was the bit that I was not completely terrible at – marathon running.

The first half of the marathon was really scenic, following a route around the lake and the impressive Sherborne Castle. But then we got to experience the 'joy' of running on a dual carriageway (to be fair, it was closed to traffic). This was fairly soul-destroying, and by that point in the race I was really starting to feel rough. My blood sugar was all over the place and I was struggling with feeling sick and shaky. I suddenly remembered that I had shoved some of the biscuits from the hotel I had stayed in the night before into

## IRONMAN IS A TRIATHLON?

my bum-bag. Moments later, I was feeling 100% better. My race was literally saved by a couple of Custard Creams and a Bourbon. Never underestimate the power of a good biscuit.

I was on my last lap, about to return to the event HQ, when I heard cheering and beeping from the other side of the dual carriageway. I looked up, thinking it was for someone else, but then saw the Olympian, Liz Yelling, and her husband Martin driving past. I was a little stunned when I realised they were actually shouting at me, 'C'mon Claire, you can do it!'. I had met them both on my second training camp, held by then Ironman athlete (now awesome running photographer) Ian Corless, but I never thought that they would remember me. This gave me a huge boost and I picked the pace up and pushed on to the finish line.

When I was almost there, a man started running next to me. For a moment I had no clue who he was, and was about to suggest that he buggered off when I realised it was actually my older brother, Nick. He was wearing a jacket I had never seen and in my fatigued state, I just hadn't recognised him. 'Hey sis, you're doing so well', he said. I grinned; it wasn't often that I got praise from my big bro.

After a few minutes though, I suddenly had a flashback to the competitors' race pack (which I had read so often that I had almost memorised it). 'Nick, you mustn't run with me, it might be seen as outside assistance', I said. I was panic-stricken – imagine getting DQ'd now... In hindsight, I don't really think the organisers of Ironman UK were particularly worried about a back-of-the-pack first-timer, but still, rules are rules.

As I got to the finish line, I could hear the announcer shouting,

## IRONMAN IS A TRIATHLON?

'YOU ARE AN IRONMAN!'. I got massive goosebumps, a rush of adrenaline and felt a little sick. For a moment, I wanted to stop, turn and run the other way. Finishing felt overwhelming, and it also meant the end of this awesome and equally horrible experience. I couldn't believe I was actually going to do it.

I rounded the corner of the finish tunnel and I saw my family all waiting; my kids and nieces then ran to meet me. By this point I had a lump in my throat and was finding it so hard to breathe. The kids grabbed my hands and literally pulled me over the finish line. It was one of the best moments in my life. I received my medal and was hugged by everyone, tears of happiness streaming down my face.

Then my brother handed me a phone. 'It's Mark,' he said. My ex-husband had called to say well done. I broke down in tears again, as it meant so much to me that he had wanted to do this, even after everything we had been through.

As I walked back through transition to collect my bike and kit bags, one of the marshals said to me, 'Well done, love. Nobody can ever take this away from you'. She was right and I have never forgotten that.

## LIFE LESSON
# 'IF YOU'RE GOING THROUGH HELL, KEEP GOING.'
# - WINSTON CHURCHILL

Winston was the king of quotes, but I think that one is my favourite.

So many times in my life, I have sat with my head in my hands, thinking that I couldn't go on. Things are just too hard. After my marriage with Mark broke down and I was forced to make massive life changes in a short space of time, I found myself at this point. I had underestimated how hard the break-up would be, and I was so busy trying to make sure that the kids were OK and my ex was coping that I didn't release how badly I was doing myself.

I was barely eating, drinking too much and I had even started smoking again. All this while having to get used to living in a rented house and starting a new job. So why continue my Ironman training? Why keep doing something so hard when I could barely cope with day-to-day issues?

I used to ask myself this on an almost daily basis when I was out running or riding my bike. Nothing felt good anymore; my energy levels were so low from my poor diet and I suffered daily hangovers from my excessive drinking. Why not just give up on the idea of completing my first Ironman?

I think, deep down, I knew how important it was, not just for my immediate future, but for later on in my life. So many times since then I have called upon the strength I found that day to get into the lake, when I stood on the side feeling completely alone and terrified. Somehow I made myself get into the water and start that race, despite every part of my body wanting to turn and run home.

I have sat in the dentist's chair, about to have root canal treatment, feeling very apprehensive, and reminded myself about the lake at Sherborne. And I've said to myself, if you can do that, you can do anything. The same for an operation to partially remove my thyroid, sitting in the waiting room before being called through to surgery, so nervous. I reminded myself of the water, the chill in the air, the low-lying mist and the other swimmers. And how I felt sick to my stomach with fear.

'If you can do that, you can do anything.'

So when you are going through hell, don't stop. Don't say to yourself, this is too hard, I'm going to quit. Just keep going. You will be surprised with what you can achieve, under enormous pressure and stress. And the rewards for getting to the other side are more than worth it.

## CHAPTER 4
# DOUBLE TROUBLE

In the spring of 2008, I was sitting in the office of the printers where I was working at the time. After completing my first Ironman, life had settled down and I was a little less crazy than I had been following the breakdown of my marriage. That day, I was obviously supposed to be working, but I was in fact on TriTalk, a well-known triathlon forum, looking for a new challenge. I was aware of the first ever Double Ironman that was going to be held in Lichfield that August, but annoyingly I had missed out when entries had opened and now it was full. But on that boring Monday afternoon, in that dusty room, surrounded by old brochures and leaflets, my life was about to change.

The race director had literally just posted in the forum that a place had become available. I looked around me, as if I was being watched. 'Should I?' I said to nobody. 'I mean, really... should I?' I went onto the website of the event, clicked on the 'Enter Here' button and held my breath. The registration page loaded and I began to fill in my details. When I got to the payment page, I stopped. It was a lot of money and I was now a single mum, living in a rented house with a part-time job. This was in no way a responsible thing to do.

Having acknowledged that, I rummaged around in my bag and found my 'emergency credit card'. 'Well, this is a kind of emergency,' I justified to myself. My hands trembled as I entered the numbers before I took one final deep breath and pressed the 'submit' button. 'Entry Confirmed' appeared on the screen and I jumped up out of my seat and squealed. I felt an overwhelming need for air and made my way down the stairs to the entrance. Once outside, I tried to

## DOUBLE TROUBLE

slow my breathing down and come to terms with what I had done. I had just entered the first UK Double Ironman!

A Double Ironman is exactly what it sounds like. This particular race was being held in the 'continuous' format, so the swim was 4.8 miles, the bike was 224 miles and then you had to run two marathons. The event was based in a leisure centre, which meant the swim was in a pool. For me, with my open-water issues, this was perfect. The bike section was on the quiet, country roads leading from the centre. And the run was a small lap, around a mile long, mostly on pavements with a short, wooded section.

'How do I train for a Double Ironman?' I wondered. I have been asked that question many times in my life since then, but at that point I didn't know anybody who had done one. And I had only just managed to finish a single Ironman. As usual, I didn't allow a small detail like not having any idea what I was doing stop me. During the months leading up to the event, I basically trained the same way I had done for the Ironman in Sherborne, but added in a couple of long back-to-back bike rides plus another one that went through the night. I swam the distance in the pool and ran a couple of marathons over the summer with my friends. Sporadic is definitely a word I would use for my training plan. And, as I was a single mum again, but now with two kids, a hyperactive Jack Russell and a job, fitting the training in was definitely a little more challenging.

The week of the event arrived and I was ready. I wouldn't say I was the most physically prepared athlete, but I wasn't injured, I had a support crew and I had a plan. I had worked out my lap times, the time I needed for my transitions and the cut-offs. I had typed it all out, and in true control-freak mode, I had used different colours for

## DOUBLE TROUBLE

each of the disciplines. I packed my bags and loaded the car with everything I thought I would need for a two-day triathlon. The only thing I hadn't done was buy my food supplies, but we had planned to do that once we were in Lichfield.

I was lucky enough to have my oldest and dearest friend Claire (that's not a typo, we have the same name) crewing for me on this event. We had known each since secondary school and she knew me very well. We have a very similar sense of humour, which for these types of events is essential. I picked Claire up en-route and we made the long drive to Lichfield. Once we had arrived and settled into the hotel, we made our way to the local supermarket to buy my race food. This basically involved my walking round Tesco putting anything I fancied into the trolley. Biscuits, sweets, crisps, rice pudding and Pot Noodles. For someone who had always controlled calorie intake and tried to eat 'healthily', this was heaven.

After the shopping trip, we needed to register. This was really nerve-racking for me, as I was in awe of the other, more experienced, athletes, but also the race directors, who had both completed the Arch to Arc. The Arch to Arc was a triathlon on a different level. For starters, it didn't follow the normal rules of triathlon. The run, from Marble Arch in London to Dover, was first. You then had to swim the English Channel, and if you survived and actually completed that, you finished up by cycling from Calais to the Arc de Triomphe in Paris. It blew my mind and I couldn't imagine ever being able to do something like that. Or even wanting to.

Once I was registered and in possession of my swim hat, timing chip and goody bag, we put up the small tent that we would use for storing my food and kit, and racked my bike in the tennis courts.

## DOUBLE TROUBLE

This was where I met Eddie Ette. He was the founder of Enduroman Events and the first person to complete the Arch to Arc. And I was a little starstuck. He smiled and shook my hand and wished me luck for the following day.

Once we were organised, the only thing left to do was eat in preparation for the event. As we were based in a retail park, the only real option was McDonalds. This was fine by me and Claire, and we sat down with some of the other competitors to a healthy meal of cheeseburger, fries and a strawberry milkshake. Perfect pre-race food... 'I was made for this ultra endurance shit,' I said to Claire, laughing.

The next morning, I wasn't laughing. I had barely slept and I sat, with my coffee and untouched porridge, wide-eyed in terror. What the fuck was I doing? A bloody Double Ironman. When had a single Ironman become not enough? I looked at Claire and she looked back, barely concealing her amusement. 'Come on hun, you'll be fine,' she said. We grabbed my swim kit and made our way across to the leisure centre.

Despite the swim being held in the pool, the smell of the wetsuit was bringing all my fears back to life. I wrestled with the neoprene, pulling it over my butt, and then asked Claire to zip me up. Immediately the tightness from the neck of the suit made me panic. I pulled at it, trying to give myself more space to breathe. 'Calm down', I said to myself, 'It's just a long pool swim.' I had done the distance during my training. I knew I could do it, so I why was I freaking out so much?

I lowered myself into the water. It felt warm. I looked around me.

## DOUBLE TROUBLE

I was in a lane with the other females in the race and two of them weren't even in wetsuits. 'Obviously hardcore endurance athletes,' I thought. The horn then sounded and we were off. From that moment, all my nerves disappeared and the strangest feeling came over me. I felt good. Really good. In fact, I felt like this was going to be a really good race. It's hard to explain, and I've only had that feeling a few times since, but it's like I knew I was going to finish. I berated myself for being too cocky, but it wasn't even that. Just a quiet confidence that everything was going to be alright.

The swim passed uneventfully and I was out, slightly ahead of my predicted time in 3 hours, 3 minutes and 41 seconds. Claire and I headed to the changing rooms, where she had laid everything out for me, ready. I was happy to have completed the first section of the race and was keen to get on the bike. As I walked to the tennis courts, trying not to slip over as I was still struggling with the cleats on the bottom of my bike shoes, I was greeted by Eddie. 'That's you finished the swim then?' he said. 'Yes,' I grinned. I lifted my bike from the racking and wheeled it out of the fenced area. Once I was by the road, I mounted it and I was off.

The bike course was 224 miles of quiet-ish country roads. It was pretty uninspiring, if I'm honest, but it wasn't about the views, just the miles. The lap was around 11 miles before you returned to headquarters. Lap after lap I rode, grabbing food and refilling my bottles when I needed to. Claire had made good friends with one of the other crew members and I was pretty sure that they were drinking wine during the afternoon, as their moods went from calm and focused to giggling and weirdly happy, despite being confined in a leisure centre car park for the weekend.

## DOUBLE TROUBLE

As night approached, my own mood dipped as the pain in my back began to really get me down. It had started early in the race and I would stop and stretch every lap, taking a lot of painkillers, but they weren't making any difference and I was desperate. Claire came into her own then, giving me a hug and saying, 'one lap at a time'. I cried and rode off into the night again.

At around 2am, I finished my last lap. I had been finding it hard to eat and my blood sugar levels were really low. I was still such a rookie and when I had lost my appetite, I had simply stopped eating. Big mistake. I dismounted, shakily, thrilled to be finished with the bike. I was even 1 minute ahead of my predicted time of 16 hours. I changed into my run kit in the small tent, which was fairly challenging in itself, and readied myself to run a double marathon. Claire made me a cup of tea and a Pot Noodle and I felt myself coming back to life. I was prepared this time for my legs to feel as if they didn't belong to me, so decided I would use the first few laps to walk and refuel.

The run laps were just over a mile in distance. The route had seemed simple enough when we had walked it the day before, but now with my stiff legs and low energy, all I could see in the wooded section were thousands of twisted roots, all vying to trip up tired athletes. It was dark too and our head torches only helped a little. I saw so many people stumbling and worried that I would fall and my race would be over. I took it steady.

As the sun started to rise, I could feel my spirits rise with it. I was able to pick the pace up a bit and I knew I was going to finish the race. I was going to become a Double Ironman, which was pretty damn cool. Out of the four women who had started, only three of

## DOUBLE TROUBLE

us were left as one had quit during the bike leg. Monique, who was leading the women's race, was way ahead of me, but the other lady, Fay, was struggling with an injury to her hip, made worse by tripping over some of those roots I think. But I didn't know this at the time; all I was thinking about was getting to the finish line.

During the latter stages of the run, I started to feel rough. I borrowed a cap from someone's crew so I could pull it down over my eyes to hide my face. I was struggling with the cheers and support at the turnaround of every lap. It wasn't that I didn't appreciate it, more that I had no energy to smile and converse back. I was spent and just wanted this to end. Claire was now feeding me cups of tea with copious amounts of sugar in them to try and pick me up. I was back to not eating again, something I would struggle with again and again in the years to come.

I remember going into the Portaloo at one point. I just wanted to be able to sit down and be on my own for a minute or two. But Trevor, who was doing the timing, spotted me and announced over the Tannoy where I was, just for a laugh. I was mortified and never quite forgave him for that!

I also properly met the legend that is TC (aka Anthony Gerundini) during the run. He helpfully told me that my run was 'as fast as his walk' and that I too should try power walking. I was in no mood at that point for well-meaning advice from anybody and glared at him, muttering 'thanks'. Once I was back in HQ, I said to Eddie that 'some bloke' had just told me I was running too slowly, and how much he had pissed me off. Eddie just laughed. He knew exactly who I was talking about. TC went on to become a great friend and he has never stopped giving me, and everybody else, 'helpful' advice!

## DOUBLE TROUBLE

My last lap finally came around and I neared the finish line. The same feeling I'd had at the two previous triathlons once again came over me. But this time it was even worse, as I was more fatigued, and this also meant even more than the previous events. How was I, the girl who hated sport, going to finish a Double Ironman? It just felt like some weird dream.

As I crossed the line, the race director, Steve Haywood, placed the medal around my neck. After that, to my surprise, he then shook my hand and congratulated me for being the second women's finisher. I was presented with a trophy and a cheque for £200. I was blown away. I simply had not considered my placing and it was an amazing surprise. I had completed the run in 13 hours and 23 minutes and the whole event in 32 hours, 27 minutes and 1 second!

After lying on the grass with my eyes closed for a while, Claire suggested we went back to the hotel so I could finally sleep. That sounded like an awesome idea and I slowly got to my feet. Walking like a zombie, I finally made it to the room. Claire asked me if I was hungry and I looked at her, almost in surprise. 'Ohmygod, I'm starving.' 'Right, McDonalds it is,' she said and went off to get it. When Claire returned she found me fast asleep, still in my run kit, on top of the bed. She shook me gently, saying, 'wake up, you need to eat.'

And with that, lying in a hotel bed, eating a McDonalds, with a big grin on my face, the Double Ironman adventure was done.

# LIFE LESSON
# TAKING ON MASSIVE CHALLENGES

In the summer leading up to the Double Iron Triathlon, my training wasn't exactly going to plan. Trying to squeeze everything in around two young children, part-time work and an energetic Jack Russell was proving tricky.

And for the past few weeks, it had been going back and forth in my head. Should I do it or not?

While out running one afternoon in the woods close to my house, listening to music and trying to get my mind to stop revolving, my iPod flicked onto a track which I hadn't heard for a while. It was Madonna's 'Over and Over' (stop judging me, it's a great song). Look up the lyrics and you'll see what I mean, but essentially, 'If I fall, I get up again, over and over.'

Ok, so not exactly deep and meaningful, but you get the point. What that song said to me was, stop being afraid of taking on this huge race and just go for it. If you fail, you fail.

I stopped running and looked around me. I was alone. My dog paused too and looked at me, sensing something. I took a deep breath and decided I would do it, I would attempt a Double Ironman. And from then on, I was focused and committed to the event. I made a plan for the remaining months of training and also for the event itself: timings, nutrition and crew.

Taking on massive challenges can seem overwhelming at the best of times, so how do you go from the first idea to crossing the finish line? Below are some of the processes I have used over the last ten years of doing crazy, hard stuff.

**Break it down**

The old adage about eating an elephant (one bite at a time) is perfect for when you start feeling panic-stricken about what you have just signed up for or started, be it a race, business or university course.

DO NOT LOOK AT THE BIG PICTURE!

Sorry to shout at you, but that's really important advice. If I had stood on the start line of the Double Deca (we'll come to that later!) thinking 'I have to cover 2,812 miles in 28 days using my (slightly crumbling) body,' I would have turned and run away. Probably still in my wetsuit…

Instead, I thought to myself, 'I'm going to swim a mile. And then after that I will swim another'. And so on.

When I decided to write a book, I discovered that I would need to produce 80,000 words. That didn't sound too bad, I thought. That was until I did a word count on the pages I had already written and realised that, actually, 80,000 was a shit load of words. And an awful lot of work. Even when I got to a point where the end seemed near, there was still loads to do with checking spelling, grammar and editing, ensuring it was written in a way people could understand, then trying to find a publisher.

Once again, I felt massively overwhelmed. So I took a deep breath and went through everything that needed doing, focusing on one chapter at the time, and made a list. Each time I sat down to work, I picked one item to focus on.

This technique can also be useful for day-to-day life, when you are having a bad day and trying to work through a huge to-do list. Just take the first few items at the top of the list and concentrate on those. Not helping? Just pick one thing, the easiest job on the list, and do that. Once you've completed that, pick the next one. And so on…

**Prepare your body and mind**

If you have entered a marathon, you'll obviously need a training plan. The same goes for a 10k or an Ironman. But it's not just about the physical training; you must also look at your mind and how to prepare that for the journey ahead. This is also very important if your challenge is starting a business or learning a new language.

Regardless of whether your challenge is physical or mental, think about how this new part of your life will fit in with the current one. What changes will you have to make in order to help you succeed?

If your challenge is a physical one, will you need to change your diet and take on more calories? You will probably need to get more sleep to help recovery. And what about your social life? How will this affect it?

If you have a partner and/or children, you need to think about how this will affect them. Whatever you are doing, it will eat into the time you normally spend with them. It's easier to prepare them for this before it happens, rather than creating problems when you are in the middle of things. Explain to them how important it is to you. Share your dream and the end result with them, so they feel part of it and not excluded.

Also, does your living space work? Do you need to create an office or training area in the corner of your bedroom or living room? Try to keep this space clean and organised, as this helps with feeling in control. Surround yourself with images/mood boards to keep you focused and help with motivation on tough days.

And how about finances, how will this impact them? Do you have a plan in place for not earning as much as you normally would, or for buying the equipment you need? There is nothing like the stress of a dwindling bank account to derail your dreams and send your stress levels soaring. Make a list of your incomings and outgoings and be realistic about what you will need to start a business or climb Kilimanjaro.

Are you an early bird or night owl? Working out when you are at your most productive can really help. If you are at your best in the morning, get used to getting up an hour or two earlier to really make the most of your time. If you are a night owl, then be prepared to lose those hours watching TV to work on your thesis or train in the gym.

**Bigger and scarier**

A simple thing that has helped me as my challenges got bigger has been to read and watch anything with people doing scarier challenges than mine. Before I took on the Continuous Deca in Switzerland (again, more on that later!), I lay in bed reading about Mark Beaumont cycling around the world on his own. Also, watching documentaries about rowing the Atlantic, for me, puts a lot of my worries into perspective. It makes me think, if they can brave 60-foot waves and capsizing, then surely I can do my challenge.

**Find a friend/mentor**

Whatever you are doing, there will be times when you will feel totally alone. Finding a person or people that have either done what you are trying to do, or are going through it at the same time, will help massively. In an ideal world you should aim to have two types of support during your challenge. One person (challenge friend) you can be in the trenches with, someone who has the same goal as you. And the other person (challenge mentor) should have already done it or something similar.

Your friend will be the person you can share a coffee with and moan about how hard it is, and they will totally get it. The mentor will advise you and help you work through stumbling blocks. They will also inspire you to keep pushing on.

**Keep track of your progress**

As time goes on and you move further down the road of your journey, it's easy to forget the progress you make. You may have learnt new skills or information. Or be able to bike or swim faster than you did a month ago. Whatever it is, make sure that you acknowledge these new skills and give yourself some credit. Write the achievements down on a piece of paper and stick it somewhere

where you will see it every day. This will also spur you on when you lose your mojo and the end goal seems too far away.

**Celebrate small victories**

While you acknowledge your progress, it's also worth creating some shorter-term goals within your overall challenge and ensure that when you reach those milestones, you celebrate them. Have coffee and cake with a friend, or a meal out with your partner. Go to the cinema with your children. Whatever it is, just take time to recognise your achievements.

**Run through the plan in your head**

Often when I have been organising large endurance events with complicated event plans, I have become overwhelmed and completely stressed out. One of the tricks I started using was finding a quiet room and sitting down with a pen and paper. I close my eyes and run through the whole event in my head, from the minute I turn up at the venue to packing down and driving away at the end. This enables me to really visualise it and it also throws up areas that may need attention, or remind you of things you have forgotten (use the pen and paper here!) It can also show you that there might be a better way to do certain things that you hadn't considered before. It's worth spending 20-30 minutes performing this activity, and you can do it as many times as you need to.

**Stay positive**

I am a huge believer in having a positive mental attitude. Since giving up alcohol, I have formed an awesome habit that I will never give up. This is to look for positives in every bad situation. It requires work and trust me, it's not easy sometimes, you have to really struggle to find positives when something truly awful happens. But I have never once not been able to get something good out of a shitty situation.

You will definitely hit bumps in the road during your challenge, but get into the habit of looking at this in a different light. Yes, you could have done without falling off your bike, but maybe this highlighted that you need to work on some basic skills? Or maybe your assignment keeps being rejected. Don't take it personally, just look at it as an opportunity to improve your writing. Read up and watch some YouTube videos on how to improve and become better.

Bad shit happens and when it does, take it in, acknowledge it and then find the positives. Every time.

And my final piece of advice that I want to share is something an endurance buddy once said to me…

**'Embrace the crazy and enjoy the ride.'**

## CHAPTER 5
# ULTRA CRAZY

After the Double Ironman, my ultra triathlon journey took a dark and twisty turn.

I decided to enter the Arch to Arc.

This was a stupid decision for many reasons. The cost alone, for a single mum, was one very big reason not to enter. The second reason was that I had a very real fear of the sea, and of swimming in open water, full stop. The third reason was that I felt the cold, badly, even in the summer.

The Arch to Arc is, in my opinion, the hardest triathlon in the world. And although it is a triathlon, it is mainly about the swim. Because running 90 miles and cycling 180 is very doable for most ultra athletes. Swimming the English Channel, however, is not.

I have said many, many times since I discovered and then set my heart on the Arch to Arc, that I wished I had never found out about it. It became my obsession and my nemesis.

I paid the deposit to Enduroman and, scarily, my name and photo went onto the website. The challenge was set for the following summer, but before then I needed to complete a few qualifying swims. The first of them was 2 hours long in Swan Pool, Birmingham, in October 2009. It was actually a lake, but maybe they had to name it 'pool' so people wouldn't confuse it with the ballet. I had limited 'lake swimming in the winter' experience at this point of my life and I had not really expected quite how bad it

## ULTRA CRAZY

would actually be. In fact, I was pretty excited.

I got into the lake and was relieved to find that it was fairly shallow in most parts around the outer waters where we were to swim. Initially I didn't feel too bad; my confidence was high and I wasn't struggling with panic that much. After a while though, the cold started to get to me. My longest open-water swim up until then had been the 2.4-mile Ironman in Sherborne, in August. Being so inexperienced, I had massively underestimated the difference in water temperature, both from the time of year but also from being further up north.

An hour in, I was shivering and my teeth were chattering. I checked my watch and couldn't believe I still had an hour to go. I definitely wasn't feeling so confident by this point. I gave myself a bit of a talking to and got my head down into the water again. The minutes dragged by, painfully slowly. Time seemed to slow down and I got colder and colder. Eventually, I was told my 2 hours were up and I dragged myself from the water. I was covered in swan poo and was shivering, violently. But this, apparently, was completely normal, and I was congratulated on my achievement.

Once I had changed and was back in my car, I realised how tired I felt. I couldn't believe how seriously a 2-hour swim had affected me. Of course, now I realise that this was not so much about the time or distance, but the effect mild hypothermia has on your body. It was something I had to get used to over the years to come.

The next swim I completed was a 4-hour sea swim, with proper boat support to prepare me for the Arch to Arc. It was still October, but the sea was a little warmer than the lake and I had that recent

## ULTRA CRAZY

experience and sense of achievement to draw from. Jumping off the boat into the sea, in Portland, Dorset, was more than a little scary. I was so reluctant, in fact, that I forgot to let go of the side of the boat. Almost wrenching your arm out of its socket before a long swim is particularly stupid, even for me.

The sea was calm that day and the sun warmed my back, which helped enormously with my body temperature. 4 hours is a long time to swim though and I had definitely had enough by the time I pulled my tired, cold body from the water and back onto the boat. And you wouldn't think that after spending that amount of time in the sea that fish and salty chips would be my choice of post-swim feed, but it was amazing as I sat on the shore in Weymouth, tired but happy.

Eddie and Steve, the organisers of the Arch to Arc, decided that organising a 'half Arch to Arc' training event in Lanzarote in December would be ideal preparation for me and a few other athletes taking on the monster triathlon the following year. The distances would comprise a 45-mile run, an 11-mile sea swim and a 90-mile bike ride to finish. Getting childcare to cover the week I would need for this was my first challenge, but once that was sorted, I booked my flights and started to plan for the adventure.

Eddie and his wife, Lynn, had a place near Playa Blanca in Lanzarote and it was agreed that I could stay there. I organised the hire of a bike box and set about making a list of all the things I would need for the event. It was a long list, but there was obviously a limit as to what I could travel with, so I needed to ensure I included the essentials. Before I knew it, the day had arrived and I was standing in the airport, clutching my bags and feeling more than a little

## ULTRA CRAZY

apprehensive about what was to come.

Once I arrived in the Canaries, Eddie picked me up from the airport and we drove back to the villa. I had never been to Lanzarote before; in fact, I had hardly left the UK at that point in my life. I stared out of the car window at the mountains that surrounded us as we travelled along the winding island roads. I loved the fact that the air felt warm on my skin; after leaving the freezing UK, it was very welcome. If only I could forget about the ultra distance triathlon I was attempting in a few days...

At Eddie's place, I put my bags into my room and sat down at the table with Eddie, Lynn and Steve to eat a meal that Lynn had prepared for us. Now, sitting at a table with three people who have already swum the English Channel is not the best thing to do when you are feeling a little nervous about your own attempt. Sitting at a table with two people who have already completed the Arch to Arc isn't great either. Talk about feeling the pressure.

On top of that, I wasn't feeling too good. I had started coming down with a cold in England – not the sort of cold that stops you from doing anything, but not what you want before starting such a tough challenge, one that would potentially have me in the sea for 10 hours. So it was decided to delay the start for 24 hours to give me the best chance of finishing.

To properly test the event, Eddie and Steve planned to do it alongside me. This was a real honour, but also a little intimidating as I felt so inexperienced compared to them. When the time came for us to start, we pulled our trainers on, applied Vaseline to sensitive parts (the boys, not me) and started the 45-mile run. We began the

## ULTRA CRAZY

challenge at 6pm, which would give us 12 hours to complete the run and 2 hours' rest before starting the swim at 8am the next day. In the real Arch to Arc, you would rest anywhere between 4-12 hours before starting your swim, depending on the pilot, the tides and your own goals (whether you were trying for the record or not).

Running 45 miles is never going to be easy, but doing this with the boys was a real laugh. Only on the last lap of our course at El Golfo, when all three of us had niggles and the tiredness started to kick in, did the laughing stop; until then it was fantastic. When we got back to the villa, I was feeling pretty grim. During the last 5 miles I had started to feel very sick and I hadn't taken on any fluids or food. I also had a sore foot and mentally wasn't in a great place. I tried to eat or sleep, but could do neither.

If I'm honest, the thought of swimming for 9-10 hours in the sea was scaring the shit out of me. The nearer the time came, the worse I felt. It was still dark outside and in hindsight that also played a big part in the negativity I was feeling. So I decided to pull out of the event. Telling Eddie and Steve this was very hard, and although they said they understood, the looks on their faces suggested otherwise.

We drove down to the sea and Steve and Eddie started their swim. I was feeling really bad, mentally and physically, and was finding it very hard to support the boys. I felt that I should have been swimming with them and that I had let them and myself down big time. I tried to have a sleep in the car at one point, then decided that I had to do it and made Lynn drive all the way back to the villa to get my wetsuit. I was aware that I was acting like a complete idiot, but couldn't seem to stop myself. I got in the sea and did a lap and a half before realising that there was no way I would finish in the light and that my heart just wasn't in it. I got out and gave myself a bit of a talking to, then concentrated on supporting the guys for the rest of their swim.

Once they were finished, we headed back to the villa for a rest and some food. Steve and Eddie started the bike at 9pm, with me and Lynn supporting. This part of the race was really hard for all concerned, as the weather started to get worse and worse. Watching the boys almost get blown off their bikes while getting soaked by the storm was very hard. When they would come in for a break and some food, it was all I could do to stop myself from pleading with them to stop. They looked so incredibly exhausted, but I knew they would never give up.

I went to bed feeling shattered, although fairly content, but when I woke up the next day, which was actually the afternoon, I felt very different. Something in me had changed and I knew I had to do the Lanzarote Ultra before I flew home. I went for a walk with Steve and I told him how I felt when we stopped off in a café. To his credit, he didn't even blink; he just said that he would support me no matter what, and then set about sorting out timescales and changing flight times. I then had the tricky job of explaining to various family members back home why I couldn't possibly return yet, and a fair amount of begging and apologising went on over the next 24 hours.

I have to say that from the start of this second attempt, I felt completely different, really happy and positive. It never entered my head at any time, during any part of the challenge, that I wouldn't finish.

## ULTRA CRAZY

I started the 45-mile run (again) on Thursday at 12pm; this was to give me enough time to complete it, as we all thought that with the lack of recovery, my foot injury and the blisters I got on the first run, it would take me a lot longer to finish. Apart from needing a little foot maintenance and a couple of painkillers at the 2-hour mark, I found this run to be easier than the first. I did take it a little slower, but after a while we realised that I would have to have a couple of longer breaks in order to get me back to the villa for my maximum 5 hours' rest and then a 7am start to allow maximum daylight for the swim. I didn't mind this, as my time was not an issue at this point. Finishing was the only goal.

At one point, I remember running (OK, maybe I was walking) up a big mountain and looking up at the stars whilst singing some random songs to myself. I felt a little mad, but in a good way. I was getting so much support from everybody via my phone and the Enduroman forum; I felt people really cared about what I was doing. I had a reasonably long food break at the villa and then started on the last lap of El Golfo. If there was a low point on the run, I guess this was it. Steve couldn't really stop here as it would have been too dangerous, and so it was just me running alongside the dark black lava fields, completely on my own.

It was then that a phone call from my best friend, Claire, was exactly what I needed. She convinced me that there weren't really any lava monsters, and at 34 I really shouldn't be scared of imaginary things anyway. Once I got off the coastal road, Steve was able to drive behind me again, which was a great relief to both of us.

I was on the last hour of the run when I noticed a car driving towards me. The driver didn't seem to be paying much attention to me or

## ULTRA CRAZY

my flashing head-torch, so I had to jump off the road to get out of his way. This would have been fine if it weren't for the whole spiky lava field thing going on. There is just no give in that stuff. So now I had a bloody leg, which actually hurt quite a bit. I sat on the side of the road for a minute and questioned my sanity, then got up and finished the run.

I don't know what or even *if* I ate after the run. I think I slept, but I don't recall that either. The only thing I remember is driving down to the sea and putting on my wetsuit in the car park. And then we sat waiting for it to get light. I was nervous, but not too bad all things considered. As soon as the sun started to rise, we pulled the canoe from the car roof and walked down to the water's edge.

Getting into the sea at first light, after a very long run and no sleep, did not feel great. But I was surprised how quickly I settled into my stroke. I used a few large objects to sight on, and when Steve wasn't in the canoe, he would feed me from the steps on the shore at the end of each lap.

After about 3 hours of swimming, I noticed that I was getting thrown about a bit, but didn't think much of it. A couple of my training swims had been a little rough, so I was prepared for some chop. But the next time I got to the steps, Steve asked me to get out of the water and sit down. As I sat shivering and throwing tea over myself, he broke the news that we would have to move the remainder of my swim to a smaller, more sheltered bay about ten minutes' walk away. Steve told me later that the lifeguard had instructed him that he would have stop the swim if the conditions got any worse.

I was quite pleased about this location move, until Steve worked

## ULTRA CRAZY

out that I still had to do 17 laps. I know it's all just miles and time, but having started the swim concentrated on doing 12 laps (of the bigger bay), it was now hard to get my head around the increase. The cold had started to really get to me now and my appetite just disappeared. This is normal for me, but I know Steve was worried and was doing his best to make me eat and drink.

I got colder and colder and I was barely talking by this point. It was all I could do to keep turning my arms over and trying to kick a little to warm myself up. My jaw ached from my teeth chattering so much, and my neck was raw from the salt and wetsuit rubbing at it. However, the support and messages I got from home were great; they made me laugh and took my mind off the endless laps.

With 4 laps to go, I got it in my head for some reason that Steve would tell me that I only had 2 left to swim. I looked at him, hopefully, but he told me to swim on. I was crushed. 4 laps seemed just too long at that point in the event, almost unbearably so.

Eventually, I finished the last lap and hauled myself out of the water. Almost as soon as I was on my feet, I fell down again, crashing into the shallow water. I was so dizzy after swimming for nearly 10 hours. I was, however, incredibly happy to have finished the longest and hardest swim of my life.

The run was hard, the swim was harder, but the bit before getting on my bike was the toughest part of it all.

I felt really, really bad.

Everything hurt; I couldn't eat and I felt so sick. The thought of

## ULTRA CRAZY

riding a bike over a tough, hilly 90-mile course was unthinkable. I just couldn't imagine how I was going to being able to do it. Still, I was hardly going to stop now, and at 10.15pm I got on my bike, shaking all over the place, and started to ride. Strangely, by the time I got 3 or 4 miles into the ride, I felt absolutely fine. In fact, I remember shouting to Steve about wanting some chips!

The rest of the ride is a bit of a blur. I remember seeing things that weren't there, riding some big hills and stopping for a couple of desperately needed naps in the back of the van, but not much else. Riding to the Mirador at the top of the highest mountain in Lanzarote, with the wind blowing so hard, and wondering if anybody had actually been blown off the mountain before, did stick in my mind. Steve said, watching from the van, that even *his* heart skipped a beat a few times. The only good thing about it was that because it was dark, I couldn't see the 1,000ft drop just to my left...

I cycled on through the night and into an amazing sunrise. At one point, just after it got light, I looked down at my bike computer and realised that I was doing over 40mph. 'Pretty cool', I thought at the time. But after the event, I decided that was more than a little reckless and could have had some interesting consequences.

Finally, after 44 hours and 17 minutes (and a bit of a false start), I finished the Lanzarote Ultra. I had lost weight, some hair and a couple of toenails. I laughed, cried and bled. I completely lost my confidence, but then found it again. I also learnt a lot about myself, and what I was truly capable of doing when I really want to.

It was a perfect end to a year of decent endurance training and events, and I felt super prepared to take on the Arch to Arc the following year.

After a break over the Christmas and New Year period, I got back to my training. This was mainly swimming, with some long bikes and runs to break up the monotony of the pool. Although I had completed the Lanzarote Ultra, it had highlighted the fact that my sea swimming was far too slow for the English Channel. I needed to swim at around 2mph; otherwise, I wouldn't be strong enough for the tides and would find myself going backwards. I also needed to work on my cold-water acclimatisation. So during the early months of this year, I swam intervals in the pool, working on getting faster, then would go down to the sea on Sunday mornings to brave the icy waters.

The cold-water training was particularly hard. Although I have a bit of padding on my bum and thighs, my top half has always been on the skinny side. This is the worst body type to have as an open-water swimmer, as it's your internal organs which need the heat. Wearing a wetsuit obviously helps, but for the short, cold dips from January to April, it simply wasn't worth the time and struggle putting it on, then trying to take it off when you have hypothermia and your hands or fingers don't work.

*Let me digress briefly and tell you about how my first few winter swims felt like…*

*Walking down to the prom, I look at the water and my stomach does that weird, flippy thing. That's the nerves. That's my brain telling me that I'm about to do something really stupid. And painful.*

## ULTRA CRAZY

*I stand by the beach huts, find a place to put my bag and begin to undress. As I reach a state of almost complete nakedness, normal people walk by and stare at me. And not in a good way.*

*Once I'm only wearing a very small swimming costume, I add some accessories. The purists will add nothing but a thin latex hat and some goggles. But I'm not that hardcore, so I put on some thick neoprene booties for my delicate feet and a big woolly hat. Because, let's be honest, I'm not putting my face in 6-degree water. Not today, anyway. Gloves are a good idea too, but they're maybe a step too far in the wimp department, so I put them back in my bag.*

*By this point I have run out of excuses. There is simply nothing left for me to do but walk down to the sea. Really, really slowly. Keeping my eyes locked on the water, as the small waves might suddenly turn into 10-foot monsters and wipe out whole families walking their dogs. But at least then I would have a decent excuse not to get in the water.*

*I am now at the point where I have to actually get in. I would look really stupid if I didn't. Other swimmers are already in the sea. And some of them are swimming properly, faces in the water and everything. I try not to feel intimidated by them. It doesn't work. But I can do this, I just need to get in...*

*The water is cold, but I expected that. What I didn't expect is the pain. Searing, white-hot pain which cuts through to your bones. I can hear someone making really stupid noises. And then realise that person is me. I can't seem to stop this though and actually, it helps, so the noises continue. The deeper I go, the more it hurts. And then the swearing starts. Hopefully there are no small children*

## ULTRA CRAZY

*on the beach, because now you are cursing like a crazy woman.*

*And just when I think I can't take any more, something happens that I didn't expect. The pain recedes. And in its place is a warm feeling, a good feeling. This is a little disconcerting, but I don't question it, I'll take anything over the bone-deep agony. I'm now enjoying this swim, splashing around and laughing. See, it's not so hard, what was all the fuss about?*

*This is the point where you need to be careful. It's like summit fever for cold-water swimmers. When you start feeling warm in 7-degree water, it's time to get out. And once out, you can't mess around. Get out of your swimsuit and into warm clothes as quickly as possible.*

*Easier said than done though, as I now seem to have lost all power in my hands and fingers. I also have no control over my limbs and feel a little drunk. It's like I know what I'm doing, but things feel a little fuzzy round the edges.*

*Also, from leaving the sea to returning to my belongings, I have precisely 2.5 minutes to get changed before The Shivering starts. Once it does, I can forget trying to put my jumper or socks on. And I don't even attempt underwear. That's never going to happen. Finally, about two hours later, I'm dressed. Exhausted, but dressed. I throw some hot tea over myself, and my sea swim is done!*

*I just need to walk up the zig-zags to where my car is parked. This sounds simple enough, but the hills have turned into mountains and I can't breathe. I normally run up here, but not today, Satan. Once again, normal people are staring at me, but this time because I'm wearing so many items of clothing I can barely move. And I have a*

## ULTRA CRAZY

*big, woolly hat on. And a DryRobe, obviously.*

*When I finally make it home, I lie on the sofa like I've just returned from trekking to the South Pole. I close my eyes, just for five minutes, I tell myself. An hour and a half later, I awake to find myself still in a DryRobe and sweating, profusely.*

*That is how it feels.*

---

As the water warmed up, my sea swims got longer and moved from down the road in Bournemouth to Weymouth, where the Enduroman training boat was moored. Swimming with boat support was invaluable as part of my Channel training. The most important lesson was how to be fed from a large, listing vessel without being completely being freaked out. I found it very intimidating, especially in choppy water, to have to stop next to the boat, which loomed over me, and try to grab a milk bottle filled with hot, sweet tea, and drink as quickly as possible from it. I had to be treading water while doing this and also attempt to eat half a banana or some other tasty treat. This was harder still, because I always felt sick from an hour into the swim and food was the last thing I wanted. But I knew if you don't feed, you don't finish. So I kept at it.

One positive aspect from my boat support training was that I got away from the shore and truly experienced sea swimming in all its glory, from the waves smashing me in the face to the mouthfuls of disgusting salty water that I tried, and failed, not to swallow, while constantly watching the crew on the boat and wondering when it was time for the next feed. Or better still, when it was time for the

## ULTRA CRAZY

ladder to be lowered into the water and I would be pulled out from my own personal hell that was a 6-hour sea swim.

All of these swims were hard, but some were truly confidence-destroying. These were when the winds were high and waves seemed to come from every direction, making it impossible to find any rhythm in my stroke. And when I stopped for a feed, it would be mostly sea water that I took on. I hated these training swims. And as more good swims turned into bad swims, the lower my confidence became and the worse I got. Every Sunday, I would wake up feeling dread in the pit of my stomach. As I made the drive to Weymouth, the feeling grew more intense. I would be feeling sick before I even stepped on the boat.

The last swim I did with the Enduroman boat was supposed to be a 6-hour session. Walking down to the jetty, I already knew the state of the sea. Driving along the coast, I could see I was in for a battering. 'It's the best training,' I told myself. But it was no good; I was feeling very low and fearful that morning.

When I stepped on the boat, I couldn't look any of the crew or other swimmers in the eyes. I felt like a failure before I had even got in the water. Once we were in wetsuits, hats and goggles, the boat left the harbour and drove into the open sea. It was as bad as I thought; we rocked from side to side, barely able to stay on our feet. Once in position, me and another couple of swimmers dropped over the side into the water and began to swim.

I tried. I really did. But my head was in a bad place before I even got my feet wet that day. I think I lasted an hour and a half…

## ULTRA CRAZY

One of the other swimmers was throwing up because it was so rough. But he did this barely breaking his stroke. I was in awe of him. I was pulled from the water and dumped, unceremoniously, onto the deck. The crew had lost patience with me and didn't hide their feelings that day. Once dressed, I sat shivering and feeling sorry for myself. My mind was spinning. How could I do the Arch to Arc when I couldn't even swim for 6 hours in choppy water?

Over the next few weeks, I tried again and again to swim, but all my open-water fears were back, in full force. One day, on the beach in Bournemouth, I just sat and cried. I hadn't even lasted 10 minutes that day before panic had overwhelmed me and I struggled from the waves. I knew in my heart that I was nowhere near ready to swim the English Channel in a few months' time, and I had no choice but to withdraw from the event. It broke my heart.

Around this time, I met someone I thought was perfect for me. We got on really well and he loved ultra endurance triathlon. I thought I had met 'the one'. Looking back, there were all the signs of my repeating old patterns and being drawn into another controlling, abusive relationship. But I ignored every one.

For the first three months, everything was perfect. He would do everything for me, buying me gifts and generally spoiling me whenever he could. He would make the four-hour drive from where he lived to see me as often as possible. We talked about moving in together and he put in a transfer request to move his job to Dorset. He even proposed.

Things couldn't be better. That was until the three months was up. From then on, it was almost like a switch had been flicked and he changed, quite dramatically.

I started to notice how he was jealous of my then eight-year-old son, Jake. He would make odd comments about him and always try to get between us if we were sitting together. His moods would swing wildly from being really happy to angry and depressed. And I never knew what I had done to trigger them. I would be walking on eggshells when he was like this.

The rows between us became more and more frequent and increased in intensity. He was starting to really scare me. I actively began to change my own behaviour around this time. I was hyper aware of his moods and as soon as I sensed an argument was brewing, I would withdraw and become quiet. I thought that he couldn't have a fight on his own, so as long as I kept my mouth shut, things couldn't escalate.

He was fiercely protective of his phone, but one evening when he went to the bathroom, a message popped up on the screen which was clearly from another woman, saying how much she missed him and couldn't wait to see him again. That night, I did not stay quiet and screamed at him, demanding to know the truth. Somehow, he managed to convince me that I was in the wrong and that he was not cheating. To this day, I still don't know how. He was a very clever man, and I was massively out of my depth.

The controlling behaviour only got worse from then on. He somehow made me fall out with my parents and I also started to withdraw from my friends. There were comments about my appearance and he would either lavish attention on me or not touch me for days. He was a compulsive liar too, coming up with elaborate stories which

## ULTRA CRAZY

made him look good and quite often, me bad. Throughout all of this though, he ensured he was the centre of my world and that nobody else mattered. And I let him.

Then I finally woke up.

Jake and I had just returned from swimming one afternoon during the summer holidays when I received a call from my daughter's friend's mum. Jessica had got drunk. Not just a little bit drunk either. She was in a real state. I went round to pick her up, but once I saw her, I realised that I was going to need some help. She was around thirteen then and about the same size as me, and there was no way I could lift her up. And there was no way she could walk.

I had to call my parents, whom I hadn't spoken to in a while, mainly because my mum had warned me that my boyfriend was bad news and she was concerned about my children. I had flown off the handle at this and we had fallen out. None of this mattered now though. When they heard the panic in my voice, they came straight over to help.

Once we were back home, I settled Jess on the sofa with towels and a bucket and tried to get her to drink some water. But something wasn't right. She kept slipping into unconsciousness, her eyes rolling and her speech slurring badly. I decided to call an ambulance, something I had never done before and couldn't believe I was doing now. Once the paramedics arrived, they checked her over and agreed things were serious. Jessica's blood pressure was dropping and they wanted to take her to the hospital.

The male paramedic made a comment about my not keeping a close enough eye on her and how she shouldn't have been allowed to get into this condition. I was gobsmacked, but said nothing. Of course I felt responsible, but she had never done anything like this before and I didn't see it coming.

We were then blue-lighted to Poole Hospital. I sat in the back of the ambulance, with Jess lying on the bed, muttering about her shoe, which had fallen off. I reached down to get it and she sat bolt upright and looked at me. Without slurring her words, she said very clearly, 'you love him more than you love us.'

I was stunned.

She then lay back down, once again muttering about her shoe. An icy cold feeling came over me. I knew what she said was how she had been feeling and the reason why she had got so drunk that afternoon. She was desperately trying to get my attention, to wake me up.

And boy, was I awake now. In fact, I was wide awake. What the fuck had I been thinking, putting this disgusting excuse for a man before my precious children? Things had to change.

We broke up pretty soon after that and I discovered that, obviously, he had been seeing someone else. Although I knew it deep down, that hit me hard. He continued to tell lies about me, trying to turn people I knew in the ultra triathlon world against me, which I found really hard to deal with. It made me withdraw even more. A few months later, I also found out that his new girlfriend was pregnant.

As much as I knew I had done the right thing, I felt really low and was really struggling to pull myself together. Every day I pulled myself out of bed and tried to be positive, but deep down I just felt lost. How had I allowed myself to get into this situation again?

Over the months that followed, I bounced from one crazy idea to another, entering ultra runs I had no chance of finishing and even trying to set up my own version of the Arch to Arc. When my ex heard about that, he sent me a text saying that he 'couldn't wait to watch me fail'. Those words played over in my head for a very long time after that.

My self-esteem was at an all-time low and my drinking became heavier still. I just didn't know what to do with the negative emotions that swirled around my brain from the moment I woke up and until I fell unconscious. Mainly from drinking too much.

One evening, nursing a glass of wine and feeling sorry for myself, I started looking back at all my previous relationships. Apart from Jake's dad, Mark, they had all been disasters, and three of them had been mentally and physically abusive. It was time to make a change. It was time to stop.

I decided then to avoid getting into any further relationships until I felt like I was in a better place.

And although I didn't know it at the time, that wouldn't be for another eight years.

# LIFE LESSON
# LISTEN TO THE VOICES IN YOUR HEAD

Not all of them. Not the ones that tell you that you really need a large Pepperoni pizza, potato wedges, chicken wings AND ice cream. But do listen to the ones that are trying to tell you something important.

I believe that we humans have stopped learning how to use our basic instincts.

Years back, I was out running with my Jack Russell, Honey. We were in a quiet part of the forest near where I lived, and normally we would rarely come across other people. But on this day, a man came over a hill and started walking towards us. I immediately felt something was wrong, but told myself to stop being silly and that I was just overreacting. Honey, on the other hand, being an animal, always relied on and listened to her instincts. She stopped dead in her tracks and growled loudly at the stranger. Right then, I decided to take a different path and called Honey to follow me.

What would have happened that day if we hadn't acted? More than likely, nothing. But something wasn't right about that man, and we both knew it. What struck me though was the difference between animals and humans when it comes to instincts. Dogs don't think, 'I'd better not growl at this bloke, because I might hurt his feelings, or maybe I'm just being silly'. They just feel something is wrong and react.

Now, I'm not suggesting that every time we feel something isn't right, we should bark at people. But I am saying that we need to learn to listen to those strong feelings we have got into the habit of ignoring, mainly because it's easier at the time or we want to be polite. Instincts are there for a reason.

**How can you use this advice in life?**

Are you in a relationship that isn't right? You don't need to be being physically hurt for it to be an abusive relationship. Abuse comes in many different forms. Are you drinking too much or relying on any other stimulants to get through the day? How about your diet? Too much sugar and junk food? Your instincts will tell you. You just need to be able to listen and be honest with yourself. Once you have done that, you can make the changes you need to improve your life and health.

**How can this apply to your training for races or challenges?**

Learn to be honest with yourself about your training and preparation. Are you doing enough or even too much? Is the training specific and helping you improve your weak areas, or are you just turning out the junk mileage because you enjoy long, slow runs? Is your diet right or are you ignoring a niggle which could turn into something more serious?

**When to ignore the voices**

Sometimes, when things are hard, like during the latter stages of a marathon or ultra run, or halfway through that college course or diet you started, the voices will suggest that you give up. I call these the whiny voices. They will tell you that you don't really need to lose those 10lbs, and that curves are really in right now. They will try to make you believe that you aren't really better off with the qualification which could help you improve your career. You need to be smart then and know the difference between your instincts and your mind looking for an easy way out.

During one event, which I had already failed once before, I was part-way through the swim section. It was a Triple Iron distance triathlon and I had already completed just over 3 miles of the 7-mile swim. I was feeling the cold and had started to shiver. The voices in my head began to tell me that I should give up and get out of the water. My instincts, however, knew that I needed to just keep swimming. That yes, it was cold, but I had completed this distance before and in water of a similar temperature. Yes, it was hard, but I could do it.

The voices I was hearing in the chilly, murky lake that morning weren't my instincts. They were the whiny voices, and I knew it. They were telling me that I was too cold and that I didn't need to put myself through this. And I didn't really want to finish this race anyway. That day, the whiny voices won and I found myself in the showers, peeling off my wetsuit. Later, once I was changed and sitting in my crew tent, I deeply regretted my decision.

Learning the difference (and similarities) between the voices that are trying to help you and the ones that are trying to derail you takes time and experience. But once you learn how to differentiate between them, you will be able to use them to progress through challenges and grow.

Personally, I know I need to do a lot of cold-water prep in order to succeed in certain events, because I don't manage the cold very well. But it's very hard to plunge into freezing water or spend hours shivering in the sea. So where my instincts tell me to get it done, my whiny voices tell me not to. It's sneaky, so be careful...

So to become an expert in your own voices, you just need to spend time practicing and learning. The most important thing is to listen.

## CHAPTER 6
# I BECOME A TRAMP

I remember where I was when I realised that my drinking was not normal.

I was standing in the tiny living room of my rented flat, which was situated in a rough part of Bournemouth, not known to be the safest of places. I was looking out of the small window down onto the high street below and knew in my heart that I had a problem.

I was eighteen years old.

It took me until I was thirty-nine to finally hit that clichéd 'rock bottom' when I was able to give it up – that was twenty-one years of drinking.

I became an expert at living a double life. It was exhausting, but somehow I managed it. In those years, I had two marriages, two divorces, two children; ran businesses, completed marathons, ultras, Ironman races and even a Double Ironman. I dealt with abuse, financial and family problems and I tried to cope with an eating disorder. I was the ultimate high-functioning alcoholic.

I wasted so much time and energy trying to hide this horrible, shameful secret of mine. The secret was that once I started drinking, I simply couldn't stop. In the last few years of my addiction, I became extremely self-destructive, drinking huge amounts at a time. Some mornings I was surprised that I actually woke up at all. I was drink-driving, getting into huge debt and constantly putting myself in dangerous situations.

## I BECOME A TRAMP

One afternoon, before the kids were back from school, a mate from work came round to cheer me up after we had recently found out we might be made redundant from our jobs at the local printers. He was a big drinker like me and had decided that the best way to deal with the bad news we had just been given was to drown our sorrows.

In Jägerbombs.

Despite my years of experience, I had never actually had one of these, but I was a big fan of Red Bull, so was keen to try it out. But me being me, it was never going to be just one…

A few hours later, we were absolutely off our faces. My young son came home from school with his best friend, Peter. He was a perfect little boy from a perfect family home, where I can guarantee his mother never rolled around the floor giggling or danced on the table to the Inspiral Carpets at three in the afternoon. And she definitely didn't do vodka shots while smoking cigarettes and trying to cook fish fingers.

The fish fingers got burnt. And my mate went home, leaving me to pretend that I was sober to my son and his friend, who looked a little shell-shocked, unsurprisingly. The rest of the afternoon was a blur and the next thing I remember was waking up on the sofa, the boys nowhere to be found. In a panic, tears streaming down my face, I rushed round to my neighbour and close friend, Isabel, hoping she could help.

She opened the door and there, sitting eating their tea, were the boys, alongside Isabel's own son. She never judged me and had

## I BECOME A TRAMP

even told the boys that I was ill so Perfect Peter wouldn't go home and tell his mother what had happened and what a terrible mother I was.

I truly hated myself for moments like that. And there were plenty of them. My kids always supported me though, always gave me the biggest hugs when I apologised again, holding my head in my hands, promising that I would be a better mum to them. They assured me that I was the best mum in the world and that they loved me, no matter what. I had to be better, but was caught in a trap which I just couldn't seem to break free from.

Below are some extracts from a diary I briefly kept while trying, and failing, to control my addiction. It's painful reading at times, but shows the nature of the trap I was caught in.

### *August 3rd*

*It's Saturday and I'm sat at my desk, drinking coffee. The sun is shining and I haven't had to take any painkillers today. Last night I had my 'last drink' (yeah... like I've never done that before) and this morning I poured the rest down the sink (there was quite a lot of vodka left, surprisingly).*

*Today I have to deal with the stuff I have been hiding from over the last week. I need to clean the house and generally sort myself out. Yesterday was a very low day. I had drunk about a bottle and a half the night before, slept for a few hours and then woke at 3am and finished off the rest of the wine (another bottle and a half). Obviously, I felt like shit for the rest of the day and even though I*

## I BECOME A TRAMP

*tried to hide under the duvet and ignore the phone, I couldn't. The call I took made me aware of some big problems at work and I fell apart. I couldn't hide it from my boss, but to his credit, he just got on with sorting out the mess I had made. (He phoned me later to see if I was alright, which only made me cry, again). After the work thing had been dealt with, I dropped my son off at the cinema and went to buy my depression survival kit. Not healthy food and a good book, but crisps, films and vodka.*

*I came home and got drunk again.*

*This has become my life. Depression, drinking and loneliness. I am a parent, I have my own business and also work very long hours for another company, and I have achieved quite a lot, especially in endurance challenges. But I think if people really knew what was going on, they wouldn't believe it. The happy, positive, do-anything girl is privately falling apart. I'm so ashamed of myself.*

### August 4th

*Feeling a little better... Less crazy.*

*Did a 10-mile run today. Sort of by accident; meant to do 3 or 5, but felt the need to punish myself! Have managed a little work. Completely lost my mojo – normally I'm a workaholic, but I just want to lie and read or watch TV. Not a great month to feel like this, as very busy and I have huge pressure to make things succeed. I think (I know) that this is why part of me wants to escape into a large bottle of vodka, just to try and forget everything.*

*Reading other people's drinking blogs, I realise that this is a very*

## I BECOME A TRAMP

*common theme. You don't even have to be having a very hard life, but it's easier to not feel anything too intensely, I think. Fear... sadness... loneliness... rejection. I have a lot of these feelings at the moment and it's preferable to not really 'feel' them. Obviously, the self-hatred and hangovers are not helping the situation, so I need to just feel stuff and when it gets too hard, go and run stupid miles, so I'm too tired to think and too knackered to crave. I really, really hope my enthusiasm for my work returns tomorrow, otherwise I'm in trouble!*

*Being sober is great because waking up without the horrible self-hatred and depression is bliss. Drinking sucks because I can never, ever get enough of it.*

### *August 5th*

*Very stressful day today, trying to do everything I need to do (which is A LOT). I started at 6am and won't finish till late tonight :-(*
*I went shopping for my daughter's birthday party, which is tomorrow, and I was doing OK, but then later on, when I became more tired and hungry, the cravings almost got to me. It would be so easy to say, 'well, I deserve it' or 'nobody really knows or cares whether I stop drinking or not'. But I didn't... I cooked a curry and had a bath.*

*I have my ex-father-in-law's funeral and daughter's party tomorrow, whilst trying to deal with work. Not going to be an easy day.*

### *August 8th*

*So I ended up drinking again. What a surprise. Pretty much drank*

## I BECOME A TRAMP

*from dawn till dusk yesterday, so you can imagine how bad I'm feeling today, and I have so much to do. And loads of people relying on me this weekend for an event and I'm really scared about letting everyone down.*

*What if this is how I'm going to die? Fuck it, why can't I stay stopped?*

---

One of the worst things which began to happen as I got older and was drinking more and more were the panic attacks. They got so bad, due to the huge amounts of alcohol I was consuming, that towards the end stage of my addiction, my life became unbearable.

It got to the point where leaving the house was impossible.

But I was running my own business and also around that time had a full-time job which required me to attend meetings. On one particular day, I was feeling awful and my anxiety levels were sky-high. Part-way through the meeting, I started to feel the familiar waves of panic rise. I tried so hard to squash them down, to control my breathing and ignore the adrenaline that was now flooding my body. But it was impossible and I leapt up, muttered an excuse and ran to the toilets.

Once the door was shut, I leant against it and breathed deeply. What the fuck was wrong with me? Why was I having panic attacks in a small meeting with people I knew well? It wasn't as if I was standing in front of a thousand people, giving a speech. I looked down at my hands, which were shaking; how was I going to go

## I BECOME A TRAMP

back out there and pretend I was normal? And more importantly, how was I going to continue to do my job in this state?

It wasn't just my work that the panic attacks affected either…

I was a single parent, and these issues made life very hard. I had real responsibilities – I needed to pick the kids up from various places, like school, clubs and friends' houses. I also needed to buy food and generally get shit done. I couldn't be hiding at home, with huge, self-inflicted anxiety. I became flaky, cancelling plans and making excuses. Anything to get out of being with other people. If I was home, I was safe.

At least I thought I was.

When I started getting serious panic attacks at home, on my own, I knew I was in trouble. Now I had nowhere to run. Before, my house was my sanctuary, but now, that too became hell.

During the last year of struggling with my addiction, I went away with a family friend I had known all my life. He was a father figure, in place of my own mainly absent dad. I trusted him implicitly, going to him whenever I needed advice. He was, in my eyes, one of the only men in my life whom I could trust 100%, and I thought the absolute world of him.

We were going to the Lake District as he knew the area far better than I did and I was organising an event for a high-profile clothing company that summer and wanted to get the routes right. We had booked a B&B, but for the second night of our stay, they were full, so did we mind sharing a room? My gut feeling was that it was not

## I BECOME A TRAMP

appropriate, but I told myself not to be silly; this man had known me as a baby and was like an uncle to me. So I agreed to the second night being in a shared room, assuming he would naturally sleep on the couch or floor.

Walking the mountain trails during the day, chatting easily about races and previous adventures we had both had, was enjoyable and I put my concerns to one side. 'Not every man is bad, Claire,' I told myself. That evening we ate well and drank a lot. He was a heavy drinker too, so we indulged a little bit more than we should. The next day's walking was a little harder for me, with a sore head and dry mouth. When we got back to the B&B, he moved his suitcase into my room and my uneasy feeling returned.

I don't recall whether it was before we went downstairs to eat or after, but he sat on the bed and put his arm around me, telling me how special I was, how attractive I was and how much he thought of me. I felt sick to my stomach as I realised that he didn't see me as a daughter or a niece; he saw me as a woman he wanted to sleep with. I felt like a stupid little girl, scared, and desperately wanted to go home, but I was hundreds of miles away and in a situation I didn't know how to handle.

So I did what I did best. I pretended it wasn't happening. That night, after drinking too much again, I lay on the very edge of the bed with every inch of my body covered with a jumper, pyjamas and socks. He lay next to me in his underwear, putting his arms around me, trying to pull me closer and cuddle me. I was rigid and didn't sleep a wink.

When I think back to that night, I wonder why I didn't say

## I BECOME A TRAMP

something. Why didn't I say 'get your hands off me, stop talking like this and sleep on the floor like you should do?' Maybe I was trying to be polite, not make a fuss, and I questioned whether what I felt was very wrong *was* actually wrong. Maybe I was misunderstanding things…

The following day we drove home. That seven hours was the longest journey of my life. Once home, he kissed me on the cheek and said, 'thank you for a lovely time'. I had barely spoken to him since the night before, I was exhausted and terribly sad. I simply could not believe that he didn't know he had upset me.

After he had gone, I bought a large bottle of vodka and drank until I felt nothing. The problem with drinking though is that you wake up the next day and the problems have not gone, but have grown legs with the horrendous hangover you now have.

People closest to me started to realise that there was a problem, as I could no longer hide it. I was now very angry, not just with my 'uncle', but with all men in general. Years and years of inappropriate behaviour, physically and mentally abusive relationships, and issues with men I trusted had taken their toll. I was at the end of the road and could no longer hide what was happening to me. The alcohol was not helping and I knew it, but I drank more and more. I also started going out to pubs and clubs and began to pick fights with men. Never women, always men, and not small men either, the bigger the better. At that point, I literally had no concerns for my own safety.

And so it continued.

## I BECOME A TRAMP

I would have good weeks, and even good months sometimes, but it would always end up the same way. One morning, after a particularly bad night, I sat in my old beat-up Honda in a pub car park, shaking and crying. I knew that one of three things were going to happen if I continued like this:

1. I was going to end up in hospital
2. I was going to wake up in a police cell
3. I was going to die

I wasn't being dramatic; it was simply inevitable. And it shook me to my core.

At that point in my life, I realised that I had become that tramp on the park bench. You know the one? Sat there, drinking at nine in the morning. I used to look at them, thinking I would never be that way. I couldn't understand how someone could drink so early in the day. I wasn't like that. No, I would wait until 4pm at least before I would start drinking.

But in the last year or so of my addiction, I completely understood the tramp. As I stood in the shower, with my hands shaking, huge waves of anxiety washing over me, wondering how the fuck I was going to get through the day, a little voice in my head said, 'have a drink… Just a small one. It will stop the shakes…'

And right there and then, I became the tramp on the bench.

I didn't think it was possible to hate myself any more than I did, but I was now at an all-time low and something had to change. And so, after trying to give up countless times, I was finally able to stop.

## I BECOME A TRAMP

And stay stopped.

It was the day after Boxing Day. Christmas had been the normal mess that it always turned into. I would start with such good intentions, but as anyone with an alcohol addiction will tell you, it's the hardest time of the year as you are surrounded by the one thing you are trying to control – people encouraging you left, right and centre to 'have a drink'. Sometimes it was easier to lay low, to avoid the inevitable drama that my drinking so often created. But I would always screw it up somehow.

That day I woke up with what can only be described as the worst hangover I have ever experienced. I lay in the darkness of the early hours, clammy with sweat and my heart racing with panic. 'This is not a life', I thought, 'this is a living hell'. And the worst thing was that I was doing it to myself. Nobody held a gun to my head, forcing me to drink. I made that choice, day after day. I was caught in a trap, a vicious cycle of addiction, and I couldn't break free. I could never understand how I could complete such hard endurance events, run my business and be a strong single mum, and yet continue to be so weak around alcohol. I have never tried to commit suicide, but that morning, curled up in a ball in my bed, I honestly didn't want to go on any more. I was exhausted and broken. And I had no faith that I would ever be able to stop. Ending my life became a very real option to me around that time.

I would like to say that I saw a sign, or God spoke to me, but I'm an atheist, so that was never going to happen. In fact, nothing really happened. There was no big announcement, no 'I'm never drinking again'. There was no alcohol in the house to dramatically throw down the sink (mainly because I'd drunk it all the night before).

## I BECOME A TRAMP

And I didn't need to apologise or explain anything to anyone that day, as I was alone.

I simply made myself a cup of tea, sat on the sofa and thought, wearily, 'I'll try again'.

And that was it.

I won't say it was easy, because it definitely wasn't. The first few years, I was constantly struggling with temptation. A couple of times, I ended up buying a bottle of wine but was able to leave it, in the fridge, unopened. Until one bottle was drunk by my best friend and the other poured down the sink. I never took my sobriety for granted, not once. I knew that it could be gone in an instant; all that hard work would evaporate in the blink of an eye. I had to be constantly vigilant and on my guard for times when I would be overwhelmed by the desire to start drinking again.

One of the biggest problems I faced, now I was without my life-support, was that I had to experience my 'feelings'. This sucked, majorly. And was also something that I hadn't had to do since I was about thirteen. It is no coincidence that this was the age when I had felt so let down by some of the adults around me. The desire to get out of my head had started then and never let up. As with most addicts, I had been running from my demons my whole life. I now had to face them, stone-cold sober, and it didn't feel good.

But it wasn't just the past that I wasn't struggling with, it was day-to-day issues, like problems with my business or drama with the kids. Anything that was even a *little* bit stressful was almost too much for me, as I was so used to blurring the edges with alcohol. I

## I BECOME A TRAMP

had to learn how to be a functioning human being without leaning on a drug to help me through times when I was stressed or tired. Or any kind of emotion, it seemed. I felt like I had to be reprogrammed in some way. Nobody could help; no-one around me had the experience or understanding to support me. Like a lot of things, I had to do it on my own.

One of the biggest breakthroughs I had when I gave up drinking was making the food connection. I had in fact figured this out a long time ago, but never acted on it until I was really serious about getting sober. As someone who was constantly trying to control my calories, I realised that the hungrier I was, the more I craved alcohol. And, more importantly, if I ate a good meal during the latter part of the day, it would stop me from craving wine or vodka. When I was drinking, I knew that the buzz you got from alcohol hitting your empty stomach was pretty damn good and ruined by eating sensibly beforehand. But when I was trying to stay stopped, this became a life-saver. So I got into the habit of eating my main meal early in the day, so that when wine'o'clock came round, I was safe. Or as safe as I could be, in the early stages.

I also got a tip from someone I met on a forum who had given up a few years before me.

Eat Haribo, she had said, simply.

Bit odd, I thought.

The lady went on to explain that I would need something to replace the habit and also the sugar from my old addiction. And Haribo, or whatever sweets you like, hit the spot. A lot of people who smoke

## I BECOME A TRAMP

start to increase that habit when they give up alcohol. But as I had stopped smoking at the same time as drinking, it wasn't an option. So Haribo it was. And it really helped. Admittedly, my teeth weren't too thrilled, but in the grand scheme of things, I felt a few cavities were a small price to pay for kicking this addiction.

One thing that did take a major hit from my new lifestyle was relationships. And not just romantic ones either. Friends I had previously spent time with, drinking and dancing the night away, were now not so keen to hang out. People I socialised with who had kids stopped inviting me over, mainly because those weekends also included drinking. And as for boyfriends, I just decided that in the early years, it was better to avoid them completely, as I just figured that was never going to end well. I also simply couldn't imagine first dates, first kisses and what followed, sober. I had so many self-confidence issues that it was almost mandatory for me to be drunk in those situations. Once again, I had to reprogram myself, learn how to be human without a false sense of confidence. It was terrifying, so I put boyfriends on the back-burner.

I also avoided going out as much as I could, making up excuses whenever possible. But sometimes it was simply unavoidable, and then I had to drag myself to the restaurant or pub and sit nursing a Coke. Most social situations were fine, but Christmas parties or birthdays would be a nightmare. Quite a few drinks down the line, people would start to repeat themselves and slur their words. Conversations became tedious and I would clock-watch and look longingly at the door, wondering when I could escape without appearing rude.

The reward from enduring those nights, however, was the clear head

## I BECOME A TRAMP

I had the following day. When everyone else was suffering with their hangovers, I would go for a run or a kayak. It was moments like these when it would hit home just how life-changing this thing I had done really was. And as time went on, the more I realised that it wasn't just me who had been caught in a trap; so many people around me were stuck too.

As the scales fell from my eyes, the more I realised that alcohol wasn't how the clever marketing companies portrayed it. Beautiful, successful people, laughing and drinking. It was a drug. No different to cocaine or heroin. And it messed people's lives up and caused misery. It was also expensive and bad for your health. Once I was free, I struggled to find any positives about the thing that had once been the centre of my life.

And almost eight years on, giving up drinking is one of the best things I have ever done. It was harder than any Double Deca could ever be. Tougher than running a business, and at times lonelier than being a single parent. But totally worth it.

Oh, and when you haven't drunk for years, red wine smells absolutely disgusting.

## LIFE LESSON
# HOW TO STAY STOPPED

**Playing it to the end:**

When I crave, the first thing I do is play the scenario to the end, which is me the next morning with a horrible hangover, self-loathing and huge panic attacks. I got into this habit very early on and use it every single time I crave – visualise the end result.

**Seeing it for what it is:**

Alcohol is a drug. It really is that simple, and when you see it like that, your attitude changes. Drinking is no different to smoking weed or taking speed; it's just a socially accepted drug. I believe there will be a time when alcohol is not taking up two or three aisles in Tesco. Probably a long way off yet though!

**HALT:**

This comes from Alcoholics Anonymous, I think, but it makes total sense to me. I will crave when I am Hungry, Angry, Lonely or Tired, and when I get to that moment when I want to drink, I check which one/ones I am. It's mainly hungry, as low blood sugar is a big trigger for me.

**Feeling the feelings:**

When I first got sober, the biggest shock was having to actually feel emotions. Drinking (or any drug) is just a distraction from the moment you are in, and when you take that away, you have to feel it. I have found it fascinating to sit and really let myself 'feel' those emotions and try and understand them. Someone once said to me, 'nobody ever died from an emotion!' That's so true, but sometimes it feels like you will.

**Ride the craving:**

I always see it a bit like surfing. I'm on a surfboard and the craving is a wave. Ride it and feel it and let it pass. It always will. In the earlier months, when I was going through some really horrible stress, there were times when I said to myself, 'fuck it, I'm getting drunk later', but when that later came, I wouldn't want to blow all my hard work. I still use that technique every now and again, knowing that the craving will have passed by the time I can drink.

**Progression:**

This addiction WILL progress. You may think that you are not that person who has to drink in the morning, or whose hands shake, or who hides bottles around the house. I thought that too. Trust me, you will get there in the end! It's scary, and the sooner you understand that you are that person, the easier it is.

# CHAPTER 7
# A BRUTAL BUSINESS

Being in business, especially running one on your own, is not dissimilar to taking part in an ultra distance event. There will be a moment, probably during the night, when you will stop and wonder what the fuck you are doing and why you thought it was a good idea to even start it. Again, as with long races, you will need strong self-belief and the will to push on. You need to ignore the voices in your head telling you to stop, pack it in and stick to safer ambitions. It takes real guts to start something, be it a business or a 100-mile race, but it takes serious endurance and determination to stay the course, especially when things don't go the way you planned.

I didn't mean to start Brutal Events. I didn't sit down and make a business plan at my kitchen table (I don't even own a kitchen table). I also didn't take that business plan to my bank manager to ask for a loan, mainly because I knew I wouldn't get one. And I definitely didn't have any previous event management experience, whatsoever.

Brutal started purely accidentally.

Life had been a little unsettled since I had broken up with my ex and pulled out of the Arch to Arc. Before I had felt like the ultra endurance community was my family, a group of like-minded people with whom I could be myself. And now I didn't feel like I deserved to be amongst them. I felt lost and untethered. Drifting from one thing to another, trying to find something that made me feel right again.

## A BRUTAL BUSINESS

That morning, I was driving to North Wales, somewhere I had never been before, to run the Snowdonia Marathon. I rattled along in my old Ford KA, music blaring, completely unaware of what was about to happen. I drove past an adventure centre, rounded the corner and this incredible view unfolded in front of me.

It was like someone had just switched the lights on. I blinked, then opened and closed my mouth a few times. I had never seen scenery like this. It was, quite literally, breathtaking. I kept driving, a little slower now, and reached down and switched off my music. I turned another corner, and there was more. A stunning lake and huge, imposing mountains filled my vision. Then, to my surprise, tears filled my eyes. I wiped them away quickly. Embarrassed, as if people could see me.

Turning at the sign to Llanberis, I started to climb. The hill got steeper, forcing me to avert my gaze from the mountains and concentrate on the winding road. Higher and higher I drove, until I reached the top of the pass. Now I was driving down a steep decline, my foot hovering over the brake nervously. My eyes flicked from the road to the views on either side of the car. There were more mountains, with white streams of water rushing off them. And huge rocks lay scattered about the land, as if giant creatures from The Lord of the Rings had been fighting with them.

I made my way down the side of the pass and through a small village. My Satnav told me that I was only ten minutes from my destination. Getting closer, a large lake came into view, followed by another one. Severe looking purple rocks towered over them. I kept driving and eventually passed a large piece of stone with the words 'Llanberis' carved into it. I had arrived. Once I had found the

## A BRUTAL BUSINESS

car park, I got out and stretched my body, stiff from the long drive. There were hundreds of runners milling around and the familiar nervous energy filled the air.

Almost as soon as I had joined the queue for race registration, the skies went dark and the weather changed from blue sky and sun to wind and driving rain. Then, as quickly as it had changed, the sun returned again. Between then and the start of the race, we had three more storms. Then there was even more crazy weather. One minute we would be running along with the sun beating down on us; the next we were being pelting by icy rain. I loved the unpredictability of it. I also loved how tough it made the event. Running up the sides of mountains became even more challenging with the wind almost blowing you off your feet and rain running down the back of your jacket.

I finished the race in 5 hours and 11 minutes and I loved every second of it. Driving home with a huge smile on my face, I felt like things had shifted and something missing had returned. But how could I keep this feeling, I wondered to myself as I drove back down south, away from the mountains which had made such an impact on me. And now, navigating the dark lanes of Dorset, an idea that had been forming over the previous weeks, about setting up my own ultra triathlon, pushed into the forefront of my mind. What about setting up a race in Snowdonia? 'Don't be stupid', I said out loud, snapping myself out of my thoughts.

But that was the moment when The Brutal Triathlon was born. Over the following weeks and months, it evolved from an idea to an actual event, with a logo, distances and routes. Soon, and not without some trepidation, I announced my idea on the ultra triathlon

## A BRUTAL BUSINESS

forum. Most feedback was positive, some not so. My ex-boyfriend jumped in with spiteful comments about how this had been his idea and that I had stolen it. Initially this upset me, but with my new-found strength, I typed a carefully thought out reply and pressed the 'submit post' button. I didn't hear much from him after that.

Gwynedd Council requested that I attend a meeting, called ESAG (Events Safety Advisory Group). This was a little daunting to say the least. At the time, I was cleaning people's houses to make ends meet, so I arranged with my mum to have the kids overnight. Then I rushed through my early morning job and jumped in the car to make the six-hour drive to Llanberis. I was exhausted when I finally arrived and I was also quite nervous. I shook my head to myself; what was I thinking? Setting up an event in another part of the country, with no experience or money behind me? I had done some pretty stupid things in my past, but sitting in the council offices, with my hands still smelling of bleach, I came to the conclusion that this was one of the stupidest.

'Claire, you can come through now,' said a man in a grey suit. Holding out his hand, he introduced himself and despite his overall dull appearance, he had a twinkle in his eye that I liked immediately. Once in the room, I was surprised first by how big it was and secondly by how many people were in there. At least ten men sat in a semi-circle in front of me. I was introduced as Claire from The Brutal (I loved how the name sounded with a strong, Welsh accent) and I was then invited to start my presentation.

'My what?'

'Your presentation. The proposal about your event,' the council man said, his eyes narrowing slightly as he looked me over.

'Ah, of course,' I replied.

My brain was spinning. There had been nothing about this in the emails leading up to the meeting. I had thought it would just be me and a couple of guys chatting over the logistics and permissions for the race. But here I was, standing in front of a group of men – and wait, there was a fireman and a paramedic. And, oh shit, a policeman too. What the fuck had I got myself into? But at that moment, I knew that I had to blag like I had never blagged before. This event was happening; that was the only thing I was sure of. I didn't know when or even how at that point, but The Brutal was on.

Somehow, I managed to get through my 'presentation'. This involved me blushing and stumbling through my idea until the representatives of the council departments were, it seemed, kind of on the same page as me. Then there followed a lot of questions. Questions that I had never even thought of. And questions I didn't have answers to. Fortunately, this group of Welsh civil servants and emergency service employees had a good sense of humour. Once the formal part of the meeting was over, I was able to relax and laugh with them. Mainly about the absurdity of my idea.

Over the next 12 months, these meetings became a regular fixture in my diary. Did I have more than other event organisations? Probably. Maybe they could sense my inexperience, or perhaps it was just council procedure. I didn't ask; I just did as I was told. Those meetings, however, were a great experience for me. I absorbed everything and learnt so much about what you need to do to set up a race in North Wales. They helped with contacts and even the

## A BRUTAL BUSINESS

routes, suggesting at one point to reverse the run section around the lake, as it would be safer to climb *up* the slippery slate steps rather than down them. I put my ego aside, took notes and made changes.

My biggest stumbling blocks were competitor numbers and medical cover. The medical cover I needed, for the scale and complexity of my race, would require more than the St John's Ambulance people parked next to the event. No, the medics I wanted would be the type who climbed mountains and weren't phased by not sleeping for days at a time. I emailed some companies and as the quotes started to come in, realised I had a major problem. The prices were for thousands and thousands of pounds. At the time, the event was still on a very small scale. I had only planned to hold a Double Ironman triathlon, but when the costs started to mount up, and the entry numbers remained low, it was clear that I needed a serious rethink.

The first plan of action was to increase the number of race distances, which would hopefully increase participation numbers. So I added a Half and Full distance to the already planned Double and waited. It had the desired effect and the entries started to come in. I relaxed a little, as I now had a little more money in the budget. But it was still not enough to cover the vast medical quotes which covered my desk.

Just through chance, a friend of a friend got in touch and said that he might know someone who ran his own business. I knew that he was struggling a little and might be open to some kind of a deal…
I got the contact details from him and set about writing an email. The reply came back quickly and a meeting at their premises in Wrexham was set up. The owner, Brian, was an excitable man, full of enthusiasm and energy. He was keen to get involved and had

## A BRUTAL BUSINESS

already devised a plan. He suggested that we went into partnership; he would handle the medical side of the business and I would deal with the rest. We would run the first event and then look to setting up others the following year.

This was a turning point for Brutal. Without making this decision, I'm not sure how or even if I would have been able to go forward. I lacked experience, not only in events, but in business as a whole. All I knew was that Brutal had to happen, and I was prepared to do anything to ensure it did.

Working with Brian was an interesting experience. It was hard not to get carried away with him as he discussed the ideas for future events. But there were definitely times when I felt he was trying to take control. Sometimes I would have to bow to his knowledge. But on other occasions, I would fight to retain something that I felt would be integral to the race.

As the first ever Brutal Triathlon got closer, I became so stressed. I worked hours into the night to ensure that every detail was checked and every potential problem had a contingency. There was so much to think about, so much to remember. The day before registration, I packed the van to make the long drive to North Wales. On the way, I had to pull over onto the hard shoulder because I was having an anxiety attack. I sat in the van, trying to control my breathing. I was completely overwhelmed by what I was about to do. 150 or so athletes were relying on me to set up and run this event. At that moment, all I wanted to do was drive back home and hide under my duvet.

Once I was on the event field, I set about trying to focus on doing

## A BRUTAL BUSINESS

one thing at a time. But I found myself constantly being pulled in different directions, and I couldn't see how I was going to get everything done in time. On the plus side, the large marquee I had hired was in the process of being erected, and the fencing and barriers were on their way. The portable toilets arrived and gradually the soggy, community field began to look more like an event HQ.

The event registration was being held in Electric Mountain, a little further down the road. This is a visitor centre focused around a hydroelectric station and housed a café, shop and a number of large rooms available for events or exhibitions. One of the rooms we used for athletes to come and be checked off the list and given their goody bags. The other was for the compulsory race briefings which all athletes and crew had to attend later that evening.

I found registration the hardest task of all. There were so many people milling around, all excited and nervous. And they all seemed to want to talk, and mainly to me. I was so incredibly stressed at that point that I found it almost impossible to be the happy, relaxed race director I felt I should be. I remember escaping to the toilets and splashing cold water on my face in an attempt to try and cool down. I just wanted it to be over.

Eventually, all the competitors, family and friends disappeared to local bunkhouses, B&Bs, hotels and campsites. My crew and I made our way back to the event field. It had been raining while we'd been away and the field was getting a little damp. We still had work to do and when most of the others went off to their tents to try and get some rest before the long weekend, Brian and I set up the marquee. We placed the chairs around the outside to allow competitors to put kit on them and set up the tables in the middle. At

## A BRUTAL BUSINESS

the end of the marquee, we built a basic kitchen area, complete with toaster, tea urns and a microwave, to allow the crews to make the athletes hot food and drinks throughout the weekend. Afterwards, we stood back and admired our work. And with only a few hours until the race started, we got our heads down.

Sleeping in a freezing cold marquee, lying on top of a trestle table, was never going to provide the best rest in preparation to run an endurance triathlon for 150 competitors. But over the next two and a half days, that's exactly what I had to do. The minute my phone alarm went off, I jumped off the table, like a coiled spring, my adrenaline levels stupidly high for 5am. I grabbed my to-do list, which had fallen to the ground and was now lying in wet grass, and reminded myself of what I needed to do before everyone arrived.

Starting the generators, then putting the tea urns on, was the first and most important job. I had about an hour before the athletes began to arrive and chaos ensued. Bleary-eyed crew pulled back the gaps in the marquee and stood blinking in the florescent lights. Once our caffeine levels were restored and instructions were given, we all set about getting ready to start the event.

From 5am, the marquee became a mass of nervous, partially dressed competitors. The marquee really wasn't big enough, but this would be the one and only time that everyone would actually be in there at the same time. At 6:30am, Brian shouted a 15-minute warning that everyone needed to be moving down towards the lake, ready for the start.

I grabbed my clipboard and started making my way down towards the water. At that point, I realised in horror that the grass was

## A BRUTAL BUSINESS

crunching under my feet. Was it so cold that there was ice on the ground? How cold was the water going to be? In my panic, I wondered if I was actually going to kill people…

l watched anxiously as the mist rose from the lake, thinking 'Shit, what have I done?'. After a short safety briefing, the swimmers attempted to warm up. At 7am, the horn sounded and 150 athletes started their race. I watched quietly from the side, with a mix of emotions. I felt the heavy weight of responsibility, but also a small sense of satisfaction from seeing more than a year and a half of very hard work play out in front of me.

The rest of the weekend was a blur of sorting out problem after problem. It was relentless and exhausting. I didn't eat or sleep. People would put cups of coffee in my hands on an hourly basis and I was so grateful for that. I had planned on leaving the field a few times to shower and have a nap, but that never happened and I remained in the same clothes I was wearing on Friday.

Once people had started completing the race, I stood on the finish line, terrified that I might miss someone. So from Saturday afternoon until the early hours of Monday morning, I never strayed far from the gantry. I wore ski trousers and a DryRobe and as many layers as I could underneath them. And a woolly hat. I had medals hanging out of my pockets; each pocket had a different distance, as the slower Half finishers were still reaching the line as the speedy Full distance racers were beginning to come in.

As Saturday turned into Sunday, the bulk of the competitors finished and headed home. The only athletes left now were a handful of Doubles. These guys (no women entered that first year) had swum

## A BRUTAL BUSINESS

4.8 miles, cycled 224 miles, completed their Snowdon ascent, and were now on the lake lap section, which would bring the run total to 50-ish miles. They were beyond tired and looked more like zombies as they stumbled through race HQ on each of the 8 laps. One by one, these incredible men would finish and I would place medals round their necks, often shedding a tear with them, feeling more like a proud mum than a race director.

Darkness fell and Sunday became the early hours of Monday morning. Everyone had finished except one man. All the crew had retired to their sleeping bags and I was left, sitting on the bonnet of my van, watching the tiny light of the final Double competitor's head-torch move along the distant path. He was on his last lap and I now allowed myself to relax, feeling my shoulders drop as I breathed a deep sigh of relief. It was almost done. From that first idea, developed in the bedroom of my tiny house in Dorset, I had successfully created The Brutal Extreme Triathlons.

Over the next nine years, Brutal Events took me on the most incredible rollercoaster ride. There were huge highs, but also big lows, moments when I would be holding on, trying not to scream. Like the time when I was organising the Oner Ultra Trail Run for the first time. I had been working on this event for a few years, whilst it had been run by another company (Votwo Events), so I had a good idea of what I was doing. Or so I thought. I had decided to buy a marquee from a company in Germany. It looked robust enough and I would be saving myself thousands by not hiring a heavy duty one from the professionals.

My crew and I erected the new marquee the afternoon before the race. Once we were done, I stood back and admired our work and

## A BRUTAL BUSINESS

my shiny white event HQ. I even put a photo on Facebook saying that we were ready to go. Which in the world of events is practically an invitation to the weather gods to fuck you up. And fuck me up they did. After I had finished setting up registration and all the other jobs, like checking the athlete trackers and ensuring the timing was set up, it was decided that I would leave the race HQ to get a decent night's sleep before the event started.

This was the first time I had ever left a race HQ the night before an event, and the last.

I was woken up by Dom's mum. Dominic was a hard-working crew member, liked by everyone. His mum, Christine, was the same. She shook me, gently, saying, 'Claire, wake up, there's a problem at the race HQ.' The minute she said that, I was awake. I sat bolt upright, asking what had happened.

'There's been a storm and there's some damage to the marquee.'

We all dressed quickly and jumped into the car to drive the fifteen minutes to the venue. It was a very long drive. I was sitting in the back, trying hard not to panic. Dom arrived before us and Christine's phone rang when we were still five minutes away. The conversation was quiet and over quickly. She turned to me and said, 'I'm sorry Claire, it's all gone.'

All gone? My brain tried to process the statement, but I couldn't make sense of it. What was all gone?

When we finally arrived at the small car park where the marquee and other gazebos had stood, ready for the 80 or so athletes to

## A BRUTAL BUSINESS

turn up later that morning, I finally understood what Christine meant. The marquee and the other tents had disappeared. I looked around the car park in total confusion. Where the fuck were they? There were tables and chairs, boxes of T-shirts and race food all lying around in puddles. But no marquee. I walked around picking up toilet rolls and packets of crisps in a vain attempt to tidy up, but the whole time all I could think was, 'ohmygod, ohmygod…'

There had been a massive, freak storm during the night, and as we were on the coast path and very exposed, the tents hadn't stood a chance.

This was a real turning point for me. As I stood there in the dark, holding a loo roll, with tears rolling down my face in total shock, I could hear a quiet voice saying, 'Claire, snap out of it. Wake up and sort this shit out.'

I realised, after a while, that the voice was mine, in my head. Yes, I had good people around me, but I was the boss; they were looking at me to deal with this, to sort it out. I took a deep breath and pulled myself together. I looked around the car park that we had hired from the local pub. I looked at my phone and wondered if the landlord was awake at 4am. Probably not, but he soon would be.

I hammered on the door and after a fair wait and a bit of banging, the door opened and the landlord stood, bleary-eyed and confused. I explained briefly what had happened and then asked the million-dollar question, 'Do you have a room I can use for the race?' He went quiet for a moment and then said, 'Yes, you can use the studio.' I let out of huge sigh of relief and thanked him. It was going to be alright, I could make this happen. We had about two hours to be ready for registration.

The 'studio' turned out to be a very small room which had very little in the way of facilities. There was a tap in the corner, a rough concrete floor and lumps missing from the walls. But it didn't matter; we had a place to put registration documents, timing and trackers. We set up another gazebo we had managed to save from the water's edge and after a lot of hard work from my crew, The Oner Ultra Trail Run was, once again, ready.

Over the following years, there would be a constant turnover of gazebos. The locations I chose to hold events were always remote and blustery, often on mountainsides and coast paths. And the event tents I bought, which were named 'Rhino Gazebos' because they were so tough, still didn't stand a chance. Even the professional marquees I hired for the bigger events would often be pushed to their limits.

I developed a disorder that I named 'Marquee Anxiety', which I joked about, but it actually felt quite real. As soon as the wind would pick up, tent sides would start flapping and metal frames would begin to creak, my stress levels would rise and my heart rate increase. When gazebos go, you need to get the fuck out of the way. I remember one Brutal Triathlon when we had been nearing the end of the event, and a sudden storm arrived and literally picked the timing tent up with me sitting in it, clinging on to thousands of pounds' worth of equipment and swearing loudly.

The weather didn't just break equipment of course; it affected the events too. One of the biggest changes I had to make to an event was in August 2014 when I held Jurassicman Extreme

## A BRUTAL BUSINESS

Triathlon on the south coast. This was a beast of an event, with a sea swim starting in the choppy waters of Budleigh Salterton. The competitors would then have to cycle a very hilly 112 miles from Devon to Dorset. Once they had arrived at transition, one of the UK's hardest marathon courses waited for them: 26 miles over the Jurassic Coast, finishing in Lulworth Cove.

The day before it began, I was on the run route, putting out some course signs, when I received a call from the Environmental Agency. They asked me if I was the race director of the Jurassicman, and I replied that I was.

'You are cancelling the event?' they asked.

'Erm, no…' I replied.

I had been keeping an eye on the weather in the days leading up to the event, but I hadn't looked at it for the past 24 hours.

'You aren't aware of Storm Bertha hitting the south coast this weekend? You will need to make changes to your event,' the voice stated at the other end of the phone.

After the call had ended, I phoned Richard, who was helping to run the event, and asked him to come and pick me up. Once I was back at base, I had to redesign the whole event from a triathlon to a duathlon, with the swim becoming a run from the car park and then back to transition. The bike remained the same, but the run section changed from the dangerous coast path to laps which were still tough and hilly, but away from the exposed cliff edges.

## A BRUTAL BUSINESS

The next day, when the athletes pulled on their trainers to start the run, we all looked at the sea they should have been getting into. The water was a muddy brown colour and huge waves crashed onto the shore. The noise from the wind and water was almost deafening, and there was no doubt that we had made the right, and only, decision.

Another event that was massively changed by the weather was The Pig Ultra Duathlon. This event had always been a little challenging to organise, due to the fact it was held on the side of Cadair Idris, one of the highest mountains in Wales. But this year promised to be the worst ever. This time I was *super* aware of the weather leading up to the event, with the BBC app on my phone displaying black arrows for the whole weekend. I was so stressed, but hoped that it would ease off to enable us to run the event.

We had set up the HQ by Friday night, and all that was left for the Saturday was signing the long bike and run routes. Together with Matt, a good friend and permanent member of the Brutal crew, we sat eating some fish and chips, laughing and chatting about normal event shit. Once it was dark, we hit our sleeping bags, Matt in his tent and me in the back of my large Luton van. I lay there for ten minutes or so, wondering if I would get away with the promised weather warnings for the next few days. There was no signal on the event field, so I couldn't check for any updates. I decided not to worry about things that I couldn't control. 'What will be, will be,' I thought as I drifted off to sleep.

I woke up in the early hours of the morning to the sound of the wind howling, the van rocking side to side. I just lay there, wrapped in the warmth of my sleeping bag, wishing that this wasn't happening, again. Maybe it's not as bad as it sounds, I thought, hopefully.

## A BRUTAL BUSINESS

At that moment there was a loud crash and everything went black. It took me a few moments to realise what had actually happened. The black gazebo, which we had set up on the side of the Luton for protection from the predicted winds, had broken; the sides had come free and flipped over the roof of the van, turning my world dark, but also, as I quickly realised, exposing all the race equipment and T-shirts that had been stored in it.

I broke free of my sleeping bag and pulled on some warm clothes as quickly as I could in the dark, tripping over the boxes and other equipment in the back of the van. Hauling up the back door, I jumped down onto the grass of the event field and quickly realised that not only was it as bad as it sounded, it was actually far worse. The wind was incredibly strong and I was acutely aware of the infrastructure that was, remarkably, still standing. How long would it stay up? I grabbed some of the boxes of T-shirts and threw them into the back of the van, when a sudden gust almost knocked me off my feet. The metal work, from the now naked gazebo, strained and pulled at the pegs in the ground. I felt very vulnerable at that moment and hid round the back of the Luton.

I looked towards Matt's tent, which was moving around, alarmingly, in the wind. I wondered if he was able to sleep through that. Quite possibly, knowing Matt…

I made a break from the shelter of the van and ran over to the tent. I called his name a couple of times and after that didn't work, I basically screamed at him over the noise of the gales. His head appeared at the door of the tent and he took one look at my face and said, 'give me a minute.'

## A BRUTAL BUSINESS

Once Matt was up, we saved as much of the kit as we could and then took shelter in his car. We decided to drive down to the village to get a phone signal in order to try and make some plans. When we had parked and realised, to our dismay, that it was still too early for any coffee shop to be open, we sat and looked at the weather report. It was not good news; the high winds and rain were set to continue for the next 36 hours at least. With 24 hours until the event started, that was going to make it impossible to put up any tents or bike racking. Signing the run course was not impossible, but as it was a very tough 10-mile run, it wasn't something I wanted to do if there was any chance the event might not go ahead.

Apart from the HQ area and run course, my main concerns were the first run, which went up Cadair Idris, and the bike course, which was very exposed to the elements on some sections. I think I knew in my heart what I needed to do, but it took me a good forty-five minutes of going back and forth trying to avoid the inevitable.

I had to cancel the race.

I had never had to cancel an event so close to the start before, and I knew it wasn't going to be an easy thing to do, but I had no idea how hard it was going to be. From the moment I sent out the email to tell competitors, I experienced what can only be described as a shit storm of replies. There were a few people who understood and were also sympathetic to the situation I was in. But a lot of athletes were not happy and weren't shy in telling me either. Not many people seemed to understand that if I went ahead and put on an extreme duathlon in forecasted bad weather, therefore knowingly putting people (my own crew, as well) at risk, I could find myself in court if there was an accident.

## A BRUTAL BUSINESS

I learnt a lot of lessons from that event and made changes to ensure that the business was protected should that happen again. I also tried to grow a thicker skin, as I knew this wouldn't be the last time I would have weather issues and complaints from competitors. I needed to grow up, in a business sense, and stop taking things so personally. It was hard though when my business was my baby. Over the years that followed I gradually learnt to become tougher and less emotionally attached.

There were many more incidents over the years, some funny, but some far more serious. Like the accident one of the Full distance Brutal triathletes had at the top of Pen-y-Pass. The competitor came off his bike, due to a mechanical issue, and literally smashed a large hole in his head. When I got news of this, in race HQ, I went cold and had to hide in one of the medic tents for five minutes while I got myself together. It's hard to explain just how responsible you feel as an organiser – even when things happen that aren't actually your responsibility.

He was airlifted to hospital and we were all incredibly relieved when news came back that he was in recovery. A few years (and a lot of rehab) later, I'm pleased to say, he returned and finished the event he started, which took a lot of guts. I worried about him for the whole event and was so relieved when he crossed the line and I was able to put a medal around his neck.

Other fun and games have included a tour boat operator driving through a live event, narrowly missing swimmers and forcing me to call the police; lake owners not informing me of huge inflatable theme parks being installed in the water where I was holding a night swimming event. I've had producers of car commercials trying to

## A BRUTAL BUSINESS

close roads where a 48-hour triathlon was being held because they wanted to film Bradley Wiggins driving with North Wales in the background. There have been times when I've made the tough decision to hold the swim in water so choppy that swimmers have crawled out, green and throwing up on the beach. There have also been times where I've had to completely change a live event bike course, during the night, due to storms, while ducking as gazebos flew overhead and rain flooded the field we were in.

All of these things are part of event organisation and I learnt valuable lessons. Some, however, are bigger than others, and can completely change how you run your business.

About a week before the fourth year of running The Brutal Triathlons, I was trying to get hold of the guy who normally chip-timed the event. Timing, I had discovered when I first set up the business, was another large but very necessary cost. For a 2-day event, it was pretty expensive, so just to make my life harder, in 2015 I had decided to hold a Triple version of the event, to run alongside the other distances, but adding another day.

My timing guy was super chilled, which I later discovered was a valuable personality trait when timing events. But it made my life harder in the run-up to race day. He would always pull through though, turning up with a big smile, wearing flip-flops, driving a hire van. He would start to unload all the mats and computers he needed to time the triathlons and plonk himself down in a corner of the marquee, where he would stay for the duration of the weekend.

That year, though, he was not returning any phone calls or emails that I sent, each one becoming more desperate as the event got closer. Eventually, I had to come to the conclusion that he had gone bust. Or been abducted by aliens. Either way, I was fucked. And, as so many times before, my gut feeling told me what I needed to do. But I really, really didn't want to do it. I needed to buy my own timing equipment and learn how to use it.

Five days before the longest triathlon I had ever organised.

I made a few more desperate phone calls to other timing companies, resulting in most of them laughing as I told them where it was, when it was and more importantly, how long the race was. 'Sorry love, not a chance,' was the general answer.

My gut feeling, once again, reminded me of what I needed to do. I typed 'race timing equipment' into Google and sat back and looked at the results. A few stressful hours and a lot of calculations later, I had ordered thousands of pounds' worth of kit. And I had a large manual to read.

With the help of the timing company (RaceResult) and my stepfather, we managed to successfully provide results for The Brutal Triathlons. Even through there was a moment when I stood in the middle of the event field in the early hours of the morning with tears running down my face. Mainly due to lack of sleep, but also because I felt so out of my depth with not only being the sole race director, but now the event timer as well.

But I never regretted buying the timing kit. I learnt so much and also saved a lot of money over the years by bringing this in-house. And I did actually enjoy the geeky side of this new skill of mine. The only downside was the extra pressure it added on me during the events,

## A BRUTAL BUSINESS

and there were definitely times when I needed to concentrate on event directing but instead was glued to the timing.

Looking back, I am proud of how I took a very stressful situation and turned it into a positive one. It was not only business-changing, but life-altering too. I realised then what I am truly capable of turning my hand to, and also how sometimes life puts you in situations that you need to recognise as opportunities to step up.

There are some things which happened while running events that I wasn't so proud of and definitely didn't need to repeat. One of them was with my van. And how I loaded it. Or over-loaded it, should I say.

Before each event, I needed to sort a huge amount of kit required and pack it into a van. When I first started the business, I somehow managed to fit it all into a transit. But after a few years, I was forced to buy a larger van. I was very proud of my new Luton and it also made a big difference being able to store the larger items in there permanently, rather than in various places around my house and garden.

Now, for all the events, bar one, I needed some of the event kit. But for The Brutal Triathlons, I needed ALL of it. Gazebos, bike racking, boxes filled with medals, food and T-shirts, a PA system and speakers, hundreds of road signs, four huge swim buoys, anchors, generators (I often wondered how my life had taken such a strange turn that I now owned not one, but three generators) and a massive, lime-green finish gantry.

Oh, and eight large buckets filled with concrete.

## A BRUTAL BUSINESS

The buckets were for the swim buoys, to keep them upright, due to their cylindrical shape. Basically, the buoys looked like huge, green TicTacs, but without the buckets, they would lie flat on the water rather than stand upright. Nobody tells you this stuff... Anyway, my stepfather made me the buckets and from that point on, I drove around with concrete. In buckets. Because that's what you do in events.

Another thing nobody tells you (probably because it's one of those things that is obvious, but obviously not to me) is that vehicles have weight limits. If I'm being really honest here, I just thought, if the van is big enough, then surely you can fill it up.

That is very much not the case.

So, a few days before the event in North Wales, I loaded my Luton and, grabbing my coffee and phone, jumped in the cab ready for the long drive. I had noticed how the tyres looked a little low on air and made a mental note to check them at the service station en-route.

About an hour or so into the drive, I was on a busy motorway when I noticed a traffic policeman parked at the side of the road. They were often there, but this morning I remember wondering what they were watching for *specifically*. I would soon find out, because to my horror I suddenly found him behind me and the 4x4 he was driving displaying the words 'PULL OVER' in flashing red letters.

The policeman pulled in front of me and indicated that I was to leave the motorway at the next junction. What had I done? I hadn't been on my phone and I wasn't speeding (for a change). I briefly considered making a break for it and then remembered that I was

## A BRUTAL BUSINESS

a grown woman with two children and a business to run, and that trying to escape from the police is frowned upon. So instead, I indicated to pull off onto the slipway.

The policeman's sign now changed to 'FOLLOW ME' and he led me to a location I had never been to. A place called a Weigh Bridge. Suddenly, the pieces started to fit together, and as I was told to position my van on some metal plates, I got a very, very bad feeling that I was going to be in a LOT of trouble.

After the van had been weighed, the policeman walked back to me. I could tell it wasn't going to be a nice conversation by the look on his face. I smiled, weakly, at him. He did not smile back.

'Mrs Smith, you are THREE TIMES over the weight limit. Did you know that?'

I was genuinely shocked and could be completely honest with him when I replied that, 'No, officer, I had no idea.'

Once again, his face didn't hide his feelings. 'I see. Please park up and come into the office.'

Driving slowly to park, my thoughts raced. I suspected that I was in for a large fine and some points on my licence (to keep the other three company). What I didn't expect was what happened next.

After being officially cautioned (which is not ideal, especially as I had developed verbal diarrhoea at that point and everything I blurted out, the officer calmly wrote down in his little black notepad), I was told that I wasn't going anywhere until I had found a further two

## A BRUTAL BUSINESS

Luton vans to unload the kit into.

I blinked.

'Wait, you want me to find two other vans, right now?'

'Yes, Mrs Smith. You aren't going anywhere until you have.'

'But, but… I've got an event to set up, a triathlon, people, lots of people are coming… I… but, how?' I stammered.

The policeman looked at me and sighed. 'I *literally* do not give a fuck,' is what his face said.

What he actually said was, 'That's down to you, Mrs Smith, you are not to leave until we have checked and cleared all three vehicles.'

I went back to my cab and had a little cry.

Then I pulled out my phone and got to work, muttering about stupid safety laws and my being such an idiot.

An hour later, two black Luton vans appeared and we set to work distributing the kit between the three of them. Once cleared by the policeman, we drove off, in convoy, to North Wales.

Overall, that mistake cost me, with van hire (to and from the event) and the fine issued later by the court, over £3,500. But it gave my event crew a really, really good laugh, which is the most important thing.

## A BRUTAL BUSINESS

Starting, and more importantly, staying in business has taught me so much. As a director of a company, you never switch off and you make mistakes constantly. You learn, you grow, you cry, you get mad and you really want to give up sometimes. It's the best and worst thing you will ever do. But it's worth it all when you can look back and realise that your company has changed people for the better. Furthermore, it has pushed people past their limits and on to finding new and exciting ones. This business has also created friendships and memories which will last a lifetime (and in one case, a marriage and new family).

I love how Brutal grew from a tiny idea and went on to become recognised, around the globe, as the hardest triathlons in the world. It taught me that with perseverance, support from family and friends and a lot of hard work, you can build something truly amazing.

You just have to never, ever, give up.

## LIFE LESSON
# GETTING SHIT DONE

The power of self-belief comes from actually doing things – not from a post on Facebook.

You can understand the concept of self-belief; you can even really think you believe in yourself. But if you don't really feel deep down that you can do it, then it won't make any difference and there is a good chance you will fail.

What changes things is when you start to succeed. But how do you get to that point?

Success comes in all shapes and sizes, and I have become overwhelmed in the past by setting myself huge goals and then failing to reach them or giving up beforehand. I believe this is a form of self-sabotage; I think I was trying to reinforce negative feelings about myself: 'See, I told you I was rubbish!'

I spent a few years like this, going round in circles. Entering stupidly hard events, not training for them properly, and then either pulling out beforehand or turning up and trying to blag it. Either way, I was caught in a vicious circle.

To break the habit, I started making a real effort to finish things. Not big, scary events, but simple tasks at work, home and also during my training. I then realised that there were times when I would run for 50 minutes instead of the 60 I had planned, or only complete half of the accounting work I needed to do. But as I began to make the effort to finish what I started, I noticed a change in myself. The good feeling that I would get at the end of a tough brick session would set me up for the day. Completing the cold-water training that I needed, but really didn't want to do, made me feel awesome. Even cleaning out my van properly gave me a sense of calm and I felt I was in control.

Completing simple tasks helped me get back into the habit of finishing what I started. I was reinforcing positive actions and, in turn, breaking the vicious circle I was caught in.

I was given a valuable piece of advice back when I first started my event business. I was really stressing out over the weather reports on Snowdon and a colleague said, 'control what you can and let go of the rest'. What he basically meant was, I couldn't control high winds on a mountain, but I could plan for what would happen if they got beyond a level deemed safe.

This really helped me cope with feeling overwhelmed, and also made a lot of sense to me. It stuck with me and I started applying it to other areas in my life. You can't control other people's reactions to you, but you can control how you behave in return. You can't control your car breaking down, but if you already have plans in place to deal with this happening, it makes a stressful situation a lot easier. How you react to your teenager telling you they've starting smoking is in your control. You can scream and shout at them, which will do nothing other than ensure they will never tell you anything again, or you can react calmly and let them talk about it.

This also helps in an endurance event setting. You can't control getting a puncture or your chain snapping, but you can ensure that you have had your bike serviced pre-race and that you have spare wheels or a bike (if possible). And you definitely can't control the weather during the race, but by bringing kit for every eventuality and also making sure you have trained in all the conditions you are likely to face, this gives you the best chance of getting to the finish line.

Pre-event (whether I'm organising it or taking part), I sit down quietly and run through the whole thing in my head. I try and visualise everything and make notes on what could go wrong and how I can prepare for that situation happening. More than likely, the race will go smoothly and you won't need any of the back-up plans you made, but knowing they are in place will help you start the race in a calm and controlled state.

You can apply the above to any situation that is causing you to worry, like giving a presentation at work or taking an important exam.

# CHAPTER 8
# SUFFERING FOR OTHERS

Sometimes I give myself I break from personal racing and give something back by raising money for charity. I have the upmost respect for people who raise large sums of money for good causes, as I know how hard it can be.

The first idea I had was when my uncle died in his early fifties of a brain tumour. I decided it would be perfect to set myself a little goal of five Ironman triathlons in a gym…

**The GymQuin – 22 December 2016**

'So, explain to me again what it is you're doing.'

I sigh. When I came up with the GymQuin, I had no idea it would confuse people so much. 'So, I'm swimming 12 miles in a pool, cycling 560 miles on a gym bike and then running 131 miles on a treadmill.'

'WHAT??? But that's crazy!!!'

'Ummm, yeah. I guess it is…'

The swim section was held at my gym as it has a nice pool and on a good day you can have a lane to yourself. We arrived around 6am and while I got ready, my crew (Martin and Rob, whom I met at my events and went on to become good friends) got the nutrition and everything else needed on the poolside.

## SUFFERING FOR OTHERS

I had planned on a 9-hour swim with 30 minutes of breaks for food. Rob and Martin took turns to count the laps and let me know when each mile was completed. I was also counting, as I always do, but the more fatigued I became, the less reliable my totals were. Still, I found that keeping count (even if it was wrong) kept my mind off other things.

Towards the end of the swim, I started feeling a bit rough. Being immersed in chemicals for so long isn't good for you, and my asthma and allergies started to play up a little. But apart from that, I felt alright and the day went reasonably fast. Lou (another good friend I met while marshalling a local triathlon) swam with me for a few hours in the morning and Rob in the afternoon. I was treated to a Starbucks Latte when I had 3 miles to go, but by then my appetite had gone and I was feeling a bit sick.

What did I think about during 9 hours of going up and down the pool? I have no idea. I broke the laps into sections of 64 and just focused on that part, stopping myself from looking too far ahead. I had been worried that as I hadn't really trained for a 12-mile swim, I might feel some soreness or other injuries, but apart from the expected tiredness, I felt good. I put this down to my recent and regular attendance of Pump classes. We do a lot of upper body work with weights and I felt so much stronger because of this.

I was so pleased to get out of the pool for the final time and enjoy a hot shower. But a quick look in the mirror was a truly terrifying moment. My goggle marks looked like someone had literally drawn thick lines around my eyes with a red Sharpie and my eyelids were swollen, making me look like I had been in a fight. I avoided mirrors from that point on…

**Top:** Mum and me. With older brother Nick and mum.
**Middle:** '*Stand there and look normal*' - school photo with Nick.
Me and my awesome hair / teeth. With my cousin Emma as Brownies.
**Bottom:** My family. A day at the beach.

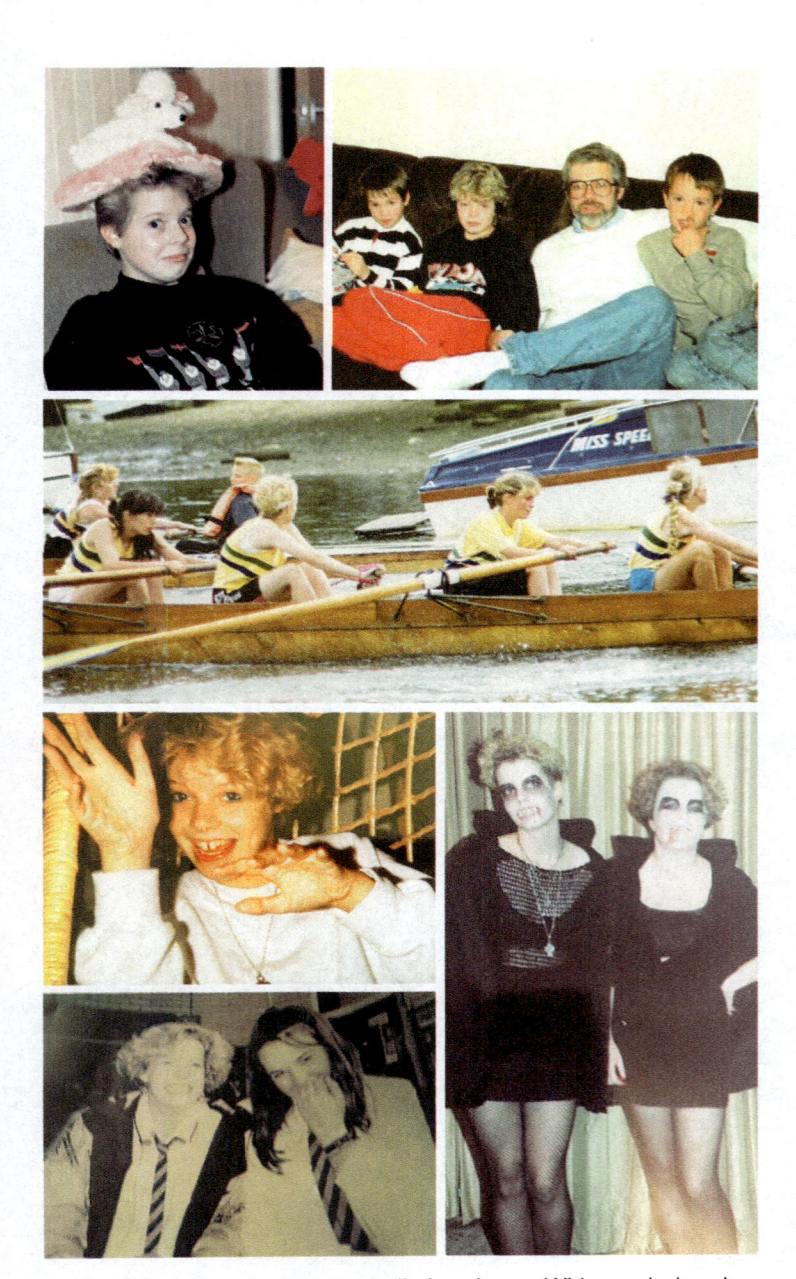

**Top:** Modelling the latest poodle headwear. With my dad and stepbrothers, sometime in the 80's. **Middle:** My first regatta in Christchurch, my teenage years. **Bottom:** Last day of school with best friend Claire Northcott, 1991.

**Top:** New mum with Jessica, 1997.
**Middle:** London Marathon / New Forest Marathon, 2005/6.
Wedding day with Mark and the kids, 2004.
**Bottom:** Des with Jacob, 2002. Me and the kids, 2009.

**Top:** First triathlon, Wimbleball 70.3 in 2006
**Middle:** Second triathlon, Sherborne Ironman in 2007
**Bottom:** At the finish with my kids and nieces.

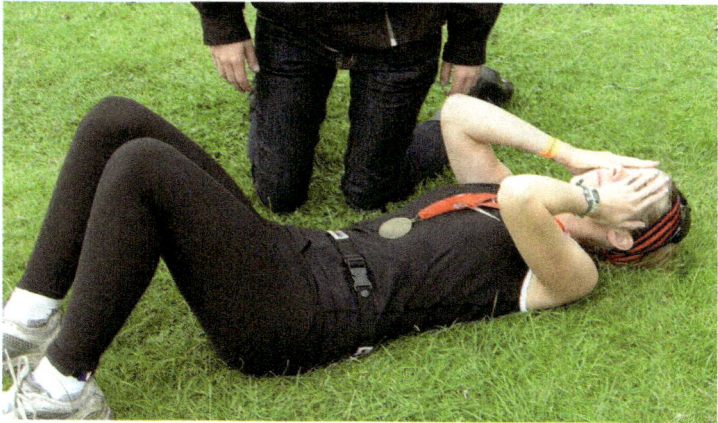

**Top:** Enduroman Double Iron with Claire crewing for me, 2008.
**Middle:** My first Double finish after 32 hours and 27 minutes of racing. **Bottom:** Relieved to be finished and 2nd place trophy in my hand.

**Top:** Lanzarote Ultra Triathlon during the 45-mile run (2nd attempt), 2008. **Middle:** Bike leg almost finished, Lanzarote 2008.
**Bottom:** During first 1x10 Deca attempt, 2015 (DNF on day 3).

**Top:** The first Brutal Extreme Triathlon in 2012.
**Middle:** Aerial view of the Llyn Padarn swim start, Llanberis.
**Bottom:** The "bike cage" in transition. Me and TC (aka Anthony Gerundini) on one of his many Brutal Tri wins.

**Top:** One of the best parts of being a race director - presenting medals. **Middle:** Double Brutal finisher Graham Smedley with Justin the Brutal Squirrel. Hugging Koen Van Meeuwen after his Double Brutal Finish. **Bottom:** Stunning views of the bike course at Llanberis Pass (photo: Kathi Harman).

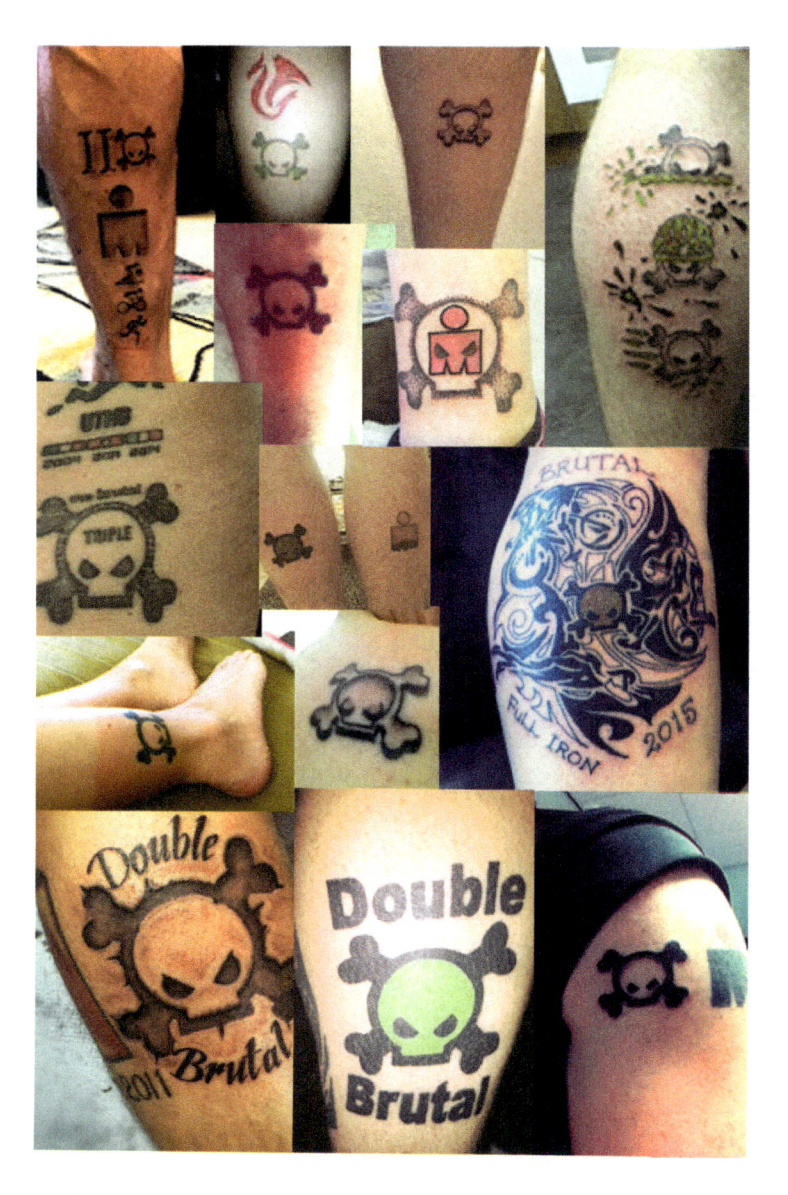

The many post-race Brutal tattoos from previous competitors.

**Top:** Another Brutal Triathlon finish line. **Middle:** In full race director mode, 2013. With Dom, his parents and Sascha during The Oner, 2014. **Bottom:** Me and fellow race director Jim wish Justin a happy birthday during DecaUK, 2019.

**Top:** Channel Five Documentary about the Brutal Triathlon in 2013.
**Middle:** With the crew after first DecaUK event, 2017 (L-R: Matt Brown, Paul Smethurst, Jim Page, me, Justin Hounsell).
**Bottom:** Same crew, different event. Running the timing kit at HQ.

**Top:** Rescuing a pigeon during DecaUK, 2019.
Justin and Rab crewing The Brutal Triathlons, 2018.
**Middle:** Matt Brown and me on swim safety duty, DecaUK, 2017.
**Bottom:** Aerial view of the Big Brutal Swim, 2017.

**Top:** My mum and stepfather, Alan, who have helped at almost every Brutal event. **Middle:** Big brother Nick and partner, Lindsay, crewing at The Brutal Triathlons. **Bottom:** Winning the 220 Triathlon Magazine award for World's Toughest Triathlon in 2016.

**Top:** Swimmers attend race briefing before the Big Brutal Swim. **Middle:** Rab, me and Jim at the Midnight Mountain Marathon briefing. **Bottom:** The "Brutal Luton" providing both transport and accommodation.

**Top:** Another DIY Deca attempt at the DecaUK venue in York, 2017.
**Middle:** Being helped out of the swim section by Maria and Rob.
My crew, Martin, at the Dorney Deca Recce, 2016
**Bottom:** Cold water training at Bournemouth and pre-Deca porridge.

**Top:** The GymQuin run section 2016. The "run" part of the Triathlon of Horrors, 2018. **Middle:** Lou Dutch and me during the GymQuin. With friends Paul and, first ever Double Brutal Tri winner, Matt, at Cotswold 24 Hour Race, 2018. **Bottom:** Some Deca advice. With my daughter Jess at the finish of her first marathon, 2018.

**Top:** Rob and me finishing the first Fan Dance with race director Ken Jones, 2019. **Middle:** Swimming at Llyn Padarn during a Double Brutal Triathlon recce, 2011. **Bottom:** Swim training in Lanzarote in 2019.

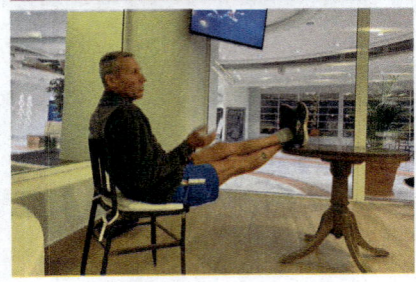

**Top / middle:** Swim training with Arch to Arc entrants in Lanzarote.
**Bottom:** Eddie Ette giving Arch to Arc advice; more swimming training with Matt, Graeme, me, Eddie and Martin, Lanzarote 2018.

**Top:** Race registration. Before Continuous Deca swim start, Switzerland, 2017. **Middle:** Rob Duddington and me during a Deca bike lap, 2017. **Bottom:** The low-hanging clouds I loved so much on the Swiss Deca bike course.

**Top:** During the 24-mile swim. On my road bike. **Middle:** Trying to manage feet issues during a 262-mile run. **Bottom:** With Shanda and Laura, my "Deca Bitches". Having a walking break during a hot afternoon. *All photos during Switzerland Deca 2017*

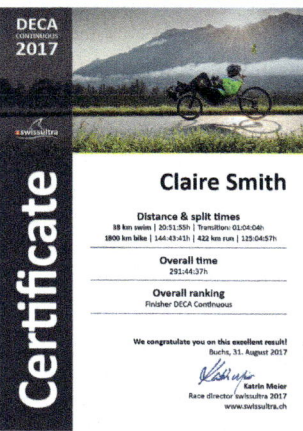

**Top:** I used both a recumbent and road bike for the 1,120-mile bike section to help manage lower back pain. **Middle:** My finisher certificate. Sharing the podium with my girls and the winner, IUTA world record holder Alexandra Meixner. **Bottom:** "Embracing the flag" at the finish. *All photos during Switzerland Deca 2017*

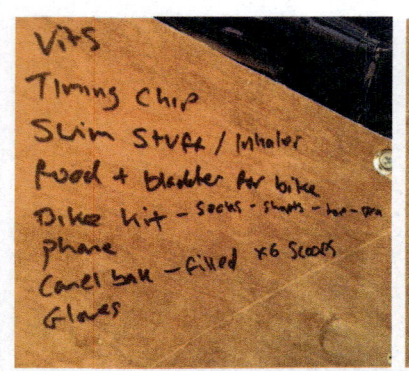

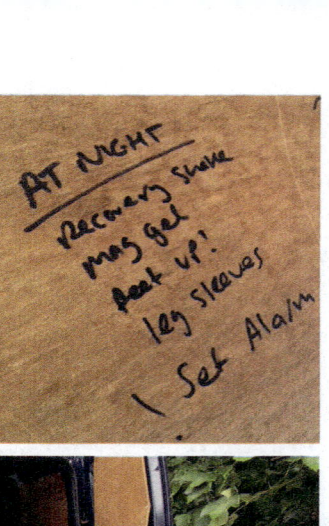

**Top:** Race notes I made on the wall on my transit van during my self-supported 1x5 Quin triathlon.   **Middle:** How I lived for a week during the event. **Bottom:** The 5 daily food bags I pre-packed before I left the UK. *All photos during Switzerland 1x5 Quin 2018*

**Top:** Day 3, pre-swim, feeling rough! Road bike only for this event.
**Middle:** All the event finishers (all distances). **Bottom:** One of many sunny afternoon marathons. Very proud of my second place trophy.
*All photos during Switzerland 1x5 Quin 2018*

**Top:** All the kit I had to take to America. **Middle:** Pre-race nerves. Jon showing the other crews how it's done. **Bottom:** The worst weather recorded in New Orleans for 100 years. Obviously.
*All photos during the New Orleans 1x10 Deca 2018*

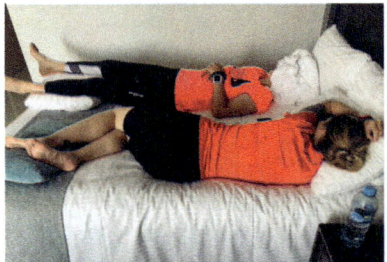

**Top:** Double the distance, double the kit. Walking down to the race start with Georgeta and Lia. **Middle:** Georgeta and me try to sleep before the 48-mile swim. My tent, race ready. Race HQ, where I spent a month of my life. **Bottom:** Me, Shanda and Laura a few days before the race. *All photos during Mexico Double Deca 2019*

**Top:** Race number and registration with the usual suspects.
**Middle:** Pre-race group shot. **Bottom:** Sometime during the middle of the swim. Joey helps me to the changing rooms at the swim finish.
*All photos during Mexico Double Deca 2019*

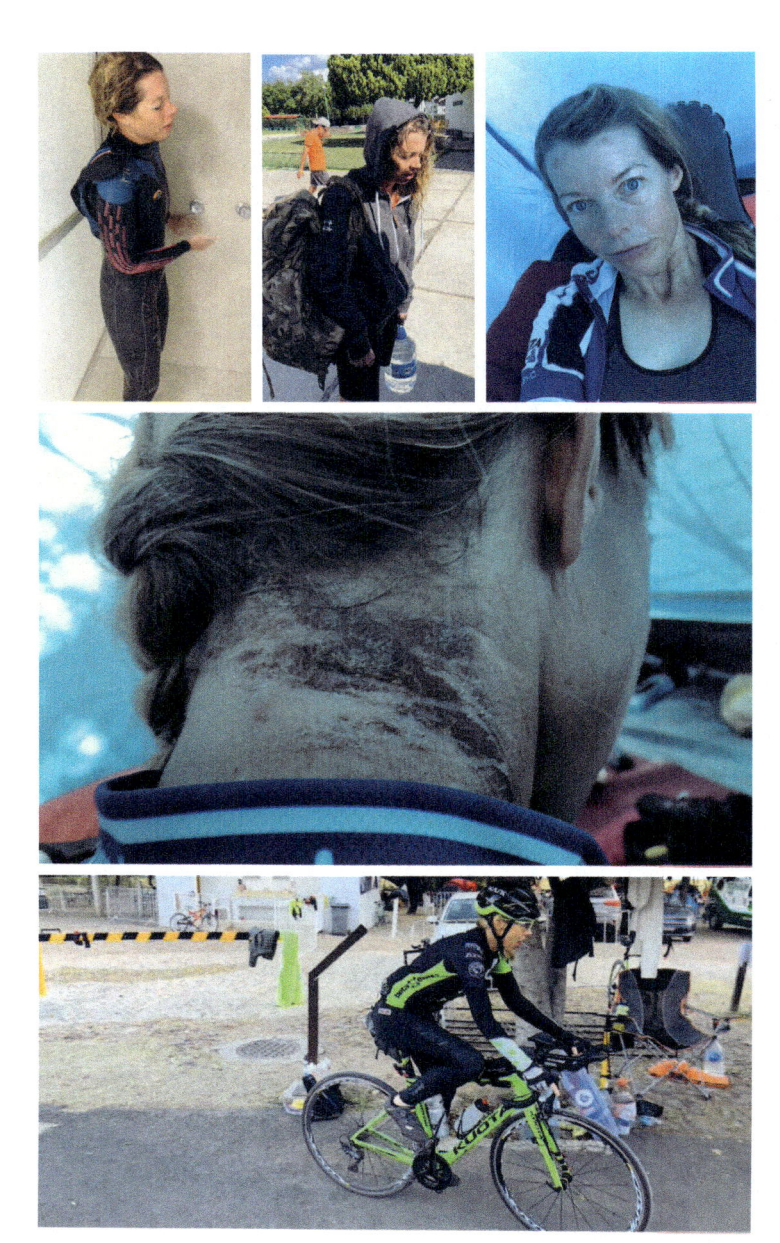

**Top:** Post 48-mile swim shower. Feeling awful but dressed! The day after the swim with a lot of sores. **Middle:** I will never complain about wetsuit chaffing again. **Bottom:** One of many laps during the 12 days I spent cycling. *All photos during Mexico Double Deca 2019*

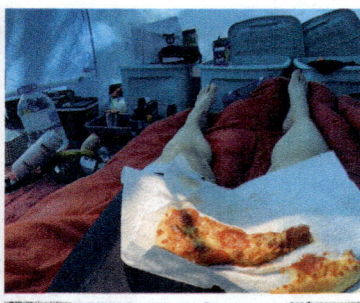

**Top:** Happy on the bike. I ate a LOT of pizza.
**Middle:** Still enjoying the bike leg.
**Bottom:** Hot afternoon breaks in the tent. With Laura and Shanda.
*All photos during Mexico Double Deca 2019*

**Top:** Daily items during the run section; music, water, pain killers, chicken noodles, race number, shoes and timing chip. My swollen left ankle during the later stages on the run. **Middle:** Shanda, me, Georgeta and Laura. Pancakes and maple syrup. **Bottom:** Getting thinner by the day, despite all the pizza and pancakes.

**Top:** Close to the end of the race, still running (sometimes).
My finisher medal and certificate.   **Bottom:** Finally finished!.
*All photos during Mexico Double Deca 2019*

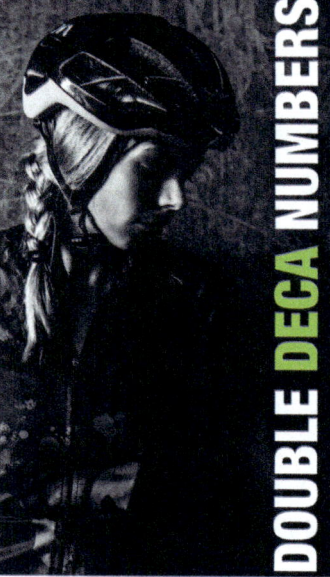

## DOUBLE DECA NUMBERS

Date stated: Friday 4th October 2019
Date finished: Friday 1st November 2019
Time taken: 660 hours, 28 minutes & 58 seconds
Position: 6th overall & 3rd female

Starters: 12
Finishers: 8

Swim distance: 48 miles
Swim time: 41 hours, 56 minutes & 49 seconds

Transition 1: 9 hours, 56 minutes & 02 seconds

Bike distance: 2240 miles
Bike time: 296 hours, 12 minutes & 16 seconds

Transition 2: 3 hours & 10 seconds

Run distance: 524 miles (20 marathons)
Run time: 309 hours, 23 minutes & 41 seconds

Daily calories required: 5,000 - 7,000
Actual daily calories: 2,500 approx.
Weight lost: 14lbs

**Top:** Flowers from the girls. Post-race junk food. Little black dresses for the presentation meal. **Bottom:** The Double Deca Stats.
*All photos during Mexico Double Deca 2019*

## START

### "I GET A BUZZ FROM SEEING PEOPLE PUSH THEIR LIMITS"

*She's the organiser of the epic Brutal triathlons and recently finished a quintuple Iron in a gym. So what drives Claire Smith to the finish line?*

I've never been in a 24hr gym before and I never will again. But last December I finished a gym-based quintuple Iron in one. It's a clammy, unnatural environment to be in. It was torture because I didn't know what time of day it was; the lights are on full beam and there's loud music continually playing. My swim was 9:30hrs and the bike 45hrs but the treadmill was where the fun began. My feet were in incredible, intense pain, so I was holding the arms of the treadmill just to take the pressure off. The total 1,130km time was 107hrs and, by the end, I didn't know where I was or what I was doing.

**Sleep deprivation is something** I'm naturally good at after working nights nursing when I was younger. I only had seven hours sleep during the gym quin. Not needing, or not being limited by, the need to go to bed is really useful in ultra triathlon.

**I mentally go into myself when** I'm suffering and don't want to speak to anyone. I think about my kids, Jake and Jess, but that makes me cry. Jess has just done her first 10km. When she finished it she said, 'Right, half marathon next!'

**CLAIRE SMITH**
Claire is the founder of Brutal Events. Races include Brutal Extreme Tri, Pig Ultra Du & Deca UK (brutalevents.co.uk).

### "I've been doing cold-water prep in an 8°C paddling pool"

And I thought, 'Oh, here we go'! They're not phased by anything they see me do.

**I used to be a lone wolf with ultras** and think I could do it alone. And sometimes I could. But I've discovered that a good crew – who know what they're doing – makes a huge difference in finishing an ultra tri. When people ask me if they need a crew, I say you don't

I've never not had chiropractor said my spine just isn road bikes, but I' give up triathlon can't ride road bi an hour, so I use

**If you want a M**
a McDonalds in McChicken sand me. I'm eating now, but a curry Noodle on the t

**I'm attempting** Iron in May. I' cold-water pre full of 8°C wate and lie in it for

---

*"The longer I go, the stronger I feel. Take the Double Deca. I had a nasty injury halfway through the run, but I flipped my mindset and it healed"* Claire Smith, first Brit to complete Double Deca Mexico

Articles from 220 Triathlon magazine - 2018 & 2020

## SUFFERING FOR OTHERS

After the boys had stopped laughing at my face, we hit the road (and the 5pm traffic) and made our way to The Gym in Bournemouth. This is an actual 24-hour gym; I kid you not, these things exist. I feel that it's important now to set the scene of what was essentially our home for the next four days.

Music – very loud, non-stop.
Lights – very bright, lots of them.
People – ever-present, working out.

So, just to be clear, the above was happening 24 HOURS A DAY – NON- STOP! Music, lights and people....

I got myself on the bike, we noted the start time, and I was off. I had my first wobble at this point; the gym was pretty busy and I was slap-bang in the main area. Other than not feeling particularly good, I also thought I looked like an actual bullfrog and felt really self-conscious. In normal events, I can put my bike glasses on and get my head down, but there was none of that here – just me sat on a bike in the middle of a busy gym. I later realised that very few of the people who came into the gym noticed us, even when we put up the giant banner that explained what I was doing.

As I started the mammoth bike ride, the guys brought all the kit up and sorted 'The Room' for my rest periods. The Room was the area where all the lost property and broken bits of gym equipment were kept – quite fitting really. It was a decent size and suited our needs; the only problem was that its lights were automatically triggered by any kind of movement, which basically meant you had to get into the camp bed and lie really, really still. Move even your little finger and the room would instantly light up, leaving you blinking and

## SUFFERING FOR OTHERS

swearing. I only had very short breaks, so this was not a massive issue for me; it got to a point that when I stopped, I fell asleep instantly. Rob was not so happy about it though.

Cycling 560 miles on a bike is always going to be challenging, but how would it be on an indoor bike? Easier, I thought... Although I had asked Chris Ette (another event organiser) what he had found the hardest aspect of his indoor Double Iron and he had said that it was having to keep turning the pedals – no free-wheeling, no cruising. And guess what? He was right. Keeping the speed at a constant rate to be able to hit the target finish of around 45 hours was really hard. And I was sweating a lot. I'm not a particularly sweaty person, but I had this weird clammy feeling the whole time. Keeping my fluids up was a must.

The seat of the bike was my main issue for the cycling section. I had chosen a recumbent bike to help with my back pain, but the saddle and back rest was so hard that Rob (who was accompanying me for some of the miles) and I both had sore bums and large bruises on our backs for days after finishing.

I was eating a reasonable amount (for me), but I remember at one point thinking that a McDonalds would be a really good idea (it was). For ultra endurance folk, eating a burger and chips is not unusual, but imagine walking into a gym and the first thing you see is a woman on an exercise bike eating a McChicken Sandwich...

The bike dragged on from 5pm on Thursday till Saturday afternoon, which even I find staggering. I watched the TV's playing music videos and the same advert for Sainsbury's over and over again. I chatted to Rob, Martin or Lou (when I say 'chatted', I mean

## SUFFERING FOR OTHERS

shouted over the music). And I rode on and on. Incredibly the gym was only completely empty for a total of twenty minutes at about 3am one night; the rest of the time there were always guys lifting ridiculously heavy weights or someone on a stepper. The cleaners would appear at some point in the middle of the night and helpfully lock the toilet doors, just when I needed them. Although, to be fair, they were really good cleaners (you notice these things when you live in a gym for nearly a week).

The last few hours were pure torture (I had no clue what was coming…). It was never-ending and I was so sick of the bike. We had changed over to a slightly more upright version for the last few hours, but it was still so uncomfortable and I kept smashing my knees on the drinks holder.

During the last 30 minutes I scrolled through Twitter and saw that a cat which belonged to someone I follow had died. He was an old cat who had lived a happy life, but I was trying to fight the tears, thinking 'don't cry, otherwise the guys will think you've lost the plot over a dead Twitter cat'. I managed to hold myself together. Little did I realise that in the next few days I would cry more than I have ever cried. In. My. Life.

Once I was off the bike, I practically skipped over to the treadmill (in reality, I hobbled over like an old man), jumped (limped) on and pressed start. I was going to smash this run and get home! Yeah baby… 5 marathons… whatever!

I have this slight issue with underestimating times and distances in the world of ultra events. I know how far I have to go, but it seems to be so much shorter in my head. This only gets worse the more

## SUFFERING FOR OTHERS

tired I get, and then suddenly I am faced with the harsh reality of another 20 hours or whatever it may be. That moment is always a good test of mental strength and character.

For most of the first half of the run, I alternated between running and walking and this seemed to work well with both timings and what I could handle physically and mentally. Visually, the treadmill was in front of the huge wall-to-ceiling windows and during the night all I could see was myself, staring back at me. I looked exhausted. Thankfully, during the day I was treated to the view of the big wheel on Bournemouth seafront instead.

At one point during the run (I have no idea what day it was), my kids came to see me. As soon as I saw them, tears came from nowhere and I pulled my daughter into the toilets, just so I could cry without feeling like an idiot. They stayed for an hour, Jess on the treadmill next to me and Jake behind on the cross-trainer. It was awesome to see them, and I felt so proud to have kids who are both fit, active and see training as a normal part of life. When they left though, I felt really down for a while.

I found that visits or phone calls from people made time go quicker, which was so necessary in this environment. I now existed in a world where even loo breaks were something I looked forward to. A couple of times, I confess, I went when I didn't actually need to, just to stop. Just to escape for a moment.

I had my first 'big' sleep of 90 minutes during the run. If it was down to me, I would not sleep at all, or at the very least, just power naps of 20 minutes. This is like hitting a reset button and stops you from falling into zombie mode, when you start to dream with

## SUFFERING FOR OTHERS

your eyes open. 90 minutes felt too indulgent and like I was losing control of my timings, but apparently sleep is important…

I woke from what felt like 8 hours to find Rob standing over me, saying my name. Not disturbing at all.

So now we have reached the part when it got very dark and twisty. It's still a real blur, and I can't really remember the order of things or whereabouts we were in terms of mileage, etc, but at roughly 3 marathons to go, the wheels well and truly fell off.

Apart from the normal aches, the main issue was my feet, which burned white-hot with pain that was indescribable. I thought it might be Plantar Fasciitis (inflammation in the sole of the foot), which I had had years ago. But that doesn't come and go; when you have it, it's there all the time. I never really found out what it was and the issue would return in other events in the future. But for now all I could do was lean on the grab rails of the treadmill to relieve some of the pressure and pain.

At this point it was noted that I was taking rather a lot of painkillers and that maybe someone else should take charge of the drug dispensing. Also, less food was being consumed and I was starting to really slow up. Even when Lou arrived and showed off her impressive Backwards Running on a Treadmill trick, it failed to cheer me up.

I had to sort myself out. I went off to my favourite hiding place (the loos) and had a quiet word. 'You have to speed up, stop focusing on the pain and stop being such a grumpy…'. I then looked at where I was in terms of distance and tried to write it down so I knew how

## SUFFERING FOR OTHERS

much I had left. I was covering 6k in an hour, so it was 1hr, 1hr, 30 mins till the end of marathon 3. Then x7 lots of 6k twice for marathons 4 and 5... (can't imagine why I failed Maths GCSE).

Simple. Sort of.

So for a while, I got it together and cracked on. Then it all went really, really bad. I never actually thought I wouldn't do it; I never thought that I would give up, but I just couldn't understand how I was going to get through the last marathon. It's hard to explain this part without sounding like a whiny, moaning idiot, but it really, really hurt at this point. Every single step killed me, and I was falling apart. I was barely speaking and then I entered The Crying Phase.

Now, I'm not proud of this part, but I feel that if you are going to write a book, then you need to be honest even when you don't want to tell people how shit you really are sometimes.

I started crying openly; not wailing, just basically sobbing. And once I had started, I really couldn't stop. I was vaguely aware of people on the treadmills near me looking at this crazy woman, speed-walking with tears streaming down her face, but I no longer cared.

Whatever it took to finish this thing.

I was getting close but still so far when Rob came into his own and calmly told me the plan. I was initially quite excited, as I thought it was going to be an awesome, painless and fast end to the GymQuin, but what it really boiled down to was this...

## SUFFERING FOR OTHERS

Rob: 'You're going to do the next hour. Then you are going to go straight into the next hour. After that you will do another hour and then you get a short break. After that you will do two more hours, then a short section, then you are finished. OK?'

Me: 'No. NO! That's not OK, it's shit. It's a shitty plan and I don't like it.'

Rob: 'Just get on with it.'

Me: More sobbing…

And as brutal as that sounds, it's exactly what I needed at that point. Sure, I could have had a sleep break, maybe some food or a shower. But what was needed was a bit of a slap and pull-yourself-together moment.

So on it went until the last 20 minutes (the worst…) and then it was over. I had finished what was undoubtedly the hardest thing I've ever done to date.

### GymQuin Stats:
Swim – 12 miles (768 lengths) = 9 hours 34 minutes
Bike – 560 miles = 47 hours 25 minutes
Run – 131 miles = 48 hours 55 minutes
Calories burnt (approx) – 7,200 (swim), 15,200 (bike) and 16,500 (run); Total = 38,900
Calories consumed – no clue but not nearly enough!
Weight lost – 4lbs
Sleep – 90 mins x2 and 20 min power naps x8; Total = 5 hours and 40 minutes (approx.)

# SUFFERING FOR OTHERS

Total time: 107 hours 49 minutes (including approx. 2 hours of transition time)

## Triathlon of Horrors - March 2018

Another particularly stupid idea of mine was The Triathlon of Horrors. This four-day event, raising funds for Sport Relief, would see me swimming the length of the English Channel in my local swimming pool. Then I would climb the equivalent of Everest on my bike by riding up and down a local hill. Finally, I would attempt the SAS Fan Dance (more on this later…) on a treadmill. With 25lbs on my back, obviously.

The first issue I had was when checking the weather forecast leading up to the start date; it looked like very cold temperatures and snow were predicted for the weekend. As I was planning to spend the first day in the swimming pool, I decided that I would change the order of the disciplines to make the most of the good weather needed for the bike. So the new plan was as follows:

Friday/Saturday: Bike the height of Everest (29,029ft) by cycling up and down a local hill (Braggers Lane in Dorset) 181 times. Which would mean I would be covering 292 miles.

Sunday: Run (although there would be very little of that happening) 15 miles wearing a 25lb pack on a treadmill, set at 6% incline to replicate the 4,000ft of elevation of the SAS Fan Dance.

Monday: Swim 1,344 lengths of a 25-metre pool, the distance between England and France.

## SUFFERING FOR OTHERS

It was an early start for the bike, and Matt, whose unfortunate job it was to crew me for this challenge, drove me the short distance from my house to the hill where I would spend the next few days cycling up and down. Shortly before we arrived, five or six deer ran out in front of the van, and we all spent a slightly surreal moment staring at each other through the early-morning mist. They eventually ran off and we continued our way to the top of Braggers Lane to set up the timing equipment which would count my laps.

I pulled my bike out of the back of the van and got my helmet and shoes on, eager to start and make the most of the light and good weather. I knew I was on borrowed time and that this challenge would become a lot harder later on tonight.

I had ridden up Braggers Lane many times before, mainly as part of the Enduroman Double and Triple Iron races that I had attempted over the years, so it was very familiar. What I hadn't experienced so much of was the selfish driving of the locals, who also knew the narrow lane well and didn't give a shit that some idiot was riding up and down it. Range Rovers and tractors towing trailers streamed past me, barely giving me an inch and a few times even forcing me off the road onto the verge. The more tired I got, the angrier I became. Poor Matt bore the brunt of my ranting and cursing during that day.

The one thing that cheered me up though (apart from my brilliant parents turning up with cheesy mashed potato) was a particularly dimwitted pheasant, who took it upon itself to be my cheerleader for the afternoon. Up and down the side of the lane it ran and while this made me a little nervous, as I expected it to run across the road at any moment, it did make me smile.

## SUFFERING FOR OTHERS

I was chipping away at the lap total and by the time I made it to sunset, I felt quite positive. The road was getting quieter and I was looking forwards to being the only one on it for a few hours. The temperature started to drop quite dramatically as night fell, so I layered up and added lights to my bike.

As it got dark, my lap times slowed. I knew this would happen, as I'm not the most confident of cyclists at the best of times, and the combo of going down a steep hill while tired added to the mix. Then the rain started – just a few showers at first, then more persistent. On went the waterproofs and my mood took a further hit. I was now very, very cold. Whose stupid idea was this?

I tried to remain positive though and listened to the audiobook of Mick Dawson rowing the Pacific as I climbed up and tentatively down the hill, over and over. Rain was now dripping down the back of my jacket. At one point, I cycled past the van and looked in to see Matt fast asleep, wrapped in a DryRobe, with the engine running. This did not improve my mood and I may have muttered some things under my breath...

The weather continued to deteriorate and with it my mood. On lap 113, I had to take shelter in the back of the van, waking Matt up in the process. I sat there shivering and soaking wet, wondering how I was going to get through the next day. At that point the rain really started coming down and the van began to rock in the wind. We looked at each other in concern. We then realised it was also snowing.

'I think we need plan B,' Matt said.

## SUFFERING FOR OTHERS

'But we don't have a plan B,' I replied.

'Then let's come up with one,' he suggested.

We decided that I would finish the bike indoors on the turbo. The storm had eased off, but the snow was now falling steadily, and cycling up and down an icy hill was only going to end one way.

To make the turbo as realistic as possible, I would set the resistance as high as possible for 12 minutes and then to an easy spin for 5 minutes to replicate the up and downhill effort. Every 'lap' I completed, Matt would pass the timing chip over the box to count it.

I had to do 68 'laps' in my little kitchen, with all my wet kit drying around me. I set Netflix up and whiled away the hours of turbo monotony. The snow continued to fall all of Saturday and I knew I had made the right call and that I hadn't had much choice. It still felt like I had given up though.

After what seemed like days, I finally finished the required amount and lay, broken, on my living room floor. Sweaty and exhausted, but it was done. Now I had a few hours to sleep before I needed to be up and in the gym to start the run section of the challenge.

I woke the next day tired and sore but ready to go. I got into my run kit and we packed my nutrition and my Bergen (an army rucksack) into the van. During the drive to the gym, I tried to cram more calories into my already depleted body. Once we had arrived, I hauled the 25lb pack out of the back and hoisted it onto my shoulders. It almost made me over-balance and fall over, it was so heavy.

## SUFFERING FOR OTHERS

Once we had taken everything up to the gym, I stood on the treadmill, my pack firmly in place and the gradient set at 6%. I was prepared for about four to five hours of pain and suffering, which compared to the bike section sounded easy, but I had a feeling it wasn't going to be.

I hit the start button on the treadmill and began to walk, increasing the speed until I hit a level that I felt was maintainable. After about an hour a few things were clear:

1. The baked bean cans I had packed my Bergen with were really making their presence known.
2. It was definitely going to be 5 hours.
3. The blisters were going to be epic!

The gym was pretty busy, due to it being a Sunday, and people were doing what they do best, staring… I had been in this situation before during the GymQuin, so I was pretty used to it, but I still found it hard. I really wished some of them would come over and donate some cash, but that seemed too much to ask.

About halfway through the distance, I began to hold onto the rails of the treadmill, as the more fatigued I became, the harder it was to stay on. I was basically starting to slide off the back. My feet were also catching on the belt, which would wake me up, as falling over on a treadmill wearing this pack would be far from ideal. Funny for the gawping gym-goers though…

After 5 hours and 17 minutes I finally hit stop on the treadmill and wrestled the pack off my back. I had deep sores under my arms and on my shoulders from the straps, and my feet were bloody from

## SUFFERING FOR OTHERS

blisters. I limped out of the gym (with Matt carrying the pack this time) and we drove home. Second part of the challenge completed!

The final section of the Triathlon of Horrors was the 21-mile swim. The furthest I had ever swum in a pool before was 12 miles, so this was going to test me somewhat. My biggest worry was my asthma, which had kicked off previously due to the chemicals and length of time I was immersed in them. During the 12-mile swim in the GymQuin, I had been coughing under the water in between taking breaths. I hoped it wouldn't come to that this time.

I started the swim in a costume as my local pool is pretty warm, but that day I was feeling anything but that. I figured I would heat up soon enough though. But after a few miles, I realised that it wasn't getting any better, so I got out of the pool to add a thermal vest. This helped a bit and I was able to forget about my body temperature and concentrate on the countless laps instead.

About halfway through, I was starting to feel cold again and this time I began to shiver. I put this down to the fatigue I was feeling after the last three days of putting my body through mile after mile of suffering. And although I felt a bit of an idiot, I completed the last part of the swim in a wetsuit. I just wanted to be warm and get this bloody thing done.

I broke the swim down into miles, counting 64 laps in my head (not often correctly, but it kept me occupied). I would stop after every mile and eat and drink whatever Matt had left for me on the poolside. My appetite reduced over the day and in the end all I was taking on were sports drinks and Jelly Babies.

## SUFFERING FOR OTHERS

After 14 hours and 21 minutes, I was finally done and struggled out of the pool, dizzy, tired, but very happy. I had raised £1,600 for Sport Relief and considering the crazy weather, felt like I had done alright. Now all I wanted was a decent meal and my bed.


**The Fan Dance - January 2019**

After completing a Fan Dance simulation on the treadmill, I was keen to see if I could do the real thing...

The Fan Dance is based in the Brecon Beacons and is part of the Fitness and Navigation phase of the selection process for the Special Forces. It is a 15-mile exercise that takes you over Pen y Fan and down Jacob's Ladder. You then continue until you reach the Check Point (CP) before you return to the start point, going back up Jacob's Ladder and over south Wales' highest mountain again.

The event company that organises this challenge for civilians offers a summer or winter version. They also hold a Single or Double option, and you can choose to wear a weighted Bergen or not. Having read this far into my book, I suspect you know which race I picked.

I entered a few weeks before the event. It was around Christmas, which is not my favourite time of year, and I was struggling with feeling a little low due to my most recent one-a-day DIY Winter Deca attempt, which ended on day 5 with tears and a chest infection. Now, in the festive season most women would perhaps go shopping for expensive shoes they don't need, or take to the sofa with wine,

## SUFFERING FOR OTHERS

chocolate and box sets. But I looked for the hardest event I could find in the UK that was taking place in the next fortnight.

It didn't take me long to stumble across the Fan Dance, and it took me precisely 0.3 of a second to decide that this was exactly what I needed. Even though I hadn't trained for it or owned any of the kit. I did, however, know the area well, as I ran some of my own events there already, so navigation wouldn't be an issue. One positive, at least.

The other good thing was that my boyfriend of the time, Jon, was in the Army, although when he discovered what I had planned, he was not too impressed. Once he was over his initial eye-rolling and 'why do you keep doing this?' stage, he set about looking at the lengthy kit list and attempting to plan some very last-minute training for me.

For the weighted version for female entrants, we had to carry 25lbs, made up of the sort of kit that you would need if you were out on the mountains.

The kit list was huge and terrifying:

**PACK AND CONTENTS**
Bergen/rucksack
Waterproof liner
Hi-viz
First aid kit
Sleeping bag
Emergency bivi
Bivi shelter

# SUFFERING FOR OTHERS

Dry kit
Base layer/T-shirt
Warm middle layer
Waterproof jacket & trousers
Roll mat
Talcum powder
Spare hat & gloves
Towel
Water bottles/hydration system (3 litres)
Gas stove burner to make a hot drink, heat food
Brew kit (tea bags/coffee)
Lighter
Emergency food rations
Flask (thermos type, not liquor) [Compulsory for winter]
Waterproof bag for valuables
Torch and spare batteries
Trainers/ trail shoes in case of damage to boots
Spare laces
Racing spoon & metal mug or mess tin
Plastic mug
Plastic sandwich box
Packed lunch: food to consume on the march
Rescue flares
Boots (Can be military or civilian trekking boots)
Trousers (Compulsory for winter edition)
Windproof jacket/SAS/Para smock/Para silk top
Warm hat or balaclava & gloves or sun hat or patrol cap
Socks of a decent quality suited to trekking and hill-walking
Emergency vitals card: name, next of kin name & cell number, blood group if known, any medical history/condition
Compass

## SUFFERING FOR OTHERS

Map segment (to be issued electronically)
Safety card (to be issued electronically)
Watch
Head torch (on person for night marches)
Spare torch (High Moon or other night event only)
Sharp knife/utility tool (can go inside Bergen or on person)
Whistle
Notebook & pencil in waterproof bag (can go inside Bergen)
Mobile phone
Spare change

**OTHER RECOMMENDED ITEMS**
Radio & ancillaries
Goggles and/or sunglasses
GPS
Lip balm
Neck buff/gaiter or scrim net
Bivi bag (different to emergency bivi)

As an extreme event organiser, I was very used to mandatory kit lists, but this was on another level. Some of the items I didn't even own. Fortunately, as Jon was in the forces, he had a LOT of kit and everything on the list.

Once everything was sorted, Jon laid out the items on his bed and we stood back and eyed the vast array of kit.

'That's never going to fit in that rucksack,' I said, matter-of-factly. Jon looked at me and sighed. 'Just watch,' he said.

And with that, he proceeded to pack the Bergen with the ease of

## SUFFERING FOR OTHERS

someone who had done it hundreds of times, and once he had finished, he offered it to me. 'Put it on.'

I took the pack from him and gasped as the weight of it shocked me. I could barely hold it; how the hell was I going to do a Double Fan Dance (one of them at night) with it on my back? I wrestled and pulled the pack until it was on my shoulders and stood, swaying, in Jon's room. 'Oh fuck, what have I done?'. Jon just laughed and called me a dickhead.

The other issue was that if you had chosen the weighted version, you needed boots. Proper hiking boots with ankle support. Obviously, I didn't own a pair and had assumed I could use my Salomon off-road running shoes.

So, a trip to Cotswold Outdoor followed and I became the owner of a brand-new pair of hiking boots and thick wool socks.

With very little time to go before the event, I squeezed in a few training sessions on the hills near my house and one longer session in the Purbecks in Dorset, specifically at Lulworth, where there are some really nasty climbs. Running with the pack was quite simply impossible. I tried, but realistically my best option for finishing the event was to walk as fast as I could. Easier said than done, when you have a huge pack on your back, which made me feel unbalanced and clumsy. My new boots rubbed and dug into my feet and ankles. When I mentioned this to my kind, supportive other half, he rolled his eyes and said, 'Normal people properly prep for events and would be wearing boots they have worn in. This is your fault, so stop moaning.' I didn't mention it again.

## SUFFERING FOR OTHERS

The training session was a relative success. I had to keep over a certain average on my Garmin to make the cut-offs. I had managed it that day, but I was very aware that the Purbecks were not mountains, and that 6 miles was definitely not 30. The best part of the training was taking the pack off. The relief was incredible and for five minutes afterwards, I felt like I was almost floating off the ground, like an astronaut in space.

I had booked a local Premier Inn for a couple of nights for the event. Anyone who knows me is familiar of my love for this particular chain of hotels. The beds are huge and comfy, and most importantly, the rooms have baths, which when you have spent hours on the coast path or swimming in the freezing waters of Dover Harbour is the most amazing thing ever.

I lugged all my kit up to my room, noticing a few other guys checking in with packs and poles. Once I had finished, I collapsed onto the bed, exhausted. Not exactly reassuring, considering it was on the first floor, but I put it down to the long drive and general tiredness you get from the kind of long-distance events that I do. I was probably anaemic too, just for a change.

There was no time to rest, as I needed to make my way to the event HQ to register and have my pack weighed. This had been stressing me out, as I had been imagining scary SAS types pushing their faces close to mine and shouting, 'THIS IS TOO LIGHT, ARE YOU TRYING TO GET AN EASY RIDE, SMITH?'. This didn't happen and the whole process went smoothly. As I attempted to get my pack back in the van, I felt like I might even enjoy tomorrow.

That night, however, I was up and down with an upset stomach

## SUFFERING FOR OTHERS

and griping pains. I awoke after a few hours of restless sleep and wondered if I had got food poisoning from the fish and chips I had eaten the night before. It seemed unlikely but why else had I felt so ill?

Once I was dressed and had everything sorted for spending a day and night in the Welsh mountains in January, I made my way once again to the race HQ. The nerves kicked in when I parked at the side of the road and saw hundreds of fit-looking people (mainly men) making their way to the start, with huge packs casually resting on their shoulders. I took a deep breath and balanced my pack on the back of the van, bent down to slip my arms through the straps and then attempted to stand. After a few failed efforts, I finally managed to get up and fix the straps firmly around my chest and waist. I was ready.

The race instructions had been very clear in stating that you needed to find the mountain log-book and sign it to ensure that the Directing Staff (DS) had a final count of who was on the hills. As an event director myself, this made perfect sense, so I have no real excuse for what happened next. I couldn't remember if the all-important book was at the famous red telephone box (which also marked the finish line) or somewhere else.

I looked around, hoping to see an obvious line of people, but could see nothing. After a while, a few people doing the same as me started walking over to a tent where, apparently, the book was. I followed them, relieved that I finally had a plan.

'Where the FUCK are you going?' a tall, intimidating man shouted. Weirdly, he seemed to be directing this question at me, despite the

## SUFFERING FOR OTHERS

fact I was in a group of four or five others.

'Erm, the mountain book? I need to sign it...' I struggled to find my words in the confusion.

'ARE YOU FUCKING KIDDING ME?' the man screamed again, this time pushing his face close to mine, so I could feel his breath hot on my face.

My confusion increased as he still seemed to be directing his anger at only me.

'YOU SHOULD HAVE DONE THIS AN HOUR AGO, YOU ARE FUCKING USELESS AND ALL OUT OF THE EVENT.'

And with that he reached down to my race number, carefully pinned on my leg, and ripped it off.

'GO ON, FUCK OFF!'

I looked around me and then back at him, waiting for someone to laugh. But nobody did. In fact, everyone looked utterly terrified, and started making excuses and begging this man to allow them to continue. He was having none of it and repeated that we were done. He marched off and left us, bewildered and wondering what to do next.

One guy, Rob, who I had been talking to (he had taken part in one of my previous events), looked at me and said, 'He doesn't own the mountain; let's just go and do it anyway.'

## SUFFERING FOR OTHERS

I thought for a moment and then looked up at him and said, 'You're right. Let's not let this grumpy bastard ruin our day.'

That moment, for me, was a perfect example of the times in life when you can make a choice. You can choose to be negative and play the victim, or look at the situation and pull out the positives from it. You then adapt your plans and move forward.

So Rob and I stood at the back of the race briefing and let the bulk of the crowd clear before starting on the route. We explained briefly to the DS at CPs along the way what had happened and why we weren't wearing our race numbers. There were a few wry smiles and nods of heads, as if this sort of thing had happened before. The tall, grumpy man turned out to be the infamous race director, Ken Jones, and he did not suffer fools gladly. Nobody stopped us continuing though, and my mood lifted as we climbed higher into the mountains.

The route itself was a simple one, up Corn Du and along to Pen y Fan. After the summit though, things changed. Descending Jacob's Ladder, which was covered in ice and snow, with 25lbs on your back and boots you have only worn three times, turns out to be pretty damn tricky. I had chosen not to take poles, as I wanted the full SAS experience (and I was scared of the DS and their scathing looks), but I could not stay on my feet. Bam! I hit the ground again and again, and each time I would struggle to pull myself up, unbalanced by the huge pack on my back. Luckily, I was surrounded by other people (the first day's event was the biggest and most popular) and we all laughed as we slipped and slid our way down the mountain.

Once off Pen y Fan, the challenge was to move as fast as possible

## SUFFERING FOR OTHERS

(in my case, this was not very fast at all) and make it to the CP at the turn point. Although we had been removed from the official event, I still wanted to complete the race within the allocated time. Speed-walking while chatting and laughing with Rob, the hour or so went quickly and I barely noticed the aching in my shoulders and back and the blisters starting to form on my heels.

When we made it to the CP, with about 10 minutes to spare, we gave the DS the same story we had been reciting along the route. Once again, we got a knowing look and the reply, 'I wouldn't worry too much, you will still get your patch when you finish.' This was good news and gave me the push I needed to turn and get back to HQ. As much as I pretended that I didn't care about being kicked off the race, I was really disappointed and was also dreading explaining to my other half how I had failed to follow some very basic instructions.

During the 7 miles back up the mountain, my body began to hurt. I realised how sore my back was and on the inclines my heels were burning as the skin was rubbed raw from the new boots. I had also decided not to wear my special hiking socks that morning, deciding instead to use my familiar running socks. This was another mistake. The climb up Jacob's Ladder was certainly easier than coming down, but I was in a lot of pain by the time I reached the top.

Once we were on the flat (after a minor navigation error), I tried to pick the pace up, keen to finish and remove my pack and boots. I had already decided that there was no way I could do the second march later that night. This had been hard enough, I decided. Soon we were descending and the famous red phone box was in sight. The tall, grumpy race director looked at me, suspiciously. 'Did he

## SUFFERING FOR OTHERS

remember me?' I wondered. I flashed him my best smile and hoped for the best.

He narrowed his eyes and barked, 'stop looking so happy!' For a moment I thought he was serious, but then I caught a look in his eyes and relaxed. I was presented with my finisher's patch and had my photo taken.

Once I had caught up with Rob, he invited me back to his van, which was an actual camper van, rather than my transit with a camp bed in the back. I hesitated for a moment, but he went on to say he would make tea and had pork pies, and I was in. I experienced a moment of pure bliss as I removed my pack and pulled at my boots. Once they were off, I inspected the damage. Blood stained my socks and my heels were a mess. I cleaned them up with a couple of wipes, while stuffing my face with sandwiches, pie and then cake, washing it down with hot, sweet tea. Heaven.

Rob then broke my happy bubble by saying, 'so, tonight's hike...?'

I looked at him in horror. 'Oh, fuck, no. Really, I can't. That was so hard. No. Just no. Fuck!'

Rob laughed. 'Really?'

I texted Jon and told him that I couldn't do the night exercise. He asked why. 'Because I don't think I can do it,' I replied. 'Of course you can,' was his response.

And that was that. I turned to Rob and said, 'OK, let's do it.'

## SUFFERING FOR OTHERS

We had a few hours' rest until the night's fun began. This event followed a different route – a climb up to the ridgeway and then down a steep gully, on to the CP and then back to Pen y Fan, this time using the morning's route. Which meant up the dreaded Jacob's Ladder for the second time.

The start was in a slightly different place as well, just down the road in a car park. A much smaller group gathered around, nervously checking kit, attaching light sticks to packs and fiddling with head torches. The DS shouted that we were to stand and wait to be called forward. Once our name was called, we would be allowed to proceed onto the route. If you missed your name, you were out. For some reason, my name didn't seem to be on this list. And as I stood waiting, getting more and more stressed, I realised that, once again, I was going to be having a conversation with the race director. I tentatively raised my hand, waiting for the bollocking I was obviously going to get.

'YOU AGAIN!' the race director shouted.

'Yes, me again. Sorry.'

'WHAT NOW?'

'I'm not on the list; I don't know why.'

'FOR FUCK'S SAKE! WHAT'S YOUR NAME? I WILL ADD YOU.'

'Claire Smith,' I muttered apologetically.

## SUFFERING FOR OTHERS

'GET DOWN AND GIVE ME 10 PRESS-UPS.'

I looked at him in horror. I could barely walk straight with this pack on my back. If I got on the ground, there would be no getting up. Let alone any kind of a press-up. Just as I was trying to work out how I was going to attempt it, I caught a look in his eye, the same look from earlier.

'I'm only joking about the press-ups,' he said, under his breath.

I breathed a MASSIVE sigh of relief. And then made my way over the bridge to start my second Fan Dance of the day.

I was hopeful that as this route was a few miles shorter and only included one ascent/descent of Pen y Fan, it would be easier. As usual, I was completely and utterly wrong. From the moment we were on the ridgeway, the wind was trying to blow me off my feet and down a very steep drop. I knew exactly how steep it was as I had seen it in the light many, many times. This didn't help.

The path was also scattered with huge, uneven rocks, and I spent the whole time getting my unfamiliar, clumsy boots caught and tripping up. Once I had survived this terrain and the howling gales of death, I pressed on to the path from hell. This route took us down the side of the ridgeway and was, quite literally, one of the worst paths I had ever been on.

I can honestly say that there were a few moments on this descent when I had to have a few words with myself. The tiny, ridiculously narrow route was covered in slippery, ice-covered rocks, and where it was so steep and I was so unbalanced, it was an incredibly slow

## SUFFERING FOR OTHERS

process. I tried very hard to not plunge to my death, or at least to a mess of broken bones and blood. In some places, I had to resign to sitting on my bum, like a three-year-old going down the stairs. Not very SAS, I thought to myself. Thank fuck the grumpy RD couldn't see me now. He would literally explode with anger, I thought to myself. This cheered me somewhat.

Once I was down and on my way to the CP, I felt a little better; surely that was the worst part over. The DS's were sitting in their vehicle and it was clear that I was one of the last people on the course. 'Get a move on,' they growled at me.

'OK,' I replied, thinking that there was little chance of any increase in speed at this point, but they probably didn't need to hear that.

This part of the course was familiar from this morning, and after a spell of flat, the trail began to rise and eventually got steeper still as I moved closer to the mountain. I was really feeling it by this stage. A few jellybeans from Rob improved my mood, but I knew exactly what I had coming up. Once we hit the really steep section, I told Rob to go on by himself. I could feel his frustration at my glacial pace and didn't want the extra pressure.

The last push up Pen y Fan was very tough that night. I remember being with a small group of people and surprisingly, a few men. I was initially at the back with the sweeper, a nice ex-forces type, who chatted away to me as if he was strolling along the prom. I, meanwhile, gasped at every breath, trying to find the air I needed to get me to the summit. I remember saying to him that 'this was my pace, and sorry it was so slow'.

## SUFFERING FOR OTHERS

'Are you going to stop?' he asked.

'No, I won't stop,' I panted at him. 'It just might look like I have.' He laughed and replied, 'As long as you keep going, that's all I care about.'

After a while, I realised that I had overtaken a few people. This briefly lifted my spirits. Until I realised how far I still had to go. I was now taking tiny steps, moving inch by inch. And my head was practically up the arse of the woman in front. This wasn't a choice, and I did apologise to her, but the problem was that she was the exact same pace as me. If I slowed, I risked falling over and I honestly didn't know if I could get up if that happened. If I went any faster, I would push her out the way. Not cool. So, my head was next to her butt. I dealt with it. To be fair, with the darkness, gales and ice-covered rocks, that was the very least of my issues.

Those last 45 minutes were a real test. There was no escape from it. I just had to put my head down and keep moving, knowing that it wouldn't last forever and I could get through it. Once I clambered, quite literally, onto the top of Pen y Fan, I grinned and let out a massive sigh of relief. I had done it. The last section was pretty much all downhill.

The wind also eased up and I picked my pace up a little. I heard a noise behind me and turned to find one of the men whom I had left behind earlier. He was over 6ft and chatted away to me for a while, explaining he was ex-forces and how much he missed that life. As we got closer to the finish, when we could see the lights of the road below, his head-torch flickered and went out.

## SUFFERING FOR OTHERS

'Fuck,' he muttered.

'No worries,' I said. 'Mine is bright enough for both of us.'

We trotted further down the mountainside until we were almost at the finish and at this point, he broke into a run and left me behind.

'Wow,' I said, to nobody in particular. 'Who said chivalry was dead?'

As I made my way into the Storey Arms, the outdoor education centre at the foot of Pen y Fan, and approached the RD for the final time, he eyed me and sighed, 'You. Again.'

I broke into a massive grin. 'I did it!'

Once I was back in my hotel room. I eased myself gingerly into a huge, hot bubble-bath. And then immediately shrieked and pulled my blistered feet out of the water. After some interesting manoeuvring, I lay back in the water, with my feet hanging over the edge of the bath, and reflected on what had been an amazing experience. From start to finish, there had been so many moments when I'd had to remind myself that nobody was going to come and rescue me; I had no choice but to keep moving forward, no matter how slowly.

And no matter how much some tall, grumpy bloke shouts at you, don't give up.

## LIFE LESSON
# STAYING MOTIVATED

Real motivation comes from within you.

It doesn't come from the Internet, Facebook or Instagram. It doesn't come in a book or podcast. And it doesn't come from a celebrity sportsman or woman.

It comes 100% from inside you.

Let that sink in for a moment. It's not to say that the books we read and the quotes we stick on our fridge or choose as the wallpaper of our phone don't help. But you need to be very clear about your goals and how you are going to reach them. Because when you lose your motivation – and that will happen, have no doubt – you need to know how to get yourself back on track with as little damage done as possible.

Here are some tips on how to keep your mojo in check:

**1. Do not procrastinate**

This is the number one reason why a lot of people give up on their goals. It is sneaky and creeps up on you. Ensure you stay on top of your to-do list and don't let it become overwhelming by getting behind on things.

**2. Take a break**

Sometimes stuff can get too much, especially if your goal is a big one. If you are feeling exhausted and broken, take a few hours, or even a day or so, to have a complete break from it all. Do some different training or don't train at all. Go to the cinema and spend some time with family and friends. Chances are you will be eager to return once you have had a mental and/or physical rest.

### 3. The why

It's easy to lose sight of the end game sometimes, and sitting down for a moment to remember why you are doing this is important and will help get you back on track. Make a short list of the reasons why you are doing this and also how you see your life changing if you complete it.

### 4. Vision board

This might make you feel like a teenage girl, but by cutting or printing out images and phrases which inspire you every time you look at them, your focus will be brought firmly back to where it needs to be. Images are strong motivators, so ensure you pick ones that really resonate with you and are specific to your goals.

## CHAPTER 9
# TEN DAYS OF HELL

I heard about the 1x10 Deca triathlon before I had even completed my first Half Ironman in 2006.

I was sitting in my living room, flipping through the pages of *220 Triathlon* magazine, and read about this event where you did 10 Ironman races for 10 days, back to back, with no breaks. I couldn't believe what I was reading and certainly had no thoughts or plans to enter one. I could barely imagine finishing the hilly Half I had coming up in a few months.

But years later and after completing the Double Iron and Lanzarote Ultra, my thoughts went back to the Deca and I started to wonder if I could finish one. I didn't know it then, but this event would become my obsession and nemesis (alongside the Arch to Arc) and would be the cause of a lot of pain, tears and DNF's (I suspect even if I had known this, it still wouldn't have stopped me).

Here's a brief explanation about Decas and their different formats. For people who don't do them (most of the population), the different styles can be understandably confusing.

Basically, there are two formats for ultra triathlons. One is the continuous and the other is the one-a-day. The continuous is where you do all the discipline distances in one go. So, taking the swim section as an example, in the continuous you swim 24 miles in one hit and in the 1x10 (one-a-day) Deca, you swim 2.4 miles every day for 10 days.

## TEN DAYS OF HELL

So, just to clarify, here are the distances for both Deca formats:
Continuous Deca: 24-mile swim; 1,120-mile bike; 262-mile run
1x10 Deca: 2.4-mile swim (every day); 112-mile bike (every day); 26.2-mile run (every day)

Also, cut-offs are confusing as they are different for both events. The 1x10 Deca is obviously 10 days. Some races have a 20-hour time limit each day, ensuring you finish every day and rest for 4 hours. Other event companies allow the athletes to use the full 24 hours.

For the continuous format of the Deca, the cut-off is 14 days. Why is it so much longer than the 1x10 format? It's been said that the continuous format is the harder of the two races.

Anyway, the year I decided to take on an ultra triathlon, the 1x10 Deca was the only race available. And it was also in Mexico! As I had only ever been to Mallorca and Lanzarote at the time, this was going to take me out of my comfort zone in every way possible. After thinking long and hard (in reality, about ten minutes), I entered the race and booked my flights.

I created some kind of training plan and I cracked on with it, feeling positive. As long as I got the miles in, I would be good. Right?

Wrong. So, so wrong.

A 1x10 Deca is hard for most folk, but if you can do a normal Ironman in a fairly respectable time, say 12-14 hours, you are on the right track. My first Ironman had taken me just over 14 hours, but that had been seven years ago and since then all I had done

## TEN DAYS OF HELL

was get slower. My Ironman time now was more like 16 hours, especially with the back problems I had. But I worked out that all I had to do was 18-20 hours a day and then get 4 hours' sleep a night. For 10 days. Easy.

What I hadn't taken into consideration was the faffing required when you are putting your body through so much. From getting changed out of your wetsuit every morning and into bike kit and then run stuff, to looking after your feet from running marathon after marathon, patching up the many blisters. Trying to eat enough, and cleaning and refilling your bottles. Punctures and mechanicals waste precious time too. It's not just about the miles…

For the Mexico 1x10 Deca, in October 2015, the swim was in a lake, the bike circled around it and the run was an out and back mile. The water in the lake was a little colder than I had expected and I struggled, as usual, with my open-water issues. The bike course was a little busy with families, which would make it hard to negotiate at peak times.

Day 1 saw me finishing in 16 hours and 32 minutes. Not too bad… Overall the day had been a good one. My back pain had been bad but it was not like I hadn't expected that. I hadn't eaten as much as I needed to though and I was definitely dehydrated from the strong Mexican sun.

Day 2 started badly, with panic attacks during the swim and shivering after. On the bike I had a couple of punctures and my appetite disappeared. Once I got to the run, my feet were throbbing so badly, it made me cry in pain. I finished in 18 hours and 44 minutes and I didn't even bother going back to the hotel that night;

## **TEN DAYS OF HELL**

I just slept in one of the tents on the lakeside.

Day 3 found me crying as I put my wetsuit on. I felt awful and just didn't know how I would make it through the day. The swim was a little better, but the back pain on my bike was terrible and at one point, I just put my head on my handlebars and sobbed. The run was mainly walking, my feet burning. That day was my last and I finished in 21 hours and 4 minutes.

I was done. I had completely underestimated how stupidly hard a Deca was. I was massively under-prepared and under-trained. I had to limp away with my tail between my legs and admit that I had really fucked up.

When I was back in the UK and after the normal period of time when you announce to the world that you are giving up triathlon forever, etc, etc, I found myself thinking two things:

1. I wanted to organise my own 1x10 Deca event, here in the UK.
2. I really, really wanted to finish one myself. Preferably before I organised one.

So I came up with the perfect plan of finding the venue where my proposed event, DecaUK, would take place, and then 12 months before the race, complete my own test. After a lot of searching, I decided to use the rowing venue, Dorney Lake, in Windsor. It was closed to the public, so traffic wouldn't be a problem. It wasn't cheap, but worth it to not have the worry of super-tired athletes on open roads.

The official race was set for the first week of October 2017. I

## TEN DAYS OF HELL

wanted September, but the venue was completely booked up with other events. I worried about the water and air temperature having a negative effect on the athletes. I also worried about my own recce and whether the cold would stop me. But as you've probably realised already, I've never been one to shy away from a challenge. I set my own Dorney Deca Recce date for the October of that year, 2016. Unfortunately, the venue was booked on the first weekend, so I had to start my test event on the 14th of October. How much of a difference would those extra ten days make to the weather and water temperature, I wondered.

Other than the temperature worries, the other thing that I had been struggling with ever since I first started in triathlon was my back pain. Now, I'm fully aware that everybody struggles with some kind of back pain on long-distance bike rides, in the same way that everyone gets sore feet during a marathon. But the pain I was suffering with seemed to be on another level. It started building from 30 miles in and became so bad by the later miles that it consumed me.

But as soon as I got off the bike, it was gone! I tried everything to eliminate or even just reduce the intense pain, but nothing worked. No painkiller or ibuprofen gel, TENS machine or heat pad; no massage or stretching, no brace or support. I even tried to ride a hybrid bike to see if the more upright position would help.

Nothing worked. And I got so frustrated that I eventually I paid for an MRI to see if that shed any light on my issue.

What the MRI showed was the lumbar (lower) part of my spine curved inwards far more than most people's, and as a result of

## TEN DAYS OF HELL

the steep curvature, my L5 nerves were being compressed, which explained the pain and also why my toes and feet went numb when I leaned forward on my road bike.

So it helped that I knew what it was, but sorting it wasn't a quick fix, or a fix at all. I learnt all I could about this new condition I had – it even had a name: hyperlordosis (I also found out that my grandma had suffered from it, but as she didn't take part in Ironman triathlons, it was never a massive issue for her!). And although Google promised me that special exercises and stretches could 'fix my back', the reality was that changing the shape of your spine when you are 40 is unrealistic.

After more fruitless Google searches, I came across the recumbent cycle. These weird-looking bikes basically put you (and your spine) in the opposite position and therefore eliminated my problem completely. I was overjoyed, thought I had finally found my answer and set about looking for one I could buy.

My first recumbent (they are known affectionately as 'bents' by their riders) was a three-wheeled tricycle that I planned to use on the Dorney Deca Recce. I named it Bender (after the robot in *Futurama*) and set about getting used to riding it. The problem was that it was very heavy and I barely got above 12mph on it. So I decided that I would switch between Bender and my road bike to help with my average speed as well as pain management over the 1,120 miles.

With all my bases covered, I was as ready as I could be. All I had to do now was try and finish 10 Ironman distances in 10 days.

## TEN DAYS OF HELL

These are my blog entries for the days leading up to, during and after the Dorney Deca Recce:

### *14 October 2016*

*I can't believe how quickly this has come round. I have found myself wishing that this weekend was just a normal few days of long training, instead of what's actually happening.*

*Basically I'm really scared, this is complete unknown territory. Have I trained enough? I don't feel like it right now. I have trained way more than before and I have made huge changes to ensure that, whatever happens over the next 10 days, I don't repeat the same mistakes I've made in the past.*

*I've got crazy amounts of neoprene for the swim, I intend to switch between Bender (the recumbent trike) and my Planet X road bike to avoid the debilitating back pain I've always suffered from and I've done all my run training on the road, so hopefully my legs/feet are better prepared this time round. I've also sorted all my work/business, so nothing is hanging over me this time round. Just 100% focus.*

*Timing wise, I intend to play the long, slow game from day 1. All I want from this is to get to the finish line. It's all I have been thinking (obsessing) about for the last 12 months and I will be listening to my (totally awe-inspiring and very experienced) support crew and eating, drinking and resting when I'm told (should be interesting…). They will also be ensuring my times are on track (my biggest pressure/worry).*

## TEN DAYS OF HELL

*16 October 2016*

*I met Martin, one of my crew, for Starbucks and Sainsbury's shopping and then my folks arrived and we got started on putting up the tents, etc. I wish we could have set up a bit earlier, so we had the chance to relax a bit. But once the wind and rain had stopped (!!!) we sorted everything and got the kettle on.*

*Once Mark 'Ugly 10 Deca' Yates had turned up, we had chips and more tea and after going through the general plan for day 1, hit the sack. I have a four-man tent to myself borrowed from Martin and super comfortable army 'cot' (not an actual cot but pull-up bed!!) from Mark. My daughter convinced me to bring the winter duvet as well as my sleeping bag and I'm glad I did. I also sleep in leggings, ski trousers and three layers on top, hat and gloves. Did I mention I feel the cold??*

*I sleep pretty well although I wake up a lot to check the time and as I thought I would be, am up before anyone else in camp. I force myself to stay in bed though, as it's cold and I know I'm going to need as much rest as possible.*

*So, in about 90 minutes, I will start the Deca. I'm stressing over how cold the swim will be (it's 'only' 2.4 miles!!) and how slow I'm going to be… but there's nothing I can do now other than keep moving forward.*

### Day 1 – 17 October 2016

*Today started with very refreshing swim. When I say refreshing, I actually mean bastardly cold but after adding yet more neoprene,*

## TEN DAYS OF HELL

*I finally finished so I could throw tea over myself.*

*The bike started with yet more 'refreshing' rain but soon cleared and was a blur of Bender and toast and marmite.*

*The run/walk felt pretty good and I have ended today with no niggles.*

*My crew have been amazing today and are growing in numbers! Ready for day two…*

**Day 2 – 18 October 2016**

*Another day, another chilly swim. I had some company from Lou Dutch and we broke the laps up with a couple of tea breaks where I mainly moaned about being cold.*

*The bike was a bit too much time on Bender and I was instructed to 'get in the pain cave and do 10 laps on road bike'. Towards the end of the day we were treated to an amazing double rainbow and then it pissed down and we got soaked…*

*The run was a mix of jogging and shuffling, but it was job done by 02:24.*

*Bring on day 3!*


**No entry for day 3….**

## TEN DAYS OF HELL

### *Day 4 – 20 October 2016*

*Well, I knew that this was going to be tough, but yesterday was a shocker.*

*The day in general was a lot colder and I massively struggled in the lake. I'm not known for my ability to handle the cold and just over halfway through the swim I just felt unbelievably cold and without much warning, I just got out.*

*After my crew got me back to the land of the living, we chatted about what to do. Mark asked if I would consider going back in the lake to finish the swim and I knew I had to. Once again, my brilliant crew helped me through and the swim was finished, albeit not in the way I wanted.*

*I got straight on the bike and over the next 8 or 9 hours (no memory) decided that I had to continue on if I had any hope of ridding this Deca monkey off my back.*

*Lou and Rob (both looking to complete the event next year) are finding the lake certainly 'fresh'. For me it's too cold for 10 days' swimming but I was desperate to get this done so a local outdoor pool became the next step.*

*The first pool swim went well yesterday and I'm now on my way to do my second. I've finished 4 days now and very much into unknown territory. I look like a bullfrog as my eyes are all weird and ugly and am feeling very sick this morning.*

*Words are not enough to explain how much my family and my crew*

## TEN DAYS OF HELL

*are doing for me…*

**No entry for day 5…**

---

*Post-Deca Recce, over a week later – 30 October 2016*

*I have just come back from my first run since the Deca recce, and on that run I thought to myself that it's time to attempt to make some sense of what happened a few weeks ago…*

*It's tricky for a number of reasons. The first being that it's hard to really recall what actually happened. The days/nights are all jumbled up and I have memories but I'm unsure of what day they belong on… The second reason is that it's still uncomfortable to think about it all. I failed. Again. And that stings a bit.*

*I will start by saying what went well with the event.*

*The courses are really good, perfect for a Deca. I completed the bike course (42 laps) 5 days running and I didn't get bored. Maybe that's because I was seeing my crew a lot. Maybe because I was enjoying the lack of cars or maybe just because I was totally in the moment, loving what I was doing.*

*The run course… well, that was slightly different and I really suffered on it, but I expected that. The Boat House lights (at the end of the lap) seem to never get any closer and I saw a lot of weird stuff that I knew wasn't actually there! But in terms of the recce, I was really pleased with how it works.*

## TEN DAYS OF HELL

*The lake is chilly obviously, but in terms of swimming, it's lovely. Very scenic and makes for a great swim.*

*The HQ area. This works very well with all the three disciplines coming back to it every lap. It means all the future Deca athletes will be properly looked after by their crew and event staff. It also works well from an event timing perspective.*

*My crew. I can't say enough good about my awesome crew: Mark, Martin, Rob and Lou. They were perfect and supported me in every way possible. I was just sad that I couldn't finish the 10 days for them.*

*So what went wrong…*

*Well, I was right in my previous blog when I said I should swim in lakes more. A LOT MORE!! I knew from day 1 that I was in trouble and that the temp was a couple of degrees less than what I had hoped and was used to. Rob and Lou dealt with it well, but I struggled on day 1 and 2 and then day 3 was just too much. I swam two thirds of the course and then just decided to get out and go home (!!!). I was definitely hypothermic at this point and Mark drove down the run course to pick me up. Once back in the tent, in two sleeping bags and two duvets, I shivered uncontrollably for about 40 minutes. I'm pretty experienced with hypothermia, but I knew that this was far from ideal!!*

*Once I had stopped shivering, I got back into the lake to finish the swim with Rob and Lou either side of me. Martin said he felt quite emotional towards the end as he watched us swim towards the bank. I personally felt pretty low still as I felt that I had let myself*

## TEN DAYS OF HELL

*down, but at least I had finished the job.*

*During the bike later that day, I came up with the idea of finding a pool nearby so I could at least keep trying. As usual my crew came through and located the venue and it was decided that the event would continue. The only real issue with the pool swim is that the travelling added about 1.5-2hrs to my day and with my glacial pace, I could ill afford to lose those precious hours.*

*The bike section was a mixed bag. Bender really sorts the back problem, but he is so goddamn heavy and I never averaged over 12mph. The road bike was much faster but with it came the inevitable pain and I would slow down with that. Still, I never once thought about stopping and apart from the last 10 laps (always in the dark and always cold) I think I enjoyed it!*

*The run was pretty good on days 1 and 2 but days 3, 4 and 5 became a real battle with the sleep monsters. I became so frustrated with myself as no amount of will power/pep talks/coffee/mini-sleeps would stop the sleepwalking. By night 5, on the last 6 laps, I fell asleep almost every minute it seemed. I was aware of my crew watching me as I fell asleep over and over. It was horrible.*

*On the morning of day 6, I was woken after 1.5hrs of sleep and I felt so ill that I knew in my heart I was done. My face was swollen, my asthma was bad and I felt like I had flu. I talked to Mark about the reality of the situation and he agreed that I had just run out of road. I cried then as my Deca dream, once again, was over.*

*Post-event, my crew spoke to me about trying again. They all agreed that with a few tweaks I really could do this and they would all be*

## TEN DAYS OF HELL

*happy to support me again if they could. This meant the absolute world to me and from that moment I started to plan my next attempt. I intend to come back stronger, faster, better acclimatised and with a new, faster recumbent in 2017 and I will finish this!*

***10 things I learnt during my second Deca attempt – 1 November 2016***

*1. I'm tougher and stronger than I thought I was.*
*2. I really need to stop ignoring the cold-water issues I have.*
*3. Even I can't argue with the sleep monsters after 3 days of sleep deprivation. They win every time.*
*4. Fruit pouches are a really good alternative to gels.*
*5. I can cry, laugh and hyperventilate at the same. But it's not a good idea.*
*6. Army ration packs are actually very nice.*
*7. I cannot be 'over-crewed' for this.*
*8. I should always eat my porridge!*
*9. Something that makes me very happy can also make me feel really sad too.*
*10. That I'm never giving up until I finish a 1x10 Deca.*

———

So another 1x10 Deca fail for me, although the DecaUK Ultra Triathlon event my team and I organised in 2017 went on to be a big success, with 14 men entering (no women) and just 5 finishing.

The next official Deca I entered was DecaMan USA, a 1x10 event held in New Orleans in October 2018. I was taking this very seriously now, as another fail was something I could not

## TEN DAYS OF HELL

bear to think about.

As training for this, I went to Switzerland to take part in a 1x5 Quin – 5 Ironman races over 5 days. The major challenge for this event was that it was so far away and I wouldn't have any support. I would also need to drive myself there and use my van as my base, basically living out of it for the duration.

The drive itself would be pretty epic. I'm known for having an extremely bad sense of direction and the thought of having to drive from Bournemouth to Switzerland by myself was a little daunting. But I had a ferry booked, a postcode for my Sat Nav and plenty of Red Bull for the 700-mile journey.

Once I had figured out how to drive on the other side of the road, the trip became easier. It took 12 or so hours to get there and surprisingly I had very few dramas. Although it turns out there are two places called Buchs in Switzerland. Both are lovely.

When I finally arrived (missing the event registration as I had to leave late due to my son Jake getting his GCSE results), I picked up my race pack, which included my swim hat and timing chip. After saying hello to some of my ultra buddies who were taking part in the longer races (feeling a pang of jealousy for a moment), I tried to find a spot to set up camp. As I was late to the party, there was little space available and I eventually found a gap at the side of a road leading to a car park.

It was quiet and out of the way, which suited me perfectly. I parked up and began to arrange my kit. The first thing I did was to sort out my bike kit bag to take with my bike down to the transition area by

## TEN DAYS OF HELL

the pool. This was in an underground garage and there were lots of bikes and bits of kit strewn around the place. I found the chair with my number on and placed my kit out ready for when I had finished my first swim the next morning. I would need to do this every day.

When I had racked my bike, I wandered back to my van to continue setting up. My clothes were in labelled boxes so I would be able to grab stuff easily. I had a camp bed and I had brought my duvet and pillow from home so I would be comfortable. I had a stove and kettle, so I could have a cuppa and make the expedition meals I had bought from home. I had also sorted five bags with all the food I needed for each day. These included canned fruit, milkshakes, crisps, some chocolate, cereal bars and nuts. I also had Weetabix, water, Coke and Red Bull.

Once I was ready, I pulled out a Sharpie pen and wrote on the inside of my van all the things I would need to remember in the coming days. These included taking my recovery shake, using my magnesium gel at night and sleeping with my legs raised. I also wrote a list of the items I needed to remember for each morning: things like my timing chip, swim and bike kit, and my mobile phone for the bike section should I get any mechanicals.

I also listed the amount of laps I had to do (swim – 38; bike – 20; run – 34), the bike cut-off (2300) and the overall cut-off (0300). I also marked five lines, so I could strike through them, prison-style.

### *My Facebook post the day before the event:*

*I'm not going to lie, I'm really feeling the pressure now. Some people think that this will be 'easy' for me. But because it's in the*

## TEN DAYS OF HELL

*one-a-day Deca format and also I'm not the fastest athlete out there, it's actually going to be very hard.*

*On top of that, there is a 20-hour cut-off and if I don't make that, I will be DQ'd. I'm obviously going into it very tired as well, which is great training for the Deca in November, but not helping with my head/nerves right now.*

*I'm going to give it everything I've got and just hope it's enough.*

### Day 1 diary:

*The swim was pretty damn cold. It's held in a 50-metre lido and the weather in Switzerland has been unusually chilly this year, leading to the water temperature being super low. Thank god, I only have to swim 2.4 miles and not 12 or 24.*

### My Facebook entry was the following:

*A good day. Enjoyed the swim, back played up from lap 8 on the bike, but no surprise here. Run went well too. Weather hasn't been good today, very wet and cold.*
*Finish time: 15:42:19.*

### Day 2 diary:

*Today on the bike when riding past the results screen on one of the laps, I see the number 2 next to my name. This puzzles me for a little while; what could it mean? Then, as I am pedalling along, I realise with a mixture of delight and dread that I'm in second place. Now, in a race with only 3 women, this may not sound like a big deal, but*

# TEN DAYS OF HELL

*it really was, because secretly not only did I want to finish, I also wanted that second place.*

*First place was out of the question, as an age grouper was properly kicking mine and the other woman's butt. But second could be possible… The issue was that the German lady (Andrea, who's lovely) was a very similar pace to me, almost identical in fact. So this only meant one thing: I was now racing. I have never properly raced anything before. Always just taking part to finish (or at least try to), so this was a new experience for me. And boy, did it sting a bit.*

### *Facebook entry:*

*A tough day. Swim very cold (not just for me!) and the bike was pain from start to finish. Run was good though and so was the weather. Bloody freezing in my van right now though.*
*Finish time: 16:44:35*

### *Day 3 diary:*

*I now understand how hard racing is when you are constantly looking behind you, wondering how far they are. Wondering if you can keep the tiny lead you have managed to build up. Today, all I did was push, with a sense of panic underlining everything. I don't eat enough. I don't have time. I don't drink enough. I don't have time. I don't even put sunscreen on. THERE'S NO TIME!*

### *Facebook post:*

*I've had better days - Finish time: 17:40:31*

# TEN DAYS OF HELL

*Day 4 diary:*

*Today I raced out of transition without even dressing myself properly. I had the wrong shorts on and no chamois cream applied. 3 laps on the bike and my bits were in, well, bits... I was also bonking massively. I stopped and had a word with myself. This was madness, I had to take better care of myself. I pulled over to the kitchen area and asked for help. Normally, I hate relying on anyone, but I was desperate. The lady told me to do another lap of the bike and she would have a meal ready for me by the time I finished. 20 minutes later, I was sat eating chicken, mash and vegetables like I hadn't eaten for weeks. 10 minutes later, feeling a thousand times better, I got on with my race.*

*Facebook entry:*

*Last night's post was a bit short, mainly because I went straight to bed. No pre-sleep curry, magnesium gel or even PJs... not good. Basically, I fell apart on the run because I hadn't eaten enough on the bike. Hopefully I will sort that today. The bike back pain as well really got to me. And the swim... brrrrrrr. Apparently the water is 20 degrees, but it certainly doesn't feel that way! Doing this without a crew is really tough. And stupid.*
*Finish time: 18:03:08*

*Day 5 diary:*

*Woke up feeling horrible and overwhelmed with what's still to do. Only one more day but I'm not sure how I'm going to get through it. The swim was better as the water had warmed a little with the sun we've had over the last few days. Today's bike was all about*

## TEN DAYS OF HELL

*maintaining my lead (although I've been told it's safe as long as I finish) but I'm still feeling the pressure. I just want to be able to tell my kids that I finished second. On the run, I start well but then stomach problems kick in. Sharp, gripping pains that make it hard to run. We then have some pretty impressive storms with huge claps of thunder that make me jump. I put my earphones in and turn my music up loud. I just need to finish this thing.*

*On the last lap, the SwissUltra crew always make you run the lap in reverse, holding your country's flag. It's a fantastic gesture, but on this event, I just want to stop and curl up in my van. My stomach hurts and I'm exhausted. I certainly don't want to pop champagne bottles, and the race director laughs and calls me a 'reserved British person', which is 100% true.*

*Finish time: 18:04:54 – Second place female*

―

Once back in the van, I didn't even bother to get changed, just pulled off my trainers and socks. Then I lay down and it felt amazing. For a moment I allowed myself to feel good. And proud. I did what I came to do, and all on my own too.

But then I remembered that this was just training for the DecaMan in a few months' time and my heart sank. I barely made it through 5 days here; how could I do 10 in New Orleans?

The next morning, I got a text from a friend I'd met on one of my events called Jon.

## TEN DAYS OF HELL

'What did you learn for the next race?', he asked.

'That I need crew,' I replied.

'When is it and for how long?'

I outlined the details of the DecaMan USA and the reply made me very, very happy.

'If I can get the leave, do you want me to come?'

'YES!!' I texted back.

And as I made the long drive home, I allowed myself to think about actually finishing a 1x10 Deca. That after the successful Quin and now having some crew on board, it might just be possible…

## CHAPTER 10
# A WILD PIG CHASE

The night before flying to America for the 2018 DecaMan, I sat eating and watching some good trashy TV with my daughter, Jess. I looked at my bags and bike box, all ready to go, and I felt strangely calm.

After the success of the SwissUltra Quin, I was eager to finally get this 1x10 Deca monkey off my back and finish it. I felt that I had been through every failure possible and experienced all that I could to help me finally get this over the line. I also had a great crew member joining me, a fellow endurance-loving mate, who knew me pretty well, was super-chilled and, from his Army background, was also very organised. Jon also had a great sense of humour, which is extremely important in these events. There are always tears with long-distance triathlons, but you need to offset those with plenty of banter, I find.

On top of that, New Orleans also promised some good weather to help me get through the 10 days. Although daylight hours would be limited because of the time of year, the temperature would be decent and that was the most important thing. The race directors were also friends and there were lots of athletes I had met over the years competing too. This was going to be one of the hardest things I had ever done, but it promised to be an amazing event and I was really excited.

I had no idea what I had coming…

We arrived at the airport long before we needed to, due to the fact

## A WILD PIG CHASE

that Jon and I are too organised for our own good. We laughed over the fact that our check-in was D and F. 'It's a sign,' I laughed, referring to the initials DNF which stand for 'Did Not Finish' in these types of events. My bags and bike box were overweight. I was not that surprised by this at all. I gave some of my shit to Jon and handed over more money to British Airways. Once we got through security (Jon setting off all the alarms), we settled into Costa's with lattes, blueberry muffins and a long wait.

Now, I'm not a great flyer – I have a sort of love/hate relationship with aeroplanes. On one hand, I get a massive buzz out of them and on the other, I'm utterly terrified. I promised myself years ago that I would never let my fear get the better of me and stop flying, but it can make for some interesting flights! My good friend, Matthew, was hugely amused by my heart rate getting over 150 BPM during take-off during a flight to Lanzarote one year.

This flight, being long-haul, had some great films, and I was able to distract myself enough to remain calm-ish, even through some turbulence. Nine hours is a long time on a plane though and not the best prep for a 10-day triathlon, what with the dehydration and sleep deprivation. But we arrived in New Orleans and then had to endure the longest wait ever through customs to finally make it outside to wait for Wayne Kurtz, the race director, to pick us up. The temperature hit us straight away: the warm air on our skin and the high humidity. I am a real lizard and love the heat, so this was bliss and eased my pre-race nerves immediately.

Wayne arrived in his truck and took us to the indoor swimming pool where the continuous Deca was well underway. These athletes were three-quarters of the way through swimming 24 miles. I looked at

## A WILD PIG CHASE

them in amazement, part-jealous and part-relieved that I wasn't doing this version of the Deca. After an hour or so, Wayne drove us 45 minutes or across what seemed like the longest bridge in the world to the race HQ. It was about midnight, so we settled into our bunkhouse accommodation and got some sleep.

Jon and I are both early risers, so we were up just after 7am to start unpacking and building the bike. Each athlete had their own area within a long line of purpose-built, temporary structures to use during the race for all your kit, food and bike. The bike and run courses went past this area every lap, making the crew's life as easy as possible.

Later that day, Wayne took us to Walmart, which was my first ever experience of this infamous mega-supermarket, and it did not disappoint. There was pretty much everything we needed, apart from tins of rice pudding, but we managed to find some alternatives. I also bought a tent, to pitch behind the crew area, as I hadn't really enjoyed the night before in the bunkhouse. I'm a really light sleeper and as I anticipated having issues during the race, felt I would be better in a tent on my own. I also need my own space and sensed that 10 days of being with people might just break me.

Once we were back at race HQ, we sorted the kit and Jon put up the tent – in about three minutes, which was pretty impressive. After grabbing some food, we wandered up the short run course and back again. It was off-road and I personally thought it was a little too rough underfoot for a Deca, but I could see that the race directors had made the best out of the situation and I obviously knew how hard it was to get all the elements of a 'perfect race' in place.

## A WILD PIG CHASE

We then decided to walk to the lake to see the swim course. This was the part I was most nervous about and thought the recce might make me feel better. The walk was a little longer than we had expected, and wearing flip-flops was a really bad idea as we both ended up with blisters. Excellent prep, once again. Lake Pontchartrain, or Lake Poncho as we called it, was huge – more like the sea, I said more than once. It even had little waves lapping the shore. And alligators somewhere in it too, apparently (although it was their hibernating season, we had been assured).

I dipped my feet into the water and felt it was a comfortable 18 degrees or so. I could cope with that, I thought. As long as it didn't get any colder...

After we got back to HQ, it was time to register and for the informal race briefing. The bike was checked over and the timing chip fitted, and I was also given a blood test. After the results came back, the medic looked at me in concern. 'You're severely anaemic, Claire,' she said. 'Almost at the point of needing a blood transfusion, in fact.'

Ah, right. I've been here before, I thought. Although this time I was surprised and a little annoyed, as I had been monitoring my iron levels and taking supplements every day. My levels had been affected by the Quin, so I had been careful to get them back up before the Deca. How had this happened?

Mentally, this rocked me a bit, as I was aware that I had no buffer for the race and my period was due in the middle of it. The worst possible time. I chatted this through with Jon and we decided to double-dose my regular iron supplement and monitor any further

## A WILD PIG CHASE

symptoms. I tried to put it out of my mind the best I could.

Once everything was sorted, we headed for bed. I got into my tent to faff with some kit and finally settled down to listen to an audiobook for a while. Although I was nervous, I felt positive. I knew I would feel better once the first swim was done. Once I felt sleepy, I turned my phone off and didn't switch it back on again for a long time, which was unusual for me and says a lot about how my mindset was over the following days.

I woke at 5am, heard Jon in the crew area and unzipped the tent to join him. Day one is always chilled, compared to the carnage that follows, and I enjoyed the temporarily relaxed atmosphere. Grabbing my swim and bike kit, we went over the cookhouse for breakfast. This was the main area for the race, where everyone would congregate, eat and drink coffee. Wayne's amazing wife, Janis, organised all the food, and she and the other staff members created a warm and friendly place for athletes and crew to hang out.

We loaded the bikes onto the trucks and drove down to the swim start, only for me to realise that I hadn't brought my swim hat. This was not like me, as I'm very organised normally. Jon found me another hat, which I promptly ripped. 'What the fuck is wrong with me?', I wondered. After the national anthem and a brief pre-race chat, we waded into the lake. The swim course was set close to shore and to my relief, we could stand up at any point during the swim. I had worn my thermal wetsuit and many layers underneath to ensure I didn't get cold, and as soon as I started swimming, I knew that I was going to be OK. No panic attacks, no temperature issues. I was going to do this.

## A WILD PIG CHASE

I got out of the swim in a time of 1:39. It was a little longer that I hoped for, but I was feeling pleased as I wasn't shivering at all (very unusual for me). I ate a cereal bar and wrestled myself into my bike kit. Once on the bike, I felt happy and settled into my steady (slow) pace – my average was around 14 mph, but I wouldn't see that speed again after this day.

After a while, I realised I was seeing a lot of athletes at the side of the road, fixing punctures. This made me nervous, as I'm not the best at sorting flats. I can do it, but I'm not fast. I had fitted the thickest winter tyres to my road bike and this turned out to be a great decision, as we had only two punctures during the whole race, compared to others who had thinner, racing tyres and also about 15-20 flats! My bike and I are not fast, but we keep on going…

Once onto the run, the temperature and humidity were still high and I was happy. Music on, I churned out the laps, run/walking all the way. I finished the day feeling good, had my recovery shake and crawled into my tent.

Day two started well with pancakes, syrup and hot tea. The swim went well again, although the temperature had dropped slightly. My pace on the bike was a little slower due to the rain, and when I say rain, I mean serious rain. Biblical downpours. This made for more punctures (not for me) and plenty of kit changes. We had brought waterproofs, but not really thinking we would have to actually use them. In fact, I had only brought my basic waterproof trousers in case of light showers, not even packing my overshoes or waterproof gloves. I ended up wearing most of Jon's kit which, thank God, was better than the crap I had brought. Jon also wore my wet kit to dry it for me. That, right there, is crew dedication!

## A WILD PIG CHASE

At one point Jon asked if I was happy and I replied, 'I would be if I saw a pig.' I think this was a reference to the fact that wild pigs had been spotted by other athletes, and Jon had even seen an armadillo. I was annoyed about the fact that I had only seen squirrels. Later in the event I did see wild pigs, plenty of them. But unfortunately, these would only be hallucinations.

Once off the bike, we found out that the run course had been changed due to rain flooding the previous one. I was really relieved as I am 'faster' on tarmac and find it easier to maintain a steady pace. The run course was now tagged onto the end of the bike course, which was a little tricky with a steady stream of bikes coming in and out of HQ, but the organisers handed out high-viz jackets and placed cones in the road to try and limit any potential issues.

The problem with the run course now was that every part of it looked similar, so I struggled to find set places to run and walk. In the last couple of long-distance triathlons I had finished, I had cues about where I ran and where I walked. This had worked well, but here there was nowhere obvious; it was all trees and bushes. This meant that my tried and tested run/walk plan went out of the window from day two.

Day three started with a real sense of foreboding. I woke in my tent absolutely freezing and my first thought was 'shit, the swim is going to be a nightmare'. Jon was up and in the crew area, getting things sorted, and once he heard I was awake, he told me to get my DryRobe on straight away. 'It's really cold,' he said, adding to my feelings of dread. We sorted the kit and headed to the cookhouse. I was feeling so bad and very negative. Jon was trying to lift my spirits, but I had been here before and had enough experience in

## A WILD PIG CHASE

low air/water temperatures to know exactly what was coming.

I was already shivering before we had even left HQ. I shivered in the car and while getting changed at the lakeside. Helpfully, the staff told us that yes, the water temperature had dropped massively from yesterday. My heart sank and I turned to Jon in panic. He hugged me and said that I could do it. I didn't agree. He kindly got my daughter Jess on the phone and I cried to her, while she said that she was proud of me and that I would smash the swim.

This was my worst nightmare come true. It was day three and I was already sleep-deprived and my body tired from finishing two Iron distances, so I wasn't handling it very well. On top of that, even though Jon repeatedly told me to not think about the next day, I was thinking about the next day. We had heard that it was going to get even colder. How could this be happening? I had flown halfway round the world to get decent weather. I could have just stayed in bloody England for this.

I pulled my goggles on, even though I was crying, and walked into the water. All the athletes gasped at the change in water temperature. I was just quiet. I looked for Jon on the jetty and made a pact with myself not to let him down; he was doing so much for me, the least I could was get through 2.4 miles. The horn went off and we all started to swim. The water took my breath away and I was aware that for most of the swim, I was making a strange, gasping noise on every stroke. This was partly down to the cold and partly down to hyperventilating. I was heartbroken.

We were supposed to swim 6 laps. Each time I would get to the end of a lap, I would stop and look to the shore, shivering violently.

## A WILD PIG CHASE

Desperately wanting someone, anyone, to tell me to stop. Nobody did. I started another lap. I got to the end once more, thinking 'that's it, I can't do any more', when I heard Jon say, 'Last lap, Claire.' 'Really?' I thought. I had been sure I had two more to swim. This made me push on and get it finished.

Once it was over, I literally crawled onto the shore and Jon helped me into the showers. I was shivering so badly, I couldn't get out of my wetsuit. I couldn't speak properly and I felt awful. Luckily, some of the other girls were in there already and were warmer, so they were able to help me out of my wetsuit and under the hot water. Once I was feeling more normal, Jon helped me get dressed and I was able to start the bike, still shivering but less so.

Once on the bike, I processed what had just happened and what this meant. I knew that I was not going to be able to push myself through that each day, especially if it was going to get colder, and as we all got more tired and lost weight. I was devastated. I pushed on through the bike, still really cold, Jon adding more layers every time I came into HQ. I remember trying to tell myself to stop being an idiot and to harden up. But in my heart, I knew I was done. How had this happened? How had it gone so wrong, so fast?

I finished the bike at around 6pm and looked at Jon. 'Can we have a chat?' I asked. I think he knew what was coming as he followed me to the bunkhouse.

'I'm going to stop,' I said. 'There's no point in continuing. The water will be even colder tomorrow and I just won't be able to do it.'

Jon did his best to convince me to keep going. We talked to the

## A WILD PIG CHASE

medic and race directors, but they just said, 'OK… we're sorry.'

I let Jon have a sleep while I got my head together. He had been helping with the race timing as well as supporting me and was exhausted. I just sat there, confused and broken.

While Jon slept, the medic came in and said, 'I'm so glad I found you, we are changing the swim to a pool, as the temperature is just too cold for the event to continue in the lake.'

I was so relieved! I hugged her and cried for probably the hundredth time that day. I looked at Jon to see if he had heard the news, but he was sound asleep. I decided to leave him to get a few much-needed hours and headed out onto the run course to catch up on the hours I had missed.

During the rest of the run, the news kept changing. Sometimes we would 'just be doing one more lake swim' and then it was back to 'it's a pool tomorrow, we just don't know when'. The race directors were doing their best to work with a situation they had no idea would occur; these were record lows in New Orleans for this time of year and totally out of the blue.

Finally, I heard that we would swim in the lake the next day, but later than normal in order to have a warmer air temperature, in the hope it would take the sting out of the water. I was not happy about it but thought, I can do one more lake swim if it means I'm still able to continue in the race. Day three ended even later as my indecision had wasted precious hours.

Day four began with Jon bringing me eggs and cheese in bed (I

## A WILD PIG CHASE

was now back in the bunkhouse, rather than the freezing tent) and laying out every item of clothing I owned, it seemed. Today was going to be seriously cold, apparently. Once dressed with countless layers and extra socks, I started the bike. My emotions were all over the place, with being extra tired and every hour bringing me closer to the final lake swim. I remember crying to Jon about it again, outside the toilet block. He must have been getting pretty fed up hearing about it by now!

As the sun came out, I started to thaw, and as the temperature rose, so did my spirits. I remember saying to Jon that 'it was going to be a good day', which in turn made him smile. Crewing is so hard, especially when your athlete is struggling. I had a puncture around this time, but luckily just as I was coming into HQ, so it was sorted, super-fast, while I ate more food.

At some point during the bike, Jon stopped me to tell me the awesome news that the lake was officially too cold to swim in and we were off to an indoor pool at 2pm. This was the best news ever and I felt like I had been given another chance at my dream. The only downside was that the pool transport was going to add at least an hour onto my day, every day. I did not have this hour to spare. This event had become the worst rollercoaster ride I had ever experienced, but I was still clinging on.

At 2pm, we met outside the cookhouse and got into various trucks and cars to be transported to the gym where the indoor pool was located. This turned out to be The Hottest Pool in the World! It suited me down to the ground, but other athletes struggled with the heat during the 2.4-mile swim. My time for that day was 1:20; I was able to draft off another couple of faster swimmers and was happy

## A WILD PIG CHASE

and warm for the first time in over 24 hours.

Once the swim was completed, I was told I had about three minutes to change and be outside. This was challenging, getting out of a wetsuit and into dry bike kit while damp and massively sleep-deprived. I skidded into the reception area, half-dressed, hair dripping, but I was ready.

Back at the race HQ, I had 4 laps left on the bike, which went well due to my feeling more positive overall. Once off the bike, I started the run, which initially went well, until the sleep demons hit and my energy levels dropped. Some rice pudding and coffee helped, and then I decided that it was Red Bull time. This did something a little odd to me and, coupled with some questionable 90's dance music, I massively ramped up my pace. For the final 8 laps, I ran like a woman possessed.

My body temperature got higher and higher, and I started stripping off my many layers, until in the end I was wearing one top, stuffed into my sports bra. I felt a little insane at this point and was kind of enjoying myself. The music was loud and I felt like I was making progress.

'Keep this pace up and you will finish 30 minutes earlier,' Jon told me. That was all the motivation I needed, and with a few more gulps of Red Bull and the music louder still, I kept cranking out the laps. At this point I was completely ignoring the little voice in my head that was telling me that I was going to injure myself by doing this. I could already feel a niggle I had brought with me from the UK starting to hurt, but did I care? Did I fuck.

## A WILD PIG CHASE

Bedtime was 3am that night. I remember nothing about it.

Two hours and twenty minutes later, I was woken up by Jon with coffee, toast and Nutella. He had been up and sorted all my kit already. Apparently I was laughing at all the instructions he was patiently giving me as he tried to get me up and ready for the swim transport. He said everything twice and still I giggled at him. Last night's madness was very much present.

Swim and bike kit ready, all the athletes were shuffled into the various vehicles for the drive to today's venue – this one apparently was an outdoor YMCA pool. I hoped it wouldn't be cold, but I needed have worried; when we arrived, I could see the steam rising from the water, not dissimilar to a spa. Day 5's swim was good as I had another couple of fast guys' feet to sit on. The swim section had now become recovery in this crazy event.

Once finished, we had a similar situation to the day before, with me panicking to remove my wetsuit and trying to get changed in record time to ensure I wouldn't miss the transport back. I was really missing Jon at these moments, when even the easiest task was challenging. Back at HQ, I tried to eat something but my mouth was so sore due to mouth ulcers developing overnight. Food today would need to be easy to eat and bland.

I started the bike at 9:30am and Jon set a goal of trying to finish by 5:30pm. Today the organisers mentioned that due to the swim venue being changed, we were a little short on the bike distance each day, so from now on we had to add on a dogleg which took in the road to the lake. The instructions were simple enough, but I'm pretty rubbish with directions at the best of times, so was not surprised

## A WILD PIG CHASE

when I found myself on a road I had never been on before. In my defence, all the roads did look very similar. I stopped, took a breath and retraced the way I came, muttering about how I was an idiot. After about ten minutes, I managed to find the correct turning and checked in with the member of staff who had been waiting patiently for me. Back at HQ, I got a well-deserved ribbing from both the race director and Jon.

The rain started again and all the waterproofs had to come out. It got worse and worse, until finally a massive thunderstorm began and we were told that the race was postponed until it had stopped. An hour later (and another hour from my rapidly shortening days) we were able to start again. I was beginning to get that familiar feeling of the event slipping out of my grasp again. I tried to push the negative feelings away, but with my back pain kicking in and my core temperature so low, I just couldn't get warm, no matter how many layers I put on.

The never-ending bike laps finally finished – not a moment too soon as I had been falling asleep on the last few. The bike course was pitch-black, fortunately with no cars, but plenty of other cyclists out there still. Their lights blinded you for a second as you tried to work out who they were. A few (mostly American athletes) would say something encouraging as they passed, 'Good job' mainly, which started to be Jon and my new favourite phrase throughout the day. Jon would hand me my gloves, after he had stuffed them down his hoodie to dry. 'Good job, Jon,' I would say. It's the little things with these events.

I got off the bike, which due to my stiffening body had become a giant task in itself. Jon had to grab the handlebars and steady me

## A WILD PIG CHASE

as I attempted to unclip my feet (which I couldn't really feel) and swing my leg over the saddle. I had so many layers on (leggings, shorts and huge waterproof overtrousers) that inevitably something got caught and I would nearly fall. Every. Damn. Time.

And time had now narrowed to living purely in the present…

*I shuffle off to the dorm to change. This is dangerous with my negative mindset now. It's dark, very warm and look, there's my bed… Jon has laid my run kit out and helps me struggle out of the soaking wet bike gear. Nobody speaks. The enormity of the impending marathon looms over me and I wonder how and even if I can finish tonight.*

*Lap after lap after lap. They all look the same. The timing mat beeping each time I limp over it. Last night's little Red Bull-assisted speed session on the run aggravated the injury I sustained six weeks ago when I fell over (running in the dark with no head torch). I take a handful of painkillers and hope it's enough to get me through.*

*The sleep monsters pull at me and now I am walking, stumbling along the road, weaving as my eyes close and I drift off. Jon decides to walk some laps with me to try and wake me up. This doesn't work and he comes up with a plan to have a couple of 15-minute power naps in the support tent. We sit down and he wraps me in a blanket, puts his arm around me to allow me to rest my head, and that's all it takes. I'm asleep. What feels like seconds later, he's calling my name, trying to get me to wake up.*

*Another few laps and we repeat it. More Red Bull, more coffee. This tiredness is beyond the power of caffeine now. This is my body*

## A WILD PIG CHASE

*saying 'enough'. The bunk-bed in the warm (and slightly festering) dorm is a welcome sight, for both of us.*

Day 6 was another day of barely conscious transport to the pool, grinding out bike laps and shuffling through the run. All while freezing and totally exhausted. The highlights of that day were an amazing burrito, cooked by the awesome Jan, and a vegan cheesecake, made by a fellow athlete, Shanda Hill.

Jon also managed to acquire some bike overshoes from another athlete, Dave Clamp, which replaced the plastic bags I was wearing to try and keep my feet warm and a little drier. I was aware that I looked like an actual tramp for most of the event, and also found it funny that I had brought my little running vests and shorts. Even suncream, sunglasses and a visor. I had such high hopes for New Orleans when I had packed in the UK.

Day 7 starts with the athlete in the next bed looking at me in confusion. I'm still in my bunk and fully dressed in last night's run kit. 'It was a late night,' I mumble. I force some coffee and pancakes down, although eating has become almost impossible now, and Jon hands me my swim kit. I look around for a free seat in somebody's truck to be taken to whatever pool we are swimming in this morning. I feel awful. Like I have flu or something. It strikes me that this is what the 'sport' I partake in is all about. You basically see how ill you can make yourself before you either fail or finish. Whichever comes first.

In the changing rooms, trying to sort my kit and wrestling with my wetsuit, I start to cry. Not sobbing, just quiet tears rolling down my cheeks as I look for my swim hat and goggles. Two other girls are

## A WILD PIG CHASE

also crying in the same way. We are broken and totally exhausted. Other athletes, from the shorter distances, look at us in a mixture of astonishment and horror. They try to comfort us, but there are no words, as what can you say? It's almost over? It's not. Everything's going to be fine? Nope. I put my goggles on, they fill with water and I laugh, as I'm not even in the pool yet.

The morning's swim is a shit show. The lane has too many swimmers in and I'm the fastest (this is a very unusual experience). I am constantly on swimmers' legs and become incredibly frustrated. I just want to swim and I literally can't. I decide to change my mindset to accept the situation and make today's swim about recovery. Although I'm still annoyed by everyone getting in my way, it helps.

Once back from the swim, we play the game of how many layers of kit can we dress me in before I can't actually move anymore. I'm wildly flicking between being positive that I can still do this to knowing that I'm completely fucked. I try not to show Jon how bad I'm feeling, but one glance at my face in the mirror tells me that that is fruitless. My puffy, bloodshot eyes say everything.

That day I spend trying to convince myself that I can still do it. I can still finish this damn event, while trying everything I can to stop myself from falling asleep on the bike. In the end I ask Jon if I can have a break. A real break. One where I sleep in the bunkhouse for a while. Was this my undoing? I fall asleep instantly and when Jon wakes me, the feeling of having to get back on the bike and complete 8 more laps overwhelms me.

But I try. I'm on the bike, it's getting dark and I'm now actually

## A WILD PIG CHASE

slapping myself hard in the face, in a vain attempt at stopping the sleep monsters that are pulling at me, dragging me under. It's now a real possibility that I'm going to fall off very soon, as I'm dropping off over and over again. I stop the bike, rest my head on my aerobars and just sob. I know it's over. I have failed again.

Back at HQ, I tell Jon that I'm done. He knows it too. He would never have stopped me though, not until I said the words. We let the race staff know and then I'm lying in my bed, struggling with a surge of panic that's now racing through my exhausted body. Jon leaves me to sleep, but instead I lie there, hating myself for being so weak.

After a while, I decide to have a shower in the hope that it will make me feel better. For the first time in days, I can take my time. Even condition my hair. All I feel is numb though. I feel like I'm caught in some kind of weird *Matrix*/*Groundhog*-type film, in a loop, never being able to escape. 'Fuck. I should have tried harder,' I say to a reflection that I no longer recognise due to the swelling in my face.

In my bunk-bed, my tormented mind finally lets go and I sleep. I'm unconscious for around 14 hours, I think. Once awake though, the negative feelings kick in straight away and I have to have a strong word with myself to put a stop to it. The only positive thing about failing, over and over, is that I have finally learnt how to deal with the emotions you are left with, once the relief of stopping goes. You have to be strict and limit the negative internal talk. You also have to learn all that you can from the event, accept your part in why you failed and understand the bits you had no control over. You need to forgive yourself and – this is the important part – move on.

## A WILD PIG CHASE

This is my sport, my passion, but it is not life or death. It's massively important for me to complete events, but perspective is required sometimes. For me, how a person deals with failure says a lot. It's easy to deal with success, but try failing at something, over and over. You learn so much about yourself and I believe it makes you a better and stronger person.

It fucking sucks big time though.

# LIFE LESSON
# FACE YOUR FEARS

Fear is a lack of control.

I used to be terrified of flying and still have massive panic attacks in open water. But I point-blank refuse to give in to either one of these fears, because if I did, I would not be able to travel to the countries I need to and take part in the ultra triathlons I love.

But it made these challenges I took on so much harder.

My fear of flying was simply down to not being in control of the situation. I always said that it would be better if I understood the workings of aeroplanes and how pilots fly them. But sitting in the cockpit wasn't an option, so I simply had to work with my fear and learn to manage it.

On the last long-haul flight I took, I wasn't in a great place, mentally. It had been an incredibly tough year and I was working through some depression. During this period, I became a little self-destructive (as is my way, being an extreme person).

What was interesting was that my fear of flying was almost non-existent that day. So what if the plane crashed? Bring it on. A little extreme, I know, but I was a bit nuts at the time. Letting go of control, or at least the feelings of control, helped me lose my fear. I can't control whether the plane stays in the air or not. That's the job of the pilots.

From then on, every time I flew, I reminded myself of the Crazy Girl

Flight and let go of control. Every time my heart rate rose, I would say to myself, 'I cannot control the plane and what happens to it'. I would then distract myself with reading, watching a film or writing. Each flight I have taken since then has become a little easier.

The open-water swimming fears are a little different. These are more in my control; there is no pilot to trust. For this situation, I have to trust myself and my ability to swim. I have to remind myself that I can actually swim, quite well in fact. I also have to remind myself that I have a wetsuit on and more than likely am swimming with a tow float. Both of these can help me should I get into trouble.

The problem with having panic attacks while out of your depth in open water is that it is damn unpleasant. I have experienced them in flat, calm lakes and choppy seas. I have been alone and with others. It doesn't seem to matter. Tiredness seems to play a part in bringing them on though. Something I try to remember.

This is what happened to me during a training sea swim in 2020…

After making some great progress in the first few days of the Lanzarote Swim Camp, I hit a bit of a blip. I had been really pleased with my training. And Eddie (the camp director) was too, which made it all worthwhile, as I was very keen to get his approval with my swimming.

On day 5, I decided to have an easy hour's swim on my own. As I walked into the water, feeling happy and confident, I had no idea that in the 60 minutes that followed, I would experience huge panic attacks and seriously wonder if I would make it back to the beach at all.

The state of the sea was very similar to the day before, which was pretty lumpy, but I had handled it well then and even enjoyed the challenge of battling with the unpredictable waves. I actually felt that after years of struggle, I had finally beaten my demons.

I swam in one direction, stopping a few times to film the fish in the reefs with my GoPro. But when I turned to swim back, suddenly everything changed. The waves were crashing into me and although I could see I was moving, albeit slowly, the familiar feeling of panic began to rise in me.

I desperately tried to ignore it. I attempted some mental games I'd used in the past, and I tried to control my racing thoughts and rapid breathing, but nothing worked. I stopped swimming, lifted my head from the water and looked at how far I was from the beach.

I realised, with a sinking feeling, that it was still a long way off.
The waves continued to knock me around. I got my head down and tried to swim. Still, the panic got worse. Adrenaline was now rushing through my body and my heart was pounding.

Shit,' I thought, 'I'm going to drown and nobody knows I'm out here.'

Head down again. My arms smashing over the waves and pulling hard through the water, trying desperately to make progress. I didn't feel like I was getting anywhere and now I was starting to shiver as well.

There was a part of my brain that knew exactly where I was and what I needed to do in order to swim back to the beach. That part of my brain also knew I was well capable of doing it. But what happened that afternoon was that I gave in to the panic. I allowed it to take control and in doing so, I put myself in real danger.

'You fucking idiot!' I shouted, so angry that I'd ended up in such a stupid situation.

Self-preservation finally kicked in and I span around in the water, looking for an alternative way out. If I swam in the opposite direction, I would be pushed towards the rocks, and there were some stone steps leading up the side of the cliff to the hotels and bars which looked down on to the sea.

Swallowing my pride (and yet more saltwater), I pushed my head back into the water and swam hard. Once I reached the rocks, I was dragged back and forth over them like a rag doll as I struggled to get out. A fisherman looked on, a bemused look on his face.

'I totally meant to do this, mate,' I called out, almost laughing as I was smashed into another rock, this time cutting my wrist.

Once out of the water, I sat on the bottom of the steps and took a moment to catch my breath. My legs were shaking and my heart racing. I shook my head and let disappointment wash over me. I was so angry that I'd put myself in a situation where I lost my precious confidence in open water. I felt like I'd wasted all my hard work.

On the walk back to my apartment, I thought long and hard about it, and realised that this is the reality when you are fighting demons. It's often one step forward and two steps back. But the only way they ever truly beat you is when you give up. So while I'm still putting on several layers of neoprene and fiddling nervously with my goggles, I'm still winning.

To help with my two huge fears, I have tackled some smaller ones over the past few years. One of them was bugs and spiders. I, like a lot of other people, used to scream whenever a large spider would tip-tap across my laminated floor of a night, or a Daddy Longlegs would bounce from wall to wall while I lay in the bath. This fear was completely irrational and it irritated me. Why was I so frightened of something so small?

These types of fears are mostly inherited from your parents and other relatives. Growing up, you are 'taught' to be scared of spiders. But in a country that has no poisonous species, this fear is fairly pointless.

So I started small, getting used to holding little spiders and bugs without making stupid noises or allowing panic to take control. After a while I progressed to larger spiders, and eventually I went to a reptile house and held a tarantula. This was quite an experience, and the feeling of actually coping with this and even enjoying the challenge helped me with understanding fear and panic. These days, I have no problems with handling spiders or other large insects, and when I have to remove one from the bath or my daughter's bedroom, I feel good that I was able to overcome my fear.

The other fear I faced was slightly more scary than the spiders. Public speaking has always been something I have shied away from as the thought of it terrified me. But again, this was an irrational fear, something I could not die from. When I was asked to talk to a group of local businessmen about taking on large challenges, and being in business myself, I said yes before I could think about it too much. I had to speak for 30-45 minutes, which doesn't sound a lot, but believe me, it is!

I practiced my talk over and over. I wrote myself notes and had cues on the slides I was showing during the evening, but the closer I got to the event, the more scared I became. I tried to think what I was actually scared about. It all boiled down to one thing. That I would have a huge panic attack and freeze. That I would go completely blank and be standing there, on the stage, blinking...

And the reality was, that could happen. But with the prep work I had put in and the visual cues I had in place, would it? The only way to find out was to just do it. The afternoon before that talk was very uncomfortable; all I wanted was for it to be over. The moments before weren't nice either. But once I had started, once that first practised introduction was safely out of my mouth, I began to relax. Fast forward to the middle of the talk, and I was laughing and interacting with the businessmen, who were keen to ask questions and seemed truly interested in what I had to say.

Earlier that evening, I had walked into the venue, my stomach full of butterflies and wishing I was anywhere but there. But a few hours later, I walked back to my van, head held high, proud of myself for once again facing my fears.

If the situation that is making you feel fear is out of your control, then let go of it. Anything you feel will not help, and panic never makes anything better.

Allow yourself to feel the fear. Understand why you are feeling it and give yourself permission to have those emotions. But once you have let the feelings run through your body, let them go and push forward.

Practice working with smaller fears – success with these will help with tackling the larger ones.

Never give up on something just because you are scared. If fear is stopping you from doing something, make a plan on how you are going to break it down to get it done.

## CHAPTER 11
# NUTELLA PANCAKES

During the long and frustrating period of constantly trying to finish a 1x10 Deca, I decided to try the continuous version of the race. I chose the SwissUltra in Buchs, Switzerland, in the summer of 2017. This was the year before I'd completed the 1x5 Quin at the same location.

I felt more confident that with 14 days to cover the continuous 12-mile swim, 1,120-mile bike and 262-mile run, I could actually finish this event. The only real issue I had was my back pain on the road bike. The three-wheeled recumbent 'Bender' was great for the pain, but too slow for the cut-offs. So I set about looking for a lighter, more race-like recumbent.

After a while spent on Google, I discovered a small shop in Edinburgh called Laid Back Bikes. The owner was lovely and promised (for a small fortune) to make me a streamlined racing machine.

A few months later I was the proud owner of a bright green Challenge Fujin SLII which I named McBender (because he was Scottish, obviously). Learning to ride this recumbent was a lot harder than the three-wheeler and it took a LOT of falling off to finally be able to ride down the road, albeit with a fair amount of wobbling. It was tougher to handle and cornering was a nightmare, but it was faster and that was all that mattered. I decided to take my road bike again, to change between the two bikes so as to help with the average speed.

## NUTELLA PANCAKES

In the lead-up to events, you are supposed to rest, eat good food and hydrate. Instead I decided to paint both my kids' bedrooms and get their floors laminated. I wasn't stupid enough to actually attempt to laminate them myself, but instead found a local handyman who was prepared to drop everything and arrive the day after I decided to do it.

'How hard can it be?', I said to myself. Just move all the furniture out of one room and into another. Three hours later, covered in sweat, dust, white emulsion and with a bruised toe, I realised it was quite hard, and pretty stupid of me to have started a week before going to Switzerland to attempt the hardest race I had ever entered. On top of that, I still had to organise an open-water swim event in North Wales for 350 people…

And if the above wasn't enough, I had also been to the dentist for some potential root-canal work. While I managed to avoid having that done, the actual filling was so deep it left me with eye-watering toothache every time I ate or drank something. Or even thought about eating or drinking something.

So, not your ideal preparation for an ultra triathlon.

The day before leaving for France found me driving home from North Wales in my large, white Luton van. I have a bitter history with white vans (I have since bought a blue transit van to attempt to break the curse). Each one that I buy seems to be programmed to kill me in some way…

I have spent many an hour sitting on the hard shoulder waiting for a recovery vehicle to rescue me after another brush with death. That

## NUTELLA PANCAKES

day, the Luton was going through its limp mode phase, when it basically gets slower and slower until I am forced to stop in a lay-by and switch the engine off for a bit. This can happen up to ten times in a journey, which is tiresome to say the least.

The Big Brutal Swim event had taken longer than normal to pack down and I was still driving home at 1am. Struggling to keep my eyes open any longer, I gave up, pulled into a truck stop and joined the long-distance lorry drivers on their break. The only difference being that they had beds and I had to lie across the timing equipment to sleep.

When I finally made it home, I found that the bathroom sink had leaked through the kitchen ceiling and our plumber friend, Gavin, had given us strict instructions not to use the toilet.

Awesome.

On top of that, my youngest cat, Samuel, needed some treatment from the vet for his cat acne (I'm completely serious) and eczema. Samuel, however, does NOT like the vet's and would literally rather kill himself than go (if you've never experienced a cat trying to force himself through the gaps in a basket, you wouldn't understand). So I had made an appointment for a home visit. The vet tried, he really did, but Samuel was still utterly terrified and shat himself, again quite literally, while the vet tried (and failed) to wrestle him to the ground. I was secretly impressed with Samuel's tenacity, but less so when I got the vet's bill. 'You're going in the basket next time,' I muttered.

Having dealt with the above (while having to secretly wee in the

## NUTELLA PANCAKES

garden), I finally got to the point when I could think about packing for Switzerland. I glanced at my watch, thinking I had a hour or two to spare, and realised in horror that we were leaving in forty-five minutes. My friend and only member of crew, Rob, appeared at this point to find me in the back of the Luton, clambering over generators and bike racking to reach the camping chair I wanted to take with us.

Rob shook his head and rolled his eyes. 'What are you doing?' he asked.

'I just…. I need… I want this!', I explained, holding up the chair, while almost losing my balance.

Once we had packed EVERYTHING I OWNED into the transit, I said a tearful goodbye to my daughter (I was tired, OK?), we drove away from my little house in Dorset and headed to Portsmouth to catch the overnight ferry to Caen to begin the long drive through France to Buchs in Switzerland.

Driving through France was not as much fun as I thought it would be. The scenery was pretty much like Wiltshire and the service stations? Damn – they are not good: dark, dirty and full of flies. And the coffee? Not a Starbucks or Costa in sight. So after paying toll after toll on the motorways, I was really pleased to drive across the border into Switzerland. The views changed to green hills and snow-capped peaks and I started to feel excited.

Once we arrived in Buchs, which is a lovely little town on the border with Lichtenstein, surrounded by craggy mountains, we checked into our hotel. I had randomly picked it from a list on the event

## NUTELLA PANCAKES

website and was pleasantly surprised with how nice it was. That night we ate in the hotel restaurant and with my nerves building, I was glad that the race started at 6pm the following day and I still had some time to myself to get my head together.

That night there was a massive storm, with thunderclaps so loud they made me jump. I love thunderstorms and little did I know, this was just a taste of what was to come over the next few weeks. After lying in bed for ages, staring at the ceiling, I tried reading some of Mark Beaumont's book about cycling around the world (Top tip – if you are doing something that terrifies you, read about somebody else doing something far more scary. It really helps).

After reading for a while, I lay there with sleep still eluding me, then looked at my left forearm. A few weeks before I had left for Switzerland, I had (impulsively) decided to get the Deca miles tattooed on me in large black numbers: 24.1120.262. It wasn't exactly a subtle tattoo, and I had to explain what it meant to the artist. Once he understood, he looked a little confused. "But you haven't done the race yet?" I confirmed that I hadn't, and as the numbers got darker and more permanent, I wondered if I would regret getting this tattoo. Now I was here and about to start chipping away at those huge numbers, I felt ready and finally was able to fall asleep.

In the pre-event information, the race organisers had explained that we would be able to set up a gazebo at the side of a road which was on the bike and run course. After we had had some breakfast at the hotel, we made our way down there. Other competitors, who were keener/more experienced than I was perhaps, had arrived early and bagged the good spots. We drove up and down the road three or

## NUTELLA PANCAKES

four times, but could not avoid the truth of the situation – we had to set up camp next to the portable toilets.

Now, I am not the type of girl to really make a fuss about this sort of thing, and looking on the bright side, it would be less distance for me to limp later in the event. However, these particular toilets were, how shall I say, different to the ones we are used to in the UK. I have no clue why, but Swiss (German) loos are basically a box with a seat, so you can see EVERYTHING, if you catch my drift. It's a good job I have a strong stomach, as these would later become an eye-watering, gag reflex-testing endurance event all of their own.

Setting up the base we would use for the event was pretty simple. Put up gazebo. Unpack contents of van into said gazebo. Rob (who I'm pretty sure has OCD) would sort everything to an inch of its life later on during the race. The only real problem we had was that the gazebo didn't quite fit onto the area of path we had ended up with (another reason we should have set up the day before). So a third of the tent was basically unusable, as if you dared to tread there, you would end up sliding down the hill into an area of scrubland behind.

I was sleeping in my van, which I have done plenty of times (albeit not for fourteen days), and as I made up my camp bed, I placed foam blocks under the far end to raise my feet during the short sleep breaks. We had tried this in previous training sessions and events, and it had worked well to reduce the swelling in my feet and knees. It wasn't very comfortable, admittedly, but comfortable and Deca are not really two words that go together.

By midday, we had finished setting up. We named the gazebo 'The

## NUTELLA PANCAKES

Cave' and the road 'Gazebo Alley', and I came to terms with the fact that this was our home for the next two weeks.

I didn't know this at the time, but during the event, my van (which I thought was my sanctuary) would actually become my prison. The four-hour sleep breaks which were supposed to be my time off were instead either hot, sweaty or shivery, cold, pain-filled, clock-watching hours of hell...

I hate race registration. I always feel like a fraud and making small talk does not come easily to me. I met the organisers (awesome, friendly folk) and made my way through to where the briefing would take place. To my horror, they were taking professional photos of the athletes. I looked down at my T-shirt, which is just a basic, stripey one from Primark, and found myself surrounded by Ironman Finisher tops and other impressively hardcore Ultra T-shirts. 'I need to change my top,' I whispered urgently to Rob, and rushed off to the van to rummage around in my bag for something more suitable. I felt even more out of my comfort zone than before.

The race briefing was mainly in German, but we got the gist of things. Puke bucket for the swim, tight turns on the bike (tricky for me and my recumbent) and laps. Lots and lots of laps. As soon as the briefing was over, we escaped to the heat of the afternoon sun to panic-buy the last few items we needed.

The last 'normal' thing I did before starting the event was to have an ice-cream (banana) while walking back to HQ to get ready for the long pool swim. I remember feeling strangely relaxed wandering through Buchs in my flip-flops. Normally triathlons start at some ungodly hour, leaving you stressed and sleep-deprived, but due

## NUTELLA PANCAKES

to the late start time and the fact that this race began in a pool (meaning no open-water panic attacks), I felt really good.

All the continuous Deca athletes milled around the poolside, flapping with goggles and hats, trying not to think about what we had coming up. 24 miles in a 50-metre open-air pool – basically the equivalent, distance-wise, of the English Channel. The organisers said the water temperature was 22 degrees, so in theory, I thought, I should be able to cope with potentially 18-20 hours of that. The reality, however, was very different.

From the minute the starter horn went off, I felt cold. I can honestly say that this was the only time in this event that I really panicked. 'Shit, what if I can't even get through the first bit?', I thought. I had visions of me posting on Facebook that I had been pulled out due to hypothermia IN A POOL SWIM!!

Rob had said to me before, that if/when I started feeling cold, to immediately get my long-sleeved top on under my suit. Feeling vaguely foolish, I pulled myself out onto the poolside and added the extra layer. Once I had done this, I relaxed a little, still a bit chilly, but knowing I could deal with it.

I'm not a great swimmer. My technique isn't too bad, but I lack power and in turn, speed. And as I've said, I really feel the cold and suffer from panic attacks in open water. So it's safe to say that this part of the triathlon is not my favourite and I'm always keen to get it done. This swim, however, was not going to be over any time soon, and I had to break it down in order to cope with it mentally.

Trying to keep track of the laps was almost impossible – I tried and

## NUTELLA PANCAKES

so did others in my lane – but every time you thought you were on track, you would look for confirmation from your support crew, only to be told that you were way off and had far more laps left to swim then you thought. This would be crushing news to a tired swimmer, and I swam away swearing many, many times. Another competitor was actually in tears at one point over the total they were told. 'No, no, noooooo, that's not right, how can that be right?', I overheard them cry. I shook my head in sympathy. At least we were all struggling with it.

I broke the distance up with four long breaks (I was stopping at the end of the lane for quick drinks and snacks as well). These stops were amazing and I would look forward to them immensely. I would crawl out of the pool and slump into a chair. Peeling off my goggles, which had started to feel like they had become part of my face, Rob would pass me hot tea and rice pudding, which I would eat as quickly as possible. As soon as the eating was done, it was time for the best bit… the hot shower! I would stumble over to the shower block and stand under the water for as long as I could, holding the wetsuit open at my neck to allow warmth to spread through my body. But as with all good things, this had to end, and I would head back to the pool for another 6 miles or so.

At about the halfway point, during the night section, I started to feel sick. I'm not sure what triggered this, but the chemicals in the water were the most likely culprit. I had been eating quite well up till this point, but for the few hours I felt so nauseous, I was unable to eat anything solid for fear it would reappear. Being sick in your mouth while swimming is not a particularly pleasant experience.

Rob tried to help me feel better by making a cup of tea at one point.

## NUTELLA PANCAKES

I took a swig and spat it straight out.

'What the fuck kind of tea is that?', I spluttered.

'I don't know, it must be the milk you bought,' Rob replied.

Confused and feeling even worse, I swam away. Rob later told me that he had accidentally used vegetable broth instead of boiling water. Easy mistake to make…

Towards the end of the swim, it became a living hell. Swimming up and down, lap after lap, unable to get out until it was done. It was the next day now and other (better) swimmers were finishing their swims. I would (irrationally and temporarily) hate them for this. Also, there were children playing in the pool next to us, laughing, having lots of fun going down the waterslides. This seemed completely wrong when we were suffering so much, just metres away. All I wanted was to see the last lap sign under the water, but it never seemed to come.

20 hours and 51 minutes later, I had finally finished the 380-lap swim. My eyes sockets were bruised from the goggles, my head was throbbing and my shoulders ached, but I was done!

After a small break in which I attempted to eat a burger and fries (I was so hungry but unable to stomach much actual food), I enjoyed just sitting in the sun by the pool. Rob was posting on Facebook how I had finished the swim and I had to threaten him with his life if he took a close-up of my now hideously disfigured face (try wearing goggles for 21 hours and see what happens). I felt so happy that the swim was done; those early panics about not being able to

## NUTELLA PANCAKES

finish seemed so long ago.

After ten minutes or so, I began to feel uneasy. 'This is a race, right? I really should be cracking on with the bike now, I think.' So we made our way to the area where the bikes were racked and then walked back to The Cave so I could change properly, feeling incredibly self-conscious of my bullfrog face (which stayed with me for over 48 hours!).

I was keen to ensure that I got some laps completed on the recumbent in the daylight, so after a few laps with Rob on the road bike, we swapped over to McBender. Before starting, I nervously looked around, not wanting anyone to see me trying to get on it.

Anyone who has ridden a recumbent bike (not many I know...) will understand that pushing off is hard, very hard. Why is it more difficult than a normal bike? I don't know. I'm sure there is some reason to do with being closer to the ground or the wheels being smaller, I have no clue, but all I knew was that it made me very nervous and never seemed to get easier. This time, however, was even worse as I was still feeling a little odd from the swim – hot and a bit dizzy – which didn't help matters.

I had chosen to bring the recumbent to ensure that I had a chance of finishing this Deca, but I felt embarrassed when I was riding it. It's hard to explain, but I could feel the other competitors looking at me, out of curiosity mostly, I think. Later, a few of them said they thought that I was disabled, that I had had an accident. Some people thought I was weird (pretty accurate) or even rude, as I didn't talk much to everyone else.

## NUTELLA PANCAKES

Later in the race I was able to explain that if I dared to move my mildly panicked gaze from the road, I would make the recumbent weave unnervingly across the already narrow path that we were riding on, almost taking out whichever unlucky cyclist was near me at the time. People stopped trying to make conversation after a while; they would remain friendly, saying hello, but due to my speed (or lack of it) and steering issues, conversation was just not an option. I would look at other competitors chatting and feel very lonely during some parts of that 1,120-mile bike.

After completing the first 9k lap of the Deca bike route on McBender without falling off, I breathed a massive sigh of relief. OK, there were places on the course which weren't particularly recumbent-friendly, like turn points (which weren't that easy on a road bike either to be fair). I tried to take the far line without putting my feet down and although I made it the first time, the next time I ended up on the floor with the bike on top of me.

Falling off a recumbent bike isn't as painful as a road bike, as you are much closer to the floor, but actually getting yourself untangled and off the ground is much harder. It seems to pin you to the tarmac and while I imagine it's fairly amusing to onlookers, it's really, really embarrassing. I decided from that moment that I would 'crab walk' my way round the timing mat to avoid the bastard bike trying to make my life any harder than it already was. Once again, I was mortified if another cyclist saw me trying to walk with the bike around the turn point.

The SwissUltra bike consists of 9k laps, and for the continuous you need to ride 200 of these to complete 1,120 miles. Sounds a lot, right? In my head (which I'm pretty sure by now you've worked

## NUTELLA PANCAKES

out isn't quite right) that sounded fine. My support crew, Rob, started talking in 'miles to go' and sharing this information with me from time to time. After a while, I informed him in no uncertain terms that I did not need to know I had 845 miles to go (or whatever I was on at the time), and my world was laps from the time I started the Deca until I finished it. How many laps I was going to do that hour, that day… Just laps. Never miles. That way I was never overwhelmed by the event. If it ever got too much, I would break it down into even smaller chunks.

There was no set plan with the recumbent and the road bike. I would ride either one until I could bear it no more: either the clumsy slowness of McBender or the searing lower-back pain of the road bike. One thing I had not prepared myself for was the impact of riding long distances on the recumbent, as I had not completed any previous long-distance, multi-day events on it before.

The positive thing about a recumbent is that, other than the obvious benefits for your back, you don't suffer from pressure on your butt, feet and hands. Almost all the ultra endurance athletes I know suffer from some kind of short to medium-term nerve damage to these parts of their bodies after races. I couldn't even open a packet of crisps after a Triple Ironman attempt. I know, truly devastating.

During the lead-up to the race, I had felt some pain above my knees, but not thought much of it. However, after riding McBender for 24 hours, I lay in my van, trying to sleep, and experienced what I then called 'The Screaming Knees'. It was a sharp, searing pain I had never felt before. Fortunately, it only hurt when I stopped, and as I couldn't stop for long, it wasn't a huge problem. It did add to the 'fun' of my sleep breaks though.

## NUTELLA PANCAKES

The 6 days of the bike section was a blur of night and day. The route was a traffic-free path which ran alongside the river Rhine, surrounded by mountains that reflected the weather we would be having that day. I particularly liked it when the clouds would almost lie on the mountaintops, like they were having a lazy day and couldn't be bothered to get out of bed.

Sometimes it would be boiling hot, then during the night the temperature would plummet, forcing us to add jackets, trousers, hats and gloves on top of our normal bike kit. The bright, hot days were my favourite; as I have said, I am a lizard by nature and prefer to be warm. You would also get the best views those days and I never tired of them. The weather was unpredictable though and the organisers had to postpone the race twice for the safety of the athletes.

The first time, the continuous athletes were all still on the bike, late in the evening. Once again, the mountains gave us the heads-up and the wind followed soon after. It was wild and made me nervous, and as I was due for my break in a few hours' time, I simply decided to take it a couple of hours earlier. After the crew had accounted for everyone (which took a while, as some of the more adventurous athletes had set off on another lap), I headed for the safety of my Ford Transit to wait out the storm.

Once it had cleared and we were allowed to return to racing again, we could see how many branches and debris littered the bike and run routes. It was definitely a good call by the organisers; I know how hard it can be to make those sort of decisions during a race and you won't always be the most popular at the time, as driven athletes can be a little unreasonable during events. But afterwards people

## NUTELLA PANCAKES

calm down and understand.

The one thing that I truly dread during these types of events is the sleep monsters. Now, I can deal with sleep deprivation like a boss. I've had a lot of experience over the years. From nightshifts in nursing homes when I was a teenager, to having a son who did not sleep for more than a few hours for the first few years of his life (Jake is a teenager now and as I sit here writing, he is still sleeping at quarter past one in the afternoon), then finally taking part in and organising multi-day endurance events. But there is a point when sleep deprivation says 'enough' and your brain tries to shut down. This is fine if you are able to take a short nap to reset, but not so good if you are halfway through a bike lap and with hours to go until you are due for another proper sleep break. This happens anytime during these types of event, but it's harder at night, as obviously you should naturally be asleep.

This one particular night I found myself nodding off on the recumbent, wildly weaving about on the path while trying to stay on the bike. It happened over and over again, as I tried various ways to wake myself up.

Slapping myself hard on the face sometimes works. Not tonight. Pinching myself and biting the inside of my cheek. That just fucking hurts and I'm still drifting off here. So tonight, Matthew, I'm going to try a new tactic. Tonight, I'm going to be Sting from the well-known 80's band, The Police. I quickly check to see if anyone is around, and once I'm happy I'm alone, I launch into a spectacular rendition of 'Roxanne'.

It did the trick and was enough to stop me hitting the deck until the

## NUTELLA PANCAKES

sun started to rise and I felt more awake again. Whatever works.

I have to say that while there were some obvious ups and downs during the event, most of the time I was relatively positive and happy (until the last few days on the run due to my feet exploding), but I remember one day I called Black Monday (I think it was a Monday but can't be 100% sure).

This day I felt truly low. I was missing my kids, particularly Jess. Rob, my crew, was great, but it wasn't the same as having someone you know give you a hug or tell you it was going to be fine. I needed female company and I was lonely (and yes, I had my period too…). I phoned my lovely mum and cried down the line, asking her, 'What was I doing?'. We chatted for a bit, while I hid from other people asking if was OK (I hate others seeing me when I'm upset) and just properly vented. Afterwards, I felt better and cracked on. Sometimes you just need to break down and get back up again.

Another moment when I was feeling tired and rundown during the bike section, I rode past an older man who was walking in the opposite direction. I had seen him a few times and he always looked grumpy and pissed off. I thought that maybe he was a local and resented us crazy ultra weirdos turning up and taking over his regular walking route every day for two weeks. That one day, however, he smiled at me. I smiled back, my heart lifted, and then I burst into tears. Just that tiny human interaction affected me so deeply (everything feels more intense in ultras).

I later found out that this man was called Walter and he was a huge supporter and part of the SwissUltra family in Buchs. He is massively loved by the athletes and crew and now me too. Some

## NUTELLA PANCAKES

people just have that thing, right?

Rob, my long-suffering crewman, got a raw deal in this event. He suffered, was sleep-deprived, had to deal with a tired, emotional female for 12 days (imagine that for a moment), and he didn't even get a medal at the end of it. He was great crew, always one step ahead and doing stuff I wasn't even aware of to try and help my progress. The one thing he was particularly good at was making Nutella pancakes. These were one of the main parts of my diet during the event and I ate them at least once a day. He also made mashed potato and melted cheese and served it with spaghetti hoops. No healthy balanced plant-based foods here; just comfort food, plain and simple.

How do you start a 262-mile run? Well, after being on a bike for what seemed like a month, I was absolutely ecstatic. Finally, I had reached the part of the event I was comfortable with. No panicky swimming and getting cold; no more stupid bikes and back pain. Just me and the road. And it was only 340 laps – not that many at all. Really.

I think it was sometime in the afternoon when I started the run. The first thing I did was walk a lap and determine which parts I would walk and which I would run. A previous Deca athlete I had met a few years back advised to me to do this and stick to it as much as possible. The obvious part I had to walk was the incline through Gazebo Alley. This was the section of the course where the bike and run course went past all the athlete support tents. It was also a road which cars leaving the public pool used, albeit slowly. It was busy, noisy and full of people. I hated having to walk through it, but a hill is a hill. The other part I walked was a small off-road section with

## NUTELLA PANCAKES

some tree roots and rocks. It seemed sensible to go slower there as this was the most likely area where I could trip over.

Once that was established, I settled into my new routine and enjoyed being able to talk to other runners, now that I was at the same height as them. I would start my day as I did the bike, at 2am, when I could enjoy the quiet of the course, with only a few athletes out and about. Rob would make me a coffee and put some breakfast on the table outside our crew tent, then he would go back to sleep until it got light.

I would plod around for the next few hours, sometimes listening to music, other times just enjoying the stillness, and complete my first half marathon. By the time I had done that, Rob would be up and making Nutella pancakes for my second breakfast of the day. After eating those and drinking some tea, I would start the next half marathon. The athlete's village would be waking up properly now and Gazebo Alley getting busier.

After the first marathon of the day was done, I would treat myself to a shower and a proper coffee from the café next to the pool. This was bliss, as I sat refreshed and resting in the sun. But being a race, you could never truly relax, and even though I was on track to finish when I wanted to, I was also aware that anything could happen. I was about to find this out in a rather painful way...

The rest of the afternoon, evening and night was spent completing the second marathon of the day and was obviously harder work than the relative ease of the morning. The temperature would rise and it was always a slog to get to 10pm when I could escape to the coolness of my transit van.

## NUTELLA PANCAKES

On a section of the run course, about halfway round, there was a gap in the trees which allowed you to see the road. It was busy with cars, lorries and public transport rushing past. People were doing normal things, going to work and shopping. To me, it was a glimpse of the outside world that we were separated from. It almost felt like if you took a few steps in the wrong direction, you would escape and burst out of the Deca bubble.

That, I guess, sums up how you feel when you are doing these long-distance events. You know there is an outside world, you used to be part of it, but now your life has shrunk down to putting one foot in front of the other, eating, drinking, sleeping and just breathing in and out. Nothing else. Maybe that's one of the reasons why I and so many others do this ultra stuff. In this crazy, fucked-up, complicated world, endurance racing makes life simple again.

As with most events, the Portaloos were a sort of plastic box of hell. You can't really avoid them, but you dread going in. As previously mentioned, the ones in Switzerland were on another level though. For some reason, instead of being like a toilet, they were more like a big, open box which got fuller and fuller with every passing day. You could literally see EVERYTHING. I have a pretty strong stomach (years of caring for elderly patients does that to you), but this had me gagging on bad days.

Every now and again, I would treat myself to the swimming pool loos. It took a little longer to get to these, so it was just an occasional treat, you understand. But they were clean, private and they flushed! Towards the end of the run, I started hallucinating a little, nothing major. Until one day, when using the posh loos, I saw Jesus. On the

## NUTELLA PANCAKES

floor of the toilet. I was a little surprised as 1) I'm an atheist and 2) Why was Jesus on the floor of a public toilet in Switzerland? Surely he has better things to do? Anyway, as with most of my hallucinations, it's easier to accept them as they are, so Jesus kept me company during my loo breaks (I didn't talk to him and he wasn't there when I returned in 2018).

So I was happy in my little routine of run, walk, eat and sleep, and I felt like I could do it forever. That was until 'The Screaming Feet' appeared.

I had had this before: the first time on my first Deca attempt; the second on a Oner Ultra Trail Run recce; and the last time during the GymQuin. It is a pain like no other and only stops when I stop. I believe it's a nerve issue, as there is no tendon or ligament damage. And the pain is not helped by any kind of painkiller (although I haven't tried morphine...), which is a big indicator.

The only way we could deal with this was rest. The pain would build and build as the laps went on and would reach a point where I couldn't handle it any more. I would then stop and lie on the floor with my feet in the air. The relief was breathtaking. I would stay there for ten minutes or so and then start again. It was relentless and just truly awful.

One thing that helped was crying (something I did lot on the GymQuin when I had the same problem), because of the endorphins released as I was sobbing. Not ideal, but whatever helps. I put my sunglasses on, pulled my visor down and got on with it. Only Rob knew how much I was suffering, although it was probably quite obvious to everyone else, looking back.

## NUTELLA PANCAKES

I wrote this for Facebook once I was home, about a memory that came back to me:

*There was a moment during the run that I will never forget, even though I don't know what day it was or even what marathon I was on. I know it was towards the end because my feet were screaming at me, so much that I was in flip-flops at that point.*

*It was the middle of the night and I was alone on the long stretch of tarmac. The wind was blowing through my hair and I was listening to Lana Del Ray's 'Heroin' track. Not the most upbeat tune I know ;-) but it was perfect for that moment.*

*I took my flip-flops off and the feeling of my bare feet on the cool, rough road was simply amazing and I had the most awesome rush of endorphins, more effective than any painkiller I know.*

*At that moment, I was so happy to be nearing the end of what was one of the most incredible experiences of my life.*

The run then became all about how many laps I could do before having to stop and put my legs in the air. When I first woke up, after my 4-hour break, I would have a good few hours to crack on. But that was it, anything after those couple of pain-free(ish) hours would then become 5 laps, then stop. 3 laps, then stop. It was soul-destroying. Particularly so when the finish came into view.

You would think that once you are 10 laps or so from being able to stop, you would just want to smash it out and finish the damn thing. But this foot pain would not let up, and even with 3 laps to go, I was forced to stop and lie on the floor once again. So frustrating.

## NUTELLA PANCAKES

The end itself was causing me more anxiety. It was just overwhelming me. I could see other athletes finishing – the second lady, Shanda Hill, had crossed the line that morning and it had almost broken me. SwissUltra make a lovely fuss when you finish. They give you a flag to carry around on your last (reverse) lap, so everyone knows you are almost done. This is a brilliant touch but in my extremely fatigued state and in incredible pain, I just couldn't handle it.

I had to say to myself, 'this is a huge achievement and you must embrace the flag'. Which is a weird thing to say, but I think I meant to not be shy, self-conscious and hide from the limelight like I would normally do. And even though all I wanted to do was to stop and go back to my van to lie down, I forced myself to be brave and truly be in that moment. I think you can see that from the photos on the finish line.

After I had completed the event, we went back to the tent and Rob put the kettle on (so British). I phoned my daughter Jess and after I had told her about finishing, she immediately launched into telling me about how the house had practically fallen down since I'd been away (my mum had banned her from telling me during the race), that she had completed a Tough Mudder 10-miler, smashed her knee up and been ill. I just sat there and smiled. Within ten minutes of finishing, I was back in the real world again.

In the days and weeks that followed the Deca, I had recurring dreams, or rather nightmares. Every night I would wake up in a panic that I was behind on my laps or that I still had hundreds to go. Also, the aches and pains in my legs were my night-time companion for quite a while before I was able to sleep normally again.

## NUTELLA PANCAKES

Other than sleep issues, I had lost a bit of weight, which was to be expected, but it wasn't too hard to put it back on again. I was a little tired and anaemic, but apart from that, I felt fine. People kept saying, 'you must be over the moon'. Sure, I was happy, but it was more of a quiet contentment I felt. Like I had done the job properly and felt at peace with it, rather than screaming from the rooftops, which folk seem to be expecting.

The confidence that it has bought me since finishing has been like a gift though. Again, it's a quiet feeling, but it's definitely there in the background. Whenever I doubt myself (which is often), it nudges me.

'Remember what you did', it says.

# LIFE LESSON
# ULTRA FAFFING

Ultra events are about just keeping going. One foot in front of the other, right?

Wrong.

This would be fine if the race had no cut-off, but as most race directors actually like to go home sometimes, there will always be time limits. Some cut-offs can be a little deceiving though. You may think that 12 days to finish 10 Iron distances sounds like you have plenty of leeway. Hell, you've got time to put your feet up and have a massage. Even have an ice cream or two...

During my first attempt at the Enduroman Continuous Triple, I arrived at the run section (having just managed to make the bike cut-off), looked at the time I had to run 78 miles in and thought 'I can do that easily'. Cut to the early hours of Monday morning and you find me having a desperate conversation with the race director, Eddie Ette. I had 5 miles to go, he had already extended the cut-off (as he tends to every year), but couldn't (and rightfully so), push it any more.

I had 5 miles to go.

We looked at the remaining time and we both knew there was no way I would make it. I reached down and undid my timing chip, handed it to Eddie, and then sat and cried in my van for half an hour. I was exhausted and heartbroken. And the worst thing was, I knew that I had wasted at least an hour during the run. Probably more.

Since then, I have worked very hard on ensuring that I have plans, lots of plans, for each event I do. This doesn't mean I finish them all, but I go into every ultra super-prepared for everything. So, below are some of the things that I have tried and tested over the past five years for taking on – and hopefully finishing – the crazy ultra shit…

**Trip Hazard**

During long events, you start fresh and clear-headed and obviously get more tired and befuddled as the hours go on. It is inevitable that you will start to struggle remembering stuff. You will find yourself on the bike without your gloves or, God forbid, missing your timing chip! These little things will seem small (not the chip), but all add up and affect your mental and physical state.

The forgotten timing chip, however, will break you…

When I have a sleep/rest break, when I'm removing kit, I will always lay it out by the door of wherever I'm resting. Be it a van, tent or hotel room, if it's by the exit, I literally cannot leave without tripping over it. (I also use this method during normal life, because I have virtually no short-term memory. Or long-term, come to that…).

**However, the timing chip goes IN THE SHOE. No matter what, always IN THE SHOE.**

Everything else – coat, hat, gloves, drink bottle, lights, all that I need – is laid out by the door. So when you do some long or multi-day sessions at home, practice it and then make it a habit.

## Lists

I bloody love lists, I do. For someone who likes to get a lot of shit done, they're essential in my everyday life.

But now I use them in events too. During the 1×5 Quin in Switzerland, when I was crew-less (or 'screwed', as my ultra buddy Joey calls it), I wrote on the inside of my van everything I needed to do before I went to sleep (get my swim kit ready, drink my recovery shake, timing chip IN THE SHOE, etc). This meant that no matter how tired I was, I kept to my routine.

And don't worry if you haven't got a Ford Transit to write on, it's fine to use paper.

## Plans

Don't get plans confused with lists. They are completely different. You need a plan for all areas of your crazy ultra shit. One for the pacing and lap times, one for your food and drink, and one for crew (if you have them).

The food/drink and crew plans can be relatively straightforward, although if you have multiple crew, you may want to build in a contingency plan in case someone can't make it. And it's also a good idea to have a 'normal' food plan and a 'when you can't eat anything any more' plan. You obviously still need to eat, so having something that your crew can fall back on is a good idea. If you have to finish the Doubletriplewhatever on Jammy Dodgers and green Jelly Babies, so be it.

The pacing and lap time plan is a little trickier, as it's almost impossible to control all the variables which will affect your pace. So I have two or three: a 'best case' plan, a 'things are still kinda OK' one, and an 'oh fuck, it's all falling apart, just try and finish' plan. I tend to end up on the latter, but by having it in place already, I still have a sense of control, which helps with keeping a positive mindset.

Also, with pacing, if you work on a walk/run plan during the run section, ensure that you stick with this at all times (or at least until you are truly unable to maintain it). So if you plan to run for 5 minutes and walk for 2, make sure you don't start running for 3 minutes and walking for 4. It's easily done and another way to lose precious time. Also, make sure your run pace isn't the same speed as your walk. Not that I would know ANYTHING about doing this. Not. At. All.

Make your plan FAFF-FREE! You always need to be moving forward. The only times you need to stop are when you are sleeping or on the loo. Don't do either of those on the go, it ends badly. When you start stopping every lap for a quick chat or find some excuse to get off the bike (mainly because you now hate it with every fibre of your being) for no real reason, you are FAFFING. Realise that you are faffing and have a strong word with yourself. Faffing leads to DNF-ing.

**Kit organisation**

This is an obvious one, but it's amazing how many people don't do it. Rather than just packing all your kit into one huge bag or loads of smaller ones, think about the type of kit you will need (if it's Wales, then just bring everything). And then sort it into bags or boxes that are clearly labelled (it'll be the middle of the night when you or your crew are rummaging around for that missing sock that you have to have).

Put your wet-weather kit in one box, and top and bottoms in separate bags too. It all saves time and helps keep your head clear. And, if you are able to, have a bag of spare stuff which you can put out the way and hopefully not need. Knowing you have a spare wetsuit or rain jacket will make you feel really smug.

The same goes for bike parts. Bag them up and label if required. Make it as easy as possible to change your cleats or fix your chain should you need to.

And when it comes to kit, think very hard before leaving items at home. Yes, your race is in the summer, but don't think for a second that you won't get a freak storm and end up putting plastic bags on your feet, because you didn't think you would need your overshoes (the bags worked really well actually, but still…).

**Communication**

If you are lucky enough to have crew, make sure you use them properly. Meet up before the race and go through your plans. Ensure they come to the race briefing and have read the info pack (y'know, that really important document the race director spends hours on and everybody reads really thoroughly?).

During the event, if they aren't doing something quite right, speak up. Unless they are experienced ultra racers themselves, they may not know that you have to have your mashed potato at an exact temperature and correct consistency. And make sure they know all your drink mixes. Write the number of scoops on the side of the container or the box. Try and make everything as idiot-proof as possible.

And, speaking of idiots, ensure you pick the right people to help you. Having rubbish crew is sometimes as bad as having no crew…

Finally, be nice to your crew. The amount of athletes I've seen ranting at their support because they haven't got the cereal bar or forgotten a certain item of kit… Remember, they're just as tired as you are, and they don't get a medal at the end of spending four days in a cold, wet field in Wales either.

## All the small things

During shorter races, you can get away with ignoring certain things. Saddle sores during an Ironman? You'll be fine. Blisters in a marathon? Whatever. But during the multi-day stuff…

Do not let these things slide. You may think that you don't have time to stop and sort your feet out. But when you have 3 marathons left, you really, really need to. Forgotten to apply chamois cream? Stop as soon as you can and deal with that. Damage limitation is a must at all times during ultra races.

And ensure these little, but oh-so-important details are on your crew plan too. That way, when you forget, someone else will be there with the Vaseline, talcum powder or sun cream (unless it's Wales, of course).

## Multiple goals

The last tip is not really about time management, but it's damn good advice I stole from another ultra athlete. Setting multiple goals is a neat trick to get you to the finish line. For the Mexico Double Deca, I had three goals. The first was just to get to the finish line. The second goal was just to get to the finish line and finish the swim in a badass time. The third goal was just to get to the finish line, a badass swim and be on the podium.

So, on this very, very rare occasion, I actually managed to reach all these goals. But there was a moment during the run when the podium went completely out the window and just finishing became the only plan. By setting multiple goals, it helps control any negative mindset you experience when shit goes down, and lets you refocus and keep moving.

So there you have it. All my years of making mistakes, trying to learn from them and going back and doing it again. And again. And sometimes again…

And you never know, one day I might actually finish the Enduroman Triple…

## CHAPTER 12
# MEXICO MINI-BREAK

In the weeks leading up to the continuous Double Deca (48-mile swim, 2,240 miles of cycling and 524 miles of running) in Mexico in October 2019, I was a mess. Not just any old mess either. A proper depressed, crying every day, wondering what I had done to my life kind of mess. My relationship with Jon, which had started after the Deca in New Orleans, had ended and I was really struggling with my business.

Before I left to attempt this monster challenge, I made a big decision to bring someone else on board to help with some of the events and also to take over some of the others. This meant giving away a large part of the business, but I was ready for that. It was time to step back. Brutal had been breaking me for a while now.

What happened with my relationship was more complicated. It was mostly down to a lack of communication, but also because we were both so used to being on our own, so used to being independent, that as soon as we had problems, we both shut down and pushed each other away.

But there was more than that. Something truly terrible had happened a few months before. Jon's best friend had taken his own life. Nobody saw it coming and it rocked our close-knit crew to the core. Rab McAvoy was one of those people whom you don't meet very often in life, and you tend not to forget once you do. He was a cheeky Scottish redhead with a cracking sense of humour and a big heart. When he left the Army, he planned on becoming a paramedic because, he explained, he loved driving fast and helping people.

## MEXICO MINI-BREAK

That summed him up completely.

I only knew him for a couple of years, but thought the world of him, and that night when he went missing was one of the worst of my life. It was simply incomprehensible that he had done this, something so final and so violent, but also that he had left us all here. This was, I guess, a selfish response, but it's how I felt for a long time. Every time I thought about him, I would ask out loud like a crazy woman, 'Why did you leave? You had plans, we all had plans *with* you!' I was angry with him for months after.

Then one day, sitting on my boyfriend's bed, I asked him the same question. Jon's answer was simple, 'He had to go, he had somewhere else to be.'

I thought about that for a while and it made sense. From then on, whenever I felt upset or angry, I would say it in my head. 'He just had somewhere else to be.' It seemed to calm the confusing emotions I felt.

But life went on, even if it felt like it shouldn't. Events had to continue, even though it was so hard because Rab was everywhere as he had been so involved in Brutal. The Oner Ultra Trail Run was Rab's first ultra run and it had been his favourite race. To honour his memory, I renamed the event 'Rab's Ultra'. Organising it a short time after his death was incredibly hard for all of the crew. And his amazingly strong wife, Emma, came to show her support to the runners. I had huge respect for her for doing this, as it must have been the last place she wanted to be.

So, I guess it's safe to say that there was a lot going on. I was doing

## MEXICO MINI-BREAK

my very best to cope with everything, but one afternoon, it all came crashing down like a ton of bricks. Overwhelmed by the latest VAT bill and faced with having to cancel yet another event that weekend, due to high winds, my stress levels were sky-high. The final straw was an argument with my daughter Jess, over something so stupid that I can't even remember it now.

I hit rock bottom.

I didn't deal with it well. I lost the ability to hide my feelings and I felt like I simply didn't give a fuck about anything. I went into super-destructive mode, eating badly, not sleeping and going running late at night, not caring if I was safe. I would drive dangerously fast, taking stupid risks on quiet country lanes. I even swam across a deep Welsh lake, on my own, in the dark.

It sounds bad, and at the time it felt like it too, but in hindsight it was a good thing. I knew it had been coming for a while and I had been doing everything in my power to avoid it. I felt like I had been driving really slowly down a long lane full of deep potholes. Carefully steering round each one, trying to avoid them, only to get to the end and then have the van explode (which, if I had been driving my old Vauxhall, was actually quite likely).

In short, this breakdown had been on the cards for some time.

So to board a flight to Mexico and take on one of the longest, hardest triathlons in the world was just plain stupid. I remember thinking I had no business even starting a race which I had not prepared for, mentally or physically. But I had become reckless. I didn't care what happened to me, so I guess this was just another stupid choice

## MEXICO MINI-BREAK

I was making.

And who even cared whether I finished or not?

I know for a fact that nobody really expected me to. Especially given my past record (with some honourable exceptions!). But there is something quite liberating about going into a massive challenge with no expectations or pressure. I even said to myself that if I pulled out, I would go on an adventure. Cycle across Mexico or become a drug lord...

**3 days to race start...**

Checking in at Heathrow had been a nightmare. My bike box was ridiculously overweight and I knew it. I was hoping the airline would just tell me off and charge me extra (which they did) but they also made a massive deal over the health and safety aspect of the box itself, and how their staff could injure themselves by lifting it. I was fully aware of this, as I had just hauled it around the airport for the last hour. Between that and my massive Bergen pack, I felt like I had pulled every muscle in my arms and back. Perfect prep for a 48-mile swim in a few days' time.

I was made to take every single item out of the bike box (I know it should only have the actual bike in there, but...) and place them all in trays to go through the scanner. I was sweating and shaking, trying to look casual, but I was mentally going through everything, trying to work out what I could leave behind if I needed to. After a long hour of intense scrutiny and many, many questions, the airport security allowed me to repack my box and it disappeared on a conveyor belt.

## MEXICO MINI-BREAK

I breathed a massive sigh of relief and allowed myself to relax before the flight to Mexico.

Once on the plane, I flicked through the inflight movies and decided on some decent ones. There was enough to keep me occupied for 10 hours. I could never sleep much on planes and although I felt deeply exhausted, both mentally and physically, I knew I wouldn't get any real rest. I also, as usual, wasn't the most relaxed flyer; the inner control freak in me was alert, ready for bits to start falling off the plane. I looked at the other passengers, already with eye-masks and travel pillows in place, with envy.

The take-off, and subsequent burst of adrenaline I always get, was a welcome distraction from the dark clouds that had drifted over me again. 'When would I stop feeling so low about everything?', I wondered. Would Mexico be what I needed to get my life back on track again, or was it another huge mistake? Well, whatever it would be, it was too late to change my mind now, I thought as the plane soared into the air.

A new continent and time-zone later, I unfolded myself from the cramped seat and stretched my stiff body. I was in Mexico! My pack and bike box were almost the first items of luggage off the plane and I hauled them from the belt. I couldn't actually believe that my kit and me were all in the right place! The race director's son, Alex, was waiting outside and we managed to fit everything into the back of his truck.

After a high-speed, 'car chase from a movie' type of drive, we arrived at my hotel, which was situated, oddly, at the side of a dual carriageway. Outside was a hot, humid chaos – cars and

## MEXICO MINI-BREAK

lorries screaming past – but once you stepped into the hotel, you were enveloped in an air-conditioned, polished-floor, mirrored-table environment. From what I had seen of León so far, this juxtaposition between areas of near poverty to lavish luxury seemed completely normal.

My room was amazing. Huge, with a separate living and kitchen area, and a massive bed and shower. Plus a view over the dual carriageway, just to remind me of where I was. I lay, sprawled on the bed, and realised that, dispute the tiredness from all the travel, I was excited to be there for the race. It was a good feeling.

After unpacking and relaxing for a while, I built my bike. Amazingly, I managed this without any help. And it seemed to actually work, but I would only find this out once I started the 2,240-mile ride the following week.

Once I had showered and sorted myself out, I met up with Shanda Hill, one of my Deca buddies from Switzerland. It's funny, you don't see these people for a year, but you fall back into an easy-going relationship straight away. Ultra endurance friends are different to others. You get so close during the races, because everyone suffers so much and conversations are just pure honesty. There's no room for bullshit when you're sitting on the floor, crying over something random, and your feet are bleeding.

Later, Georgetta and Lia arrived. Lia was attempting her first continuous Deca and looked utterly terrified. Which, selfishly speaking, made me feel better. Georgetta was doing the Double with me. We walked down to the park where the bike and run section of the race were to be held and chatted about how we were feeling.

## MEXICO MINI-BREAK

I warned them that I would probably cry even more than normal due to the recent shit that had happened. Georgetta asked me if it was really over between me and my ex. I sighed and nodded. I knew that it was, but just her saying that gave me a little spark of hope that I quickly tried to stamp out. I stared out across the lake and seriously worried that I was not going to have the mental strength for this race.

After socialising just enough so I didn't seem rude, I escaped to the sanctuary of my room, closing the door behind me, pulling off my clothes and falling into bed. It was only 6pm, and I had no idea how long I'd been awake or what time it was at home, but I desperately needed sleep. Even in my exhausted state though, insomnia had followed me from the UK. After staring at the ceiling fan for a while, I reached for my iPad and tapped the Amazon Prime icon, allowing myself to forget reality and be absorbed into the comforting ridiculousness of *Grey's Anatomy*.

**2 days to race start...**

I woke up at 4am with a ridiculous headache. I made a coffee and drank a ton of water, but it still hurt; it felt like I had a hangover. I finally gave in and took some of the painkillers that were supposed to be for the race. They helped a little. I had a shower and faffed with my kit for a while.

Later that morning, I met up with the girls and a couple of the guys who were also taking part in the race. We went to Starbucks and then to find somewhere to eat. I wasn't that hungry, but ordered potato wedges and some salad. After eating, we headed over to Walmart and looked for some storage boxes to sort our kit for the race. Most

## MEXICO MINI-BREAK

of us were unsupported, so organisation was very important. The last thing you need during the middle of the night is to not be able to find a sock or a pair of cycling shorts you desperately need.

My headache was still bad, but I was told it was the elevation (León sits at an altitude of nearly 6,000 feet), which can cause symptoms of mild altitude sickness, like headaches, tiredness and nausea. I hoped that it would ease off before the swim.

Later that evening, everyone met up at a restaurant, but I made my excuses. My head hurt so much, I just wanted to lie in the dark. I get a lot of headaches in normal life, but this was more migraine territory. I had my period too, which was a very good thing, as I normally get it during a race. Hopefully, I would have finished the event by the time I was due again.

I chatted to some friends back home for a while and went to sleep around 8pm.

**1 day to race start…**

I woke up at 5am, so a little later than yesterday. My head was still banging and now my eyes were swollen. My period was stupidly heavy, which probably meant I would be massively anaemic even before I started. Awesome.

I checked my messages from last night's group chat and felt a pang of loneliness. They looked like they had a good time, but I was really struggling with the whole social thing. I liked it for a while, but then just felt exhausted pretending that I'm this super-happy person. Inside, I felt so broken by everything.

## MEXICO MINI-BREAK

More shopping, more faffing with kit and more pre-race stressing. We were all just killing time, waiting to start the biggest race of our lives.

**Double Deca Diary: T minus 12 hours**

*Later tonight we will start the 48-mile pool swim. Yes, I'm really nervous, but also incredibly relieved that it's finally here and I can just focus on moving forwards and dealing with physical pain, rather than mental.*

*This morning we visited the race HQ area and where we will be camping within the huge park in León. The main race tent is basically a small marquee with a large kitchen area and tables and chairs. And just next to it is a scattering of tiny, one-man tents. It's funny, but in a few days this will feel like home to us all.*

All there was left to do now was to move our kit from the hotel to the park. This was going to be quite a big job, as there was a lot of kit and the hotel was about a mile away. I was thinking that we would have to lug it all down there ourselves, not ideal prep before a 48-mile swim, but Georgetta (a woman who gets shit done) organized things so that the hotel helped with their van. We loaded it up with everything and then walked down, carrying our bikes so as not to get punctures. A little while later, we had everything we needed and each of us was in our tents, setting up our 'home' for the next month.

I rather liked my little blue tent, which became far more than just a place to sleep. It had an airbed, which I raised the end of, which helps when your feet, knees and lower legs start to swell during the

## MEXICO MINI-BREAK

race. I had three large boxes at the end of my bed: one with food and race nutrition; one with wet weather and spare kit; and the last one for kit I would use every day. Other than that, I had a box with all my medical supplies in, another with charging stuff, lights and batteries. And the last one had bike inner tubes, a spare tyre and extra parts, should I get a serious mechanical.

I'd bought a yoga mat from Walmart to cover the area next to my bed and soften the hard ground and even purchased a cheap pink bath-mat as a kind of makeshift rug to make the tent feel homely. After everything was unpacked and I had my bags ready for the swim, with my wetsuit, Heatseeker vest, hats, goggles, nutrition, and also my bike kit for when I had finished, I sat back on my bed and looked around me. I was ready, I decided. There was nothing else for me to do. I zipped up my tent door and wandered across to the other tents, where the others were almost finished. Georgetta's tent was on another level to the rest of ours. We're talking glamping here and I was a little jealous.

When there was nothing left to do at camp, we walked back along the crazy dual carriageway, with trucks speeding past, workmen crammed into every available space in the back. I loved the huge lorries, with their shiny chrome front grills making ours back home look so dull in comparison. What I didn't like was the stray dogs that lay curled up alongside the road, sleeping out of the midday sun. They made my heart ache.

Back at the hotel, I headed for Georgetta's room, as I couldn't afford to keep mine for the duration of the race. Jade, who is an event medic and all-round amazing woman, had arrived. I was really pleased to see her as I had met her in a previous race and

## MEXICO MINI-BREAK

liked her immensely. She wasn't the type of lady you mess with, but had a heart of gold and would do anything for her 'ultra girls' during these races.

We ate, drank and chatted about our worries for the event, mainly focused on the huge beast of a swim we faced in a few hours. Would we even finish it? Nobody we knew had taken on something like this, so we had very little to work with in terms of advice and strategy. My plan was simple. Don't mess about too much. Keep breaks short and don't get out too many times. Basically, get it done as quickly as possible.

With a few hours to go, we tried to sleep. I failed miserably, but it was a great opportunity to lie there and think about all the things I had run away to Mexico from.

Just before 8pm, we grabbed our bags and made our way to the lobby, where the bus was waiting to take us the pool. My stomach was flipping with nerves. And as I looked around, I could see everyone else felt the same. In the van, the atmosphere was similar to a school trip. We were like noisy, unruly kids, making stupid jokes and laughing too loudly. The nervous energy charged through the small space. I wonder what the driver must have thought of us.

We finally arrived at the sports centre – it had been much further away than we expected – and climbed out of the bus. Walking into the pool area – it was basically a 50-metre lido – I got a feeling not dissimilar to the one when you get to a hotel resort, only to find a building site. It did not look like the pool in the pictures. I didn't know why I was surprised, but I was. There was also a swimming club in progress, a large amount of teenagers smashing through

## MEXICO MINI-BREAK

their sets, as we stood on the poolside feeling like we were in the wrong place.

I saw that there was nowhere to put our kit in order to protect it should it rain. We then walked over to the changing rooms and looked around in horror. They were disgusting. Dirty floors, blocked toilets and one cramped bench to change at. Still, sometimes it is what it is. Checking the time, there was no avoiding it anymore – the race would start in ten minutes. We pulled off our normal clothes and I thought, weirdly, that I would be wearing triathlon kit for the next month.

Once we were changed, we walked to the pool which was now, thankfully, empty. It looked a little swamp-like, with a slight green tinge to the water and steam rising from it, but I've swum in worse. We were given hats and assigned lanes, which would chop and change over the next few days as there was public swimming and more clubs, but for tonight, the pool was ours.

Some people jumped in, some dived, but I plopped over the side, cautiously. The water temperature was good and I was relieved. Shouts of good luck filled the warm air and then Beto, the race director, started the Double Deca.

I pushed off from the side and straight away noticed the water. It was really cloudy, and a strong, unfamiliar chemical taste seeped into my mouth. By the time I was back to where Joey, who was helping out for the swim, was standing, my tongue already felt a little numb. 'Has anyone else said anything about the water?' I asked, as my panic began to rise.

## MEXICO MINI-BREAK

Joey looked bemused. 'Not yet,' he replied.

After a few more laps, he leant down to the edge of the pool and told me that everyone was complaining now. It was a huge worry. I've done a lot of sea swimming, which destroys the inside of your mouth, but it's natural – seawater. This was different. One fellow athlete, Laura Knoblach, told me after the race that she became so paranoid at one point, she thought the water might start dissolving her eyeballs!

After an initial settling-in period, I started to relax. Right from the beginning, I made the decision to rotate in my stroke as much as I could to take the pressure off my shoulders. This was one of the best decisions I made in the race. And apart from my worries about the water quality, I feel good and positive as I churned out the laps, over and over. Friday night went quickly and I swam into Saturday.

During the swim, I ate bars, nuts and bananas, as well as some fruit jelly sweets as a treat. I drank Hydrixa, a French sports drink which I have found the most palatable over long-distance events, and I think someone made me noodles at one point, but I didn't eat that much over the 48 miles.

My mouth got more and more sore over the hours and days that followed, and worse than that, I began to sneeze. Not just once, but over and over. Sometimes, I would have to stop mid-length and hold on to the lane rope as I would sneeze five or ten times in one go. It was exhausting and I could hear others doing the same. I was also having problems with my asthma; my lungs tightened up and I struggled to breathe normally. Once again, I could hear my fellow competitors also coughing and spluttering.

## MEXICO MINI-BREAK

During the daytime, the pool was absolutely rammed with the general public and swimming lessons. Unfortunately, I was in the lane next to the lessons, which had more than twenty swimmers in every hour. It was ridiculously busy and more than once, I was kicked by someone doing breaststroke or butterfly. I longed for the time when the public swimming was over.

At some point on Saturday afternoon, Joey stopped me and informed me that I was halfway. I had completed 24 miles, and not only that, I had taken 4 hours off my previous best continuous Deca time. I was thrilled. It was a real confidence boost. Halfway, I thought. This is actually happening. I am going to finish a 48-mile swim. Joey also said that I was in the lead. I looked at him and shook my head: 'What are you talking about?"

'You're leading,' he confirmed. I shrugged and dismissed it. I was never in the lead for anything, so I just thought they were messing with me.

As the darkness of the second night fell, I began to hallucinate badly. The bottom of the swimming pool had obviously been fixed a fair few times, and there was what looked like Polyfilla in several places. There were also a lot of tiles missing and with this and the large lumps of filler, they turned into faces of creatures as I swam over them, time and time again. My eyes would flick between one shape to another, my poor, tired brain trying to make sense of it all. Laura said all she could see was Japanese ink paintings and latex gloves.

Saturday night was a real tough one. The air temperature had dropped and we were all so tired that the cold began to really affect

## MEXICO MINI-BREAK

us. I was shivering as I swam, length after length, and at one point I think I actually fell asleep in the water. I stopped at the end of the lane and looked around to see only about half the competitors in the water. I wondered where they were and in my head, I decided that they had found a warm place to sleep, like a room with beds on the floor.

I hauled myself out of the pool, my shoulders screaming and my neck red raw. I ignored the pain and went in search of the special sleeping room. After a few minutes of padding around the edge of the pool and over by the changing rooms, I sighed and looked back at the water. Jade was sitting, wrapped in a blanket, watching the remaining swimmers. I went over to ask her where I could rest.

'There is no room,' she said. 'The only thing people are doing is lying down on a couple of airbeds, over by the trees.'

I could make out a few dark shapes, covered in sleeping bags. 'Could I get 20 minutes' sleep?' I asked her.

'I will see if I can find you a space,' she said.

After a moment Jade returned and confirmed that there was a space, but I would need to share with someone. I didn't care; I just needed to stop for a little while. I had no idea who the wetsuit-covered shape was next to me; it was definitely a man though. Jade told me just to lie down as I was; all I took off was my goggles.

I honestly thought, as I lay there, that I would never stop shivering, but after a few minutes it subsided and I was able to get maybe 15 minutes of sleep. Not the best, but it would have to do, I thought,

## MEXICO MINI-BREAK

as I attempted to get up off the bed. There was a new person next to me now, but I still had no idea who it was. I walked back to the pool and sat on the edge. The water felt warmer on my feet than the air did. I was longing for the sun to rise, but I knew we still had hours of darkness yet.

I lowered myself back into the water and pushed off the side again. Lap after lap, mile after mile. At one point, one of my fellow Double Deca competitors, Al, fell fast asleep while swimming and ploughed straight into me. If you've ever had a head-on crash with someone in the pool, you will know how much it hurts. It's also a bit of a shock! Still, it woke us both up a bit. Al is a lovely guy and was so apologetic, but I laughed it off. The second time he did it, I didn't laugh so much. And the third, I wanted to punch him in the face.

As I swam on, I looked at the sky each time I took a breath, searching for any signs of daylight, willing the sun to rise, as if the power of my mind could make it happen more quickly. Eventually, the sky began to change colour, from dark blue to purple and pink, then finally, it was light blue. Sunday morning had arrived. I had no idea what mile I was on, but I knew I was going to finish that day and that's all I focused on.

My neck had now become so sore that every time I moved my head from side to side to breathe, it made me wince in pain. I touched it at one point and pulled my hand away quickly. It felt disgusting. I had also pulled some muscles around my ribs from sneezing so much, and every time I breathed in, I had a stabbing pain in my right lung. I tried not to think too much about what I had done to myself.

## MEXICO MINI-BREAK

Lap after lap, mile upon mile. It never ended. I had tried not to ask how long I had left up until now, but I was desperate. When the timing guy told me that I still had over 3 miles to go, I cried into my goggles. I had now stopped eating as my mouth and tongue were so painful. I tried to keep drinking my Hydrixa, but even that was hard to get down.

I can't describe the misery of those last few hours. The pain, the cold, the fucking relentless swimming lessons and people kicking me... all I wanted was for it to stop. Why weren't the timing guys doing their job properly? I must have done 3 miles by now. I could see the race director walking around the pool. He must be getting ready to say that I had finished, right? Nobody did anything. On I swam. I became quite irrational for the last hour. I didn't speak to anyone and I hated the timing guy with a passion. Poor bloke.

I decided that if there was a hell, then this was it. The devil would make you swim in a dark, cloudy, cold pool, filled with toxic chemicals, for the rest of eternity. Whilst your skin peeled off, layer after layer, and your ribs broke from sneezing non-stop. And weirdly – and to this day I can't explain this – I developed two painful lumps on the top of my forehead, almost like developing horns. They stayed there for the whole race.

Finally, I was told to stop. I had finished the 48-mile swim and I could get out of the pool.

I think someone helped me out. I remember trying to walk to the changing rooms and Joey having to hold me up. I remember standing in the shower, crying as the water ran over the open sores on my neck, and Jade having to help me take off all the

## MEXICO MINI-BREAK

layers of neoprene.

Everything hurt. Absolutely everything. But I was done.

Once the epic job of getting out of my wetsuit and into my bike kit was complete, I stumbled out of the changing rooms, blinking, blinded by the sunlight. I felt awful. Imagine having the flu (proper flu, not a bad cold), the worst hangover you have ever had (you know the night with the tequila? Yeah, that one…), and on top of all that, you have been in a nasty fight with someone much, much harder than you. And you didn't come out of it well. If you can imagine that, then you are close to how I felt (and looked) after that swim.

Beto, the race director, congratulated me. And I showed him my teeth in some weak attempt at a smile. Joey then gently took my arm and led me, like an old lady, to the car which was going to take me back to the park. There, waiting for me, was my bike (which I had absolutely no intention of getting on for a good few hours) and more importantly, my bed.

I half-sat, half-lay in the back seat of the car, groaning. Joey was finding this all very amusing. After a while, he asked if I wanted food. I did, I think. Actually, I didn't know. Was I hungry? I literally couldn't make a single decision. Did I want to eat in a restaurant?

'Have you seen my face?' I asked.

'Fair point,' he laughed.

So Joey decided that McDonalds would be perfect and I still

had no clue.

Back at race HQ, I shuffled over towards my tent. The timing guys (different ones to the pool) looked at me, horrified. Fuck, is it possible I look worse than I thought?

'It's OK,' Joey shouted. 'She's having a sleep before starting the bike.'

They looked relieved and went back to frowning at the laptops.

'Who else is here?' I asked.

'Nobody, you're the first one back,' said Joey.

I thought about this for a while. Some of the faster swimmers, all men, had started later than us, so it wasn't so strange that I was back first. But it still felt odd. I'm normally the last one out of the lake or pool.

Back in my tent, I sat surrounded with McDonalds. Joey sat outside and we chatted about life for a while. I could barely eat anything as my mouth was so sore, but I managed a few chips and half a burger. Joey then left to go back to helping the remaining swimmers. And I settled down to sleep.

You would think that after swimming 48 miles in 42 hours and with 15 minutes' rubbish sleep, I would have been out for the count. But no. I lay there for hours, the pain in my neck excruciating, and every time I fell into unconsciousness, I would wake up with terrible shooting pains. Jesus, what had I done to myself?

## MEXICO MINI-BREAK

At some point during the night, I gave up. The idea of having six wonderful hours of uninterrupted sleep simply wasn't happening. I sat up and flicked on a light so I could get myself ready to start the 2,240-mile bike. I pulled on my shoes, coat and helmet and sat for a while on the side of my airbed. I felt horrible. My head pounded and breathing was hard. My neck just hurt so much.

Unzipping the door, I had to steady myself on the sides of the tent. There was nobody around. Attaching my light to my helmet, I walked over to the bike racking and found my bright green Kuota. I smiled to myself. I hadn't owned this bike very long, but I already loved it. Due to my back issues, loving a bike was an unusual emotion for me. Cars and vans, yes. But not bikes. However, on the three or four training rides pre-Mexico, I had really enjoyed riding my green machine. It had been an extra £1,000 more than what I had spent in the past, but so worth it.

Pushing my bike over to the start of the lap, I looked around for someone. 'Do I just get on and ride?' I wondered. I then heard some voices and one of the timing guys walked over to me. The language barrier was a little bit of an issue, but I worked out that I needed to do an extra bit on the first lap to ensure my mileage was correct. As a race director, I knew all about this stuff – people get really funny if the overall distance isn't exact. I was never really that fussed. Another guy appeared on a bike and I was told to follow him.

I started to ride. I was really shaky and wobbled off behind him, frantically trying to get my shoe clipped in as he disappeared into the night. We went in the opposite direction to how the lap would normally run, and after ten minutes or so, the man on the bike stopped and told me we were done and I was now free to turn

## MEXICO MINI-BREAK

around and complete the laps as normal.

I breathed a sigh of relief and stood for a while on my own. I needed a moment. And I needed some food. I found the bar I had put in my jersey pocket and nibbled at it. My blood sugar was super-low, but I had no appetite and a very sore mouth. I wished I had somebody crewing me, to help. And not for the first or last time in the race, I thought of my ex-boyfriend and wished that he was here.

'Stop feeling fucking sorry for yourself, you idiot,' I said out loud. 'And get on with it.'

The Double Deca bike lap was about 5 miles long and circled a large lake. The path was smooth and had two lanes, one for cycling and one for walking and running. For the most part, park users would stay in the correct lane, but during the event, every one of us had problems with people wandering in front, crossing lanes without looking and even stopping dead, causing us to brake hard and swerve. Because of these issues, most competitors fell off at least once during the race.

When the park was busy, it was extremely stressful for us tired Deca athletes, and I hated it. But the lap itself was a really pretty, flat, interesting route. As you left the start area, you cycled past the entrance to the park, with the guards sitting around, always watching, and into Squirrel Lane. This section would be where fat Mexican squirrels would constantly race across the road, playing chicken with us, trying their very best to make us fall off.

After swerving and shouting at them, I eventually gave up and ignored them. 'If I hit you, it's your own bloody fault,' I would

## MEXICO MINI-BREAK

say to them. They didn't understand, because they were Mexican, obviously. When they weren't trying to die, they would be beating the crap out of each other at the side of the path. Watching Squirrel Wars kept me entertained for hours.

If you survived the furry little fuckers, you cycled on to The Mountain section. This was one of two hills on the course and it went over a dam. It was surprisingly steep, even on the first lap, so I knew it was only going to get harder and harder as the miles went by. Luckily, it was very short, but it was also the only part of the course where the road surface was rough, and my God, was it bad. After you came to the top of the dam, you would speed down the other side, holding tightly onto your handlebars, teeth rattling in your head, trying (and failing) to find a better, smoother route on every single lap.

After The Mountain section followed Family World. With its children's play park, cafés and ice-cream kiosks, it was a perfect place to spend an afternoon with kids. Don't worry about the sleep-deprived cyclists speeding past at 20mph. And it's perfectly fine to leave your toddler on his tricycle in the middle of the bike lane. What's the worst that can happen?

Thankfully, after the squirrels and the kids, there was a quiet section of path with a little bit of downhill and lovely views across the lake. This part found us cycling next to a farm, where every morning the Goat Man would lead his goats across the cycle path (obviously not looking beforehand) and to the lake for their morning ablutions. I always looked forward to seeing this, as Goat Man was pretty hot and always shirtless. More importantly though, he always had a baby goat with him, who you could tell was an absolute handful,

## MEXICO MINI-BREAK

leaping about all over the place and doing the opposite of everything he was told. Goat Man always looked like a tired parent, right on the edge of losing his rag.

Past the farm were more quieter paths, where you could get onto your aerobars, enjoy a little speed and some respite from looking out for livestock and children. That was until you reached another busy point of the course, where yet more families would enjoy weaving across in front of you at any given time.

There was one time when I was cycling behind a girl of about thirteen. I was about to overtake her and called out 'bika' to her (which I thought was Spanish for 'bike', but have since discovered doesn't mean anything at all). She turned, looked at me in absolute horror, pulled her bike to the centre of the path, therefore completely blocking it, and stopped dead. I have no clue why she did this and just braked hard, came to a halt, put my head on my bars and sighed.

To get back to the start point, we had to climb the second mountain (on the other side of the dam), which wasn't quite as steep as the first but also rewarded you with a cracking downhill. On pretty much every lap, I would stand up on my pedals to stretch out my legs and back, enjoying the break and feeling like a ten-year-old again, whizzing down a hill, carefree and happy.

# CHAPTER 13
# DOUBLE DECA DIARIES

What follows here are my Double Deca Diary entries, which I would send my good friend and business partner, James Page, so he could update my family and friends via Facebook.

I don't know how I found time and energy to do these, but they will, I hope, take you right to where I was and how I felt during that Double Deca in León.

**Double Deca Diary: Monday Oct 7th**

In a lot of pain this morning from the swim, breathing bad and I can't move my neck.

I tried to do some bike laps at 02:00, but kept falling asleep, so gave up and had another few more hours' kip. It's now 05:15 and I'm going to do some more.

My tent is a fucking state already!

**Double Deca Diary: Tuesday Oct 8th**

Got 200 miles in for Monday, which I was really pleased with. I'm trying to make sure I do at least that, every day. It's 0138 Tuesday now and very windy on the course, so I'm in bed with a jam sandwich (fucking weird-tasting jam here…). Planning on getting back up at 03:00.

It's 17:20 here and I'm on 150 miles. Just had boiled potatoes and broccoli for tea and getting my head down for an hour before another 50. Finding the more I do this stuff, the more plain, vegetarian food I crave.

Thought I saw a dog earlier, but it was a wheelbarrow. I was very disappointed.

The nights here are very cold. I was in my down jacket on the bike and then during the day, I need factor 50.

I am now an ultra endurance hobo. I am disgusting. My body is a mass of sores, dirt and sweat.

### Double Deca Diary: Wednesday Oct 9th

Things are getting really tough now (like they weren't before…). My back pain kicked in this morning. I thought I was getting away with it by breaking up the daily miles into shorter sections and then sleeping, but I had it from the start this morning. Going to try the TENS machine now, hopefully that will take the edge off.

Got a puncture last night. I was changing it and I discovered I had the inner tube for McBender (the recumbent bike), which is literally half the size. Luckily, Beto's crew turned up with a spare wheel.

Everyone is still coughing from the chemicals in the pool…

### Double Deca Diary: Thursday Oct 10th

It's 06:22 here and I've just done 40 miles, but now really tired. Going to grab 45 minutes' sleep to try and take the edge off it. I had

## DOUBLE DECA DIARIES

my longest sleep of 2 hours 30 minutes last night after reaching 200 miles at about 23:30. Spent the last 30m riding and chatting with Laura, which was really nice. I'm hoping today won't be quite as hot as yesterday, but I'm definitely NOT complaining about having nice weather during an event!

**Double Deca Diary: Friday Oct 11th**

Yesterday I had some stomach issues which made it hard to eat... but obviously I have to, so it was a big chicken noodle kinda day. Super-hot weather added to the problems and everyone was struggling with it.

I intended to make up for lost miles during the night section, but my body had other ideas and I had to take a lot more mini sleep breaks than I wanted to. It was really good to see the sunrise just now though.

In other news, I have just started to be able to move my neck properly again from the damage caused by the swim, so that's pretty cool... but nowhere near as exciting as finally seeing the possum I have been catching glimpses of over the last few nights. I did almost run him over, and he gave me the dirtiest of looks, but it was worth it just to see his little face.

**Double Deca Diary: Saturday October 12th**

After eating cereal for breakfast every day, I discovered that they cook fresh pancakes. Every. Single. Day. (Why haven't I realised this before?). If you get there early (about 05:00), they are hot and totally delicious with tons of maple syrup. I will have no teeth by the time I get back to the UK, but that's OK with me.

It's the weekend and there are kids everywhere. I've had three near misses already, and I'm so worried about crashing and it ending my race. Why can't people just fucking look? I'm trying and failing to stay calm. Georgetta and Shanda just scream at them. I haven't quite reached that point yet, but I'm close.

I have been on the bike since the early hours of Monday morning now, so about 6 days, and today the muscles in my neck started to fail. I have never experienced this before and when I saw 'Deca Dave' Clamp or Shanda resting their chin on the palm of their hand, elbow on the aerobars, I thought that they were just being cool for the photographer (and to be fair, it does look pretty cool…). But I now understand that it's simply to keep their head up. And by the end of the lap, I had learnt to do it too.

**Double Deca Diary: Sunday October 13th**

Busiest day yet. I just can't handle it. People everywhere. Someone is going to get really hurt. I've only done 65 miles and finally given up. I'm going to take a day off to do washing, eat and try and recover a bit. It doesn't feel right, but I can't face trying to cycle around people constantly. It's incredibly stressful.

I've just had a shower, which although the room where it is, is fairly grim, really picks me up. I've also conditioned my hair and tried to pull a brush through it. The scabs on my neck are finally coming off and disgusting as it is, I can't stop from picking at it.

I also washed a few clothes at the same time as showering. Some shorts, top and some socks. I really miss having crew. Especially a certain person. I had a little cry in the shower and then had a word with myself. Gotta stop the self-pity.

Hanging out my clothes on the line and having a bit of a tidy up really sorts my head out. I then had noodles, fruit, a few slices of pizza and some ice-cold orange soda then fell into a deep coma.

After the alarm went off, I literally sat on the side of my airbed and asked myself (for about the 100th time that week) why I was doing this. I do some more quick/crap maths and work out I need to do 220 miles a day to ensure that I'm not still on the bike at the weekend. Is this even possible? The answer is no, but that won't stop me from trying.

I have to finish by Friday night. Another Saturday in the park, heaving with people. I just can't do it.

**Double Deca Diary: Monday October 14th**

It's Monday evening and I'm on a rest break between my last 50-ish miles of today. The park has been much quieter, but I've still unfortunately had quite a few near misses with kids on bikes, etc. Also, a particularly fat squirrel decided to run into the side of my front wheel. Not his best idea and possibly his last. Normally I would have been upset by this, but my pain level was pretty high at the time, so I just rode on, swearing. But then I was overwhelmed with paranoid thoughts that someone had seen me hit the squirrel and not stop to try and resuscitate him. I spent the whole of the following lap trying to justify my terrible behaviour to nobody at all.

## DOUBLE DECA DIARIES

I started today with not two but three huge pancakes, and half a bottle of maple syrup. I have also eaten noodles, fruit and egg mayo rolls during the day. I'm now eating pizza. On the bike I'm drinking Hydrixa and snacking on cashew nuts and Cliff Shot Blox. I also only have one coffee a day, which to those who know me, is astounding, as I normally have about twelve.

My ankles and wrists are pretty swollen. This is normal for me and when things get really tough my face swells too. This morning was particularly bad and I resembled a Mr Potato Head version of myself. Luckily, it's dark when I get up so nobody gets to see this. I've also started using Compeed in a place I'm almost 100% sure it wasn't designed for. But it's helping, so whatever it takes.

The light is at the end of the tunnel for the bike. If I can stay on this brutal schedule of 200 miles a day, I might finish by Friday. That still feels like eternity right now though.

**Double Deca Diary: Tuesday October 15th**

Today some more tents have appeared around me. These are excited new athletes taking on the shorter events, like the one-a-day Deca and Quin. I'm very tired and they are fucking annoying. And noisy too, everyone fucking talks too much. And they are all foreign. They seem to have no clue that we have all been here a week already and are completely exhausted. I can barely hide my feelings as a crew member smashes her bags into the side of my tent, waking me up. As I leave, I throw her a dirty look. She doesn't notice me or my bad temper.

I am losing blood. A lot of blood. This happened in the Deca and all the other recent ultra triathlons and it's a big problem. Basically, it's caused from eating more, in terms of quantity and frequency, than I normally do. And then having to go to the toilet about 250 times every day. I'm pretty sure you don't need any more details and can figure it out from that. But I worry about how much more I can lose before I start to fall over. And if I do that, will they pull me out of the race? I'm so dizzy every time I stand up and my hair is falling out because I'm now so anaemic. But I can't tell anyone for fear of being pulled out on medical grounds.

## Double Deca Diary: Wednesday October 16th

In a world of pain today. The saddle sore that was annoying is now absolutely excruciating. It's affecting my bike position and speed and just generally fucking things up. I think I still have another 550 miles to go and I'm still desperately trying to get it done by Friday night, although now that will be early hours Saturday I think.

I'm so, so sick of the bike. It would be nice to have a little time out right now. Pop home, cuddle the kids and cats, have a cup of tea (I've not had a cuppa since the end of September! Is that even legal for a Brit?) and have some toast and Marmite.

I've also been dreaming of roast chicken dinners. The food here is great; Beto's wife, family and crew work extremely hard on providing as much as possible for everyone. But I'm missing home food. Actually, I'm just really missing home.

This afternoon we had really strong wind, which made the bike stupidly hard. I took a break as I seemed to be getting nowhere and as I lay in my bed, I actually wondered if my tent would survive.

## DOUBLE DECA DIARIES

I kept waking up to see if it had calmed down enough to allow me to get back on the bike, but it just seemed to get worse. I ended up sleeping more than I should, but feeling guilty that I wasn't out cycling.

When I finally got up, I made my way over to where I had racked my bike. I stopped on the way to use the toilet and glanced at myself in the mirror. Big, fucking mistake. My face was so swollen that I looked like a different person. I also have a strange swelling on the lower part of my stomach. Is this a hernia? I panic a little, as I seem to be falling apart quite badly. Again, I'm reluctant to talk to anyone about this, in case it's serious and they try and stop me from finishing the race. I push at the lump, in an attempt to force it back to normal, but it doesn't do anything. So I try to put it to the back of my mind.

### Double Deca Diary: Thursday October 17th

Yesterday was very tough and my mileage was down because of it. We had strong winds for the afternoon and through the night with some rain too. The winds make it so hard to make any progress, especially as I have very little power left in my legs. The saddle sores obviously added to what was a hard day.

This morning started with a few tears in the tent, as physically and mentally I'm very low now, but I had a word with myself and made a plan for the next two days, still hoping to make that Saturday 06:00 finish.

In other news, I saw three raccoons sat in a line yesterday night. Initially I thought, 'they're funny-looking cats and how weird that

# DOUBLE DECA DIARIES

they all look exactly the same'. But then the small part of my brain that is still functioning realised what they were.

All I do in my breaks, whilst I'm gorging on pancakes, is make plans that I can never keep to, goals I never reach. I break the mileage down into chunks that my brain can cope with, like: Do 4 sets of 50 miles before Friday 06:00. My phone's Notes is full of them, all half-completed.

## Double Deca Diary: Saturday October 19th

Well, I finally managed to finish the bike, but it didn't let me go without a fight.

Friday afternoon we were hit with massive storms. Thunder, lightning and ridiculously heavy rain. I was furthest away on the course and got absolutely soaked. Once back at the tent (which was a bit damp, but not too bad), I sat shivering, trying to work out how to get dry. The biggest issue was my shoes, as I had no spares. I ended up putting black bin-bags on my feet, whilst having flashbacks of the New Orleans race and the terrible weather we experienced there.

Later that night, I was back on the road, cycling up the Dam, and my eyes started stinging. I realised the park guys were out spraying some awful chemical to kill mosquitoes. They had done it a few nights ago and we had to wait for it to pass as it smells horrible. This time, as there was no wind, you could literally see the mist in the air and couldn't avoid breathing it in. I had nowhere to go and had to stop and wait, with my buff over my nose and mouth, trying not to breathe.

## DOUBLE DECA DIARIES

I biked through the night, stopping for an hour or so to rest. And by first light I had about 10 laps to go and was feeling pretty good, as the end of the bike was finally in sight. The park was starting to get busier, as it was a Saturday, but then I also realised that in the large open area just past the Goat Farm, people were setting up some kind of event.

My heart sank. Not now, I pleaded. Just let me finish and get off the bike.

A few laps later, I realised that it was a 10k run. Registration had finished and the race was just starting. Imagine 700 or so people running all over the place when you are finishing the last few laps of 2,240-mile bike and your painkillers ran out a few hours ago.

But it's done. After 296 hours and 12 minutes, I've finally finished the bike section. And now, it's just a small matter of 20 marathons. After I had racked my bike, had a few hugs and high fives from people, I treated myself to a shower. After, I sorted out my kit and tidied the tent. You know it's bad when the ants are trying to clean the floor up for you.

Once I'm sorted, I pull on my trainers and start the run section. It feels so good to be on my feet (I know that will wear off soon), with no worries about having a collision on the bike. I plan on just walking for the first afternoon, as my legs are in bad way from the bike.

I've got 15 laps done (approx. 20 miles), but then another massive thunderstorm hit us. Much bigger than yesterday and the camp, which was already very muddy, is turning into a swamp. Our tents are single skin, so not really fit for this sort of weather and the floor was totally flooded. My pet ants are either dead or have run off (do ants run?) and my sleeping-bag is a bit damp at the edges too. Hopefully tomorrow brings the better weather back.

**Double Deca Diary: Sunday October 20th**

I woke up and my bed, pillow and sleeping-bag were soaking wet. There were more storms during the night and it's really getting me down now. Physically, I feel quite ill and rundown. I'm also not sleeping very well. When I stop moving and try to rest, my hip joints scream with pain from the bike section. As I chat with the girls on the run laps, they are all experiencing the same pain. I'm also starting to feel the early twinges of shin splints and Jade applies some KT tape to my sore shin. Again, the other girls have the same problems. We laugh about it and take a photo with our blue, taped legs held out in front of us.

I started to run today. I worked out the parts of the course where I would walk and the bits where I would run. I like to get into this kind of routine on long-distance runs from the start. Nobody runs them all and I find, if you stick to the plan, you can keep a steady, consistent pace until the end. It helps break up the monotony too.

By the end of the two marathons, my feet were so sore and I was desperate to stop. Once I got into bed with my noodles, I raised my feet up and all I could feel was them pulsing away to themselves...

'You need to toughen up,' I tell them. 'We've got a long way to go.'

# DOUBLE DECA DIARIES

## Double Deca Diary: Monday October 21st

I got 5 hours' sleep last night and feel much better for it. Although the thunder woke me up again.

Struggled to get out of bed at 02:00 to start the routine, so I was a bit late to the course. I only managed 9 laps, so I will need to make it up later. I start thinking about Rab whilst running, which made me cry. At the far end of the course, on Squirrel Lane, the streetlights flash on and off like Morse code. Sometimes, I like to think it's Rab chatting to me, telling me not to be shit and other things he would say. I know it's not, but still…

Later, back in bed, I had pancakes and fruit and literally fell asleep for a moment whilst eating it. I woke up with the pancake hanging out of my mouth. I don't think I've ever done that before.

As I was getting ready to go again, I poured coffee in my trainer, which is annoying as my others are still soaking wet from the storms. I hope this weather improves soon, everything is so much harder when everywhere is wet and muddy.

30 mins break and I will start the next block of 10 laps…

Super-hot day. I managed a decent amount of laps until the heat got the best of me and I needed a few hours of kip. I did some washing and general tent admin. Made some potato and egg mayo and tried to get motivated to do more laps. I've lost track of all sense of time and I have to check my phone to find out what day it is. My run pace is painfully slow. My hips kill. My feet screaming. And I'm sleeping too much. I just want to sleep.

# DOUBLE DECA DIARIES

## Double Deca Diary: Tuesday October 22nd

I tried to go through the night, but willpower failed me. Got up at 0130 and started again. An ultra friend, Michael Ortiz, turned up with chocolate and crisps and me, him and Shanda sat on the side of the road eating and laughing about random stuff until the thunder started again. I did 4 or 5 more laps in the rain, until I couldn't stand the pain in my feet any more and I took another break. Lying here, I feel like this is never going to end.

The distance I have left to do with the pain I have right now is massively overwhelming me.

## Double Deca Diary: Wednesday October 23rd

More laps done but I'm really struggling. I cried a lot today, partly due to pain, but also because I'm hating this part of the event. Normally the run is my favourite, but I feel that I'm not making anywhere near the progress I should be. I'm also feeling really lonely. There are lots of lovely people here, but essentially I'm alone and I'm desperate to get home. The only place I feel OK is in my tent, but then I feel guilty as I should be getting the laps in.

I hate all the small talk and so much is lost in translation as most people are foreign here. I'm not really looking after myself either, not eating or drinking enough. Not showering much either. I've got my period again now and considering how much blood I've lost, I'm surprised I'm still standing. And that's not me being dramatic. Today is the first day that I have really doubted that I can finish. I'm going to try and get some sleep and run the night shift. Less people around…

## DOUBLE DECA DIARIES

### Double Deca Diary: Thursday October 24th

So much for reaching my lap quota. I had 2 left of my required amount and another ridiculous thunderstorm hit. Of course I was at the far end of the course and obviously my tent's air vent was open. Got back to a wet pillow and sleeping-bag again. I got myself dry and did the best I could to dry bedding off and called it a day.

This is the worst storm yet I think and lying in my damp bed watching the rain drip through the roof of the tent (I've placed the washing underneath – always multi-tasking) and feeling the walls almost pressing against my face, I feel a little anxious. I'm pretty tired and could do without my tent blowing away.

As I'm lying there, all I can smell is my rancid kit that I haven't been able to wash. I'm eating some soggy jelly sweets and the thunder is crashing away outside. I just need to try and sleep, so I can get up to start running again. On top of all this crazy weather shit, I also got a little niggle today. Dealt with it straight away, so hopefully it won't turn into anything serious.

### Double Deca Diary: Friday October 25th

A real low morning. My injury (inflamed tendon on the front of my ankle) is much worse and subsequently my night mileage very poor. My tent is in a real state with clothing that was dry now soaked, wet trainers and sleeping-bag.

How many more storms we will get before this race ends? And more importantly, as I'm not even at the halfway point of the run, how much will this injury affect me?

## DOUBLE DECA DIARIES

I need to stop feeling sorry for myself, so I clean my teeth, attempt a tidy up of the tent and hang a few tops on the line. Just getting a couple of things done makes me feel a little better.

It's 08:13 and I'm at 170 laps. I need to achieve 195 to reach quota today; with a very sore ankle, it is going to be a challenging day. It's amazing how quickly your moods change during these types of events. One minute you think 'yes, I can do this, one foot in front of the other and all that' and the next you are sitting on a wall sobbing, because you're in so much pain and you feel your dream slipping away from you.

Apparently there's another storm due tonight. This news breaks me, but at least I can prepare.

The promised storm arrives at 18:00, so I go out in my 'ridiculously expensive, but so worth it' Inov8 jacket and I am totally dry. I've also prepped the tent, so my bedding won't get soaked as well. Fuck you storm.

But I don't reach quota as I'm in a lot of pain, so call it a night at lap 188, which is frustrating, but I'm going to try and get a decent block of sleep to hopefully help heal my fucked body. It's even hard to sleep during this Deca stuff, as your body seems to try and sort stuff just as you are trying to sleep and I get shooting pains through my hips and legs and a general deep aching that makes it hard to lie still.

**Double Deca Diary: Saturday October 26th**

Well, today in what is basically The Hardest Thing I've Ever Done,

## DOUBLE DECA DIARIES

the area outside where race HQ is situated became the venue for León's biggest 10k race. Totally awesome! 5,000 runners, stalls, crowd barriers, really loud music and a PA!

I kid you not.

So, from 18:00 I decided to take a break until the race was done, as fighting through the crowds was almost impossible (especially as I'm limping like an idiot) and even though normally I absolutely love crowds of people (!!) my state of mind is a little delicate, to say the least right now.

My injury is really not good, but I'm staying as positive as I can. The tendon is painful all the time and now I'm getting severe shooting pains. It's also creaking/crunching. I'm elevating, icing, taking Ibru when possible.

I still have 11 laps left of my quota to do once the 10k is over, but for now I'm sat in my tent with the extremely enthusiastic race PA literally screaming a few hundred metres away and Lady Gaga blaring out. It's a good job I'm not tired...

It could be worse I guess, there could be another storm.

### Double Deca Diary: Sunday October 27th
No update.

### Double Deca Diary: Monday October 28th

So due to the pain I've had to reduce my lap blocks to 4. I run/walk 4 laps, then break for 30-60 minutes depending on tiredness, pain,

## DOUBLE DECA DIARIES

heat, time of day, etc.

After twisting my bad ankle this morning and having a 'small' breakdown afterwards, it's not been any worse than it was before, thank god. I ice it at every break and that seems to help.

But I'm scared, really scared that if this gets any worse, I might not finish this. I simply can't imagine having got so far, that I DNF. It's 1700 here and the heat is just starting to reduce. I'm currently on lap number 273 and tonight's target is 293, so that's basically a marathon by dawn... Once I reach 300, there's 'just' 5 marathons to go. This makes me want to cry. Again.

### Double Deca Diary: Tuesday October 29th

It's hard to suffer so much, to be so raw with pain and fatigue in a public park, full of joggers and families. I wish we were somewhere quieter, more private.

The good news is that my ankle is a little less painful today.

### Double Deca Diary: Wednesday October 30th

It's 03:15 and I'm on my 320th lap, which means I have 'only' 4 marathons to go... I'm going to have an hour's nap after this, then back at it.

It's an obvious thing to say, but we are all really struggling with needing extra sleeps now. Maybe because we feel the end is close? I don't know. All you want to do is eat up the miles, but your body is screaming for sleep.

## DOUBLE DECA DIARIES

It's also tricky because it's so hot during the day, it makes it hard to push too much. You think that you can make up the miles during the coolness of the night, but your brain has other ideas and just wants bed.

And then there's the question of how much sleep should I have? 30-40 minutes doesn't cut it any more, but an hour seems OK. Having a 'big' sleep of 3 hours is wonderful, but waking up from that is truly horrible and I've had some real low moments sat on the side of the airbed feeling disoriented and questioning what I'm doing. But a 3-hour sleep can bring a good '10 lap block in a decent time with relatively low pain', so it's worth it.

All we keep saying is 'it's almost over, it's almost over...'

### Double Deca Diary: Thursday October 31st

I have a marathon and two laps to go. It's 18:48 and I've had to go to bed for a few hours. In my sleeping-bag, my feet throb and sting so painfully that I lie there and cry. The pain makes spasms shoot up my legs and it feels like the bones in my feet are breaking. I wonder how I'm going to be able to complete another 22 laps before I can finally finish this.

### Double Deca Diary: Friday November 1st

I have just a half marathon to go. I just had to have a sleep after Shanda had finished, but when I awoke 90 minutes later, the blisters on my left foot had revolted and were seriously angry about yet more miles on the relentless tarmac. The pain was breathtaking and I just broke down, crying as I limped along.

## DOUBLE DECA DIARIES

Luckily Marcus, the race massage therapist, was close by and heard me sobbing like a baby. He asked what was wrong, but because of the language barrier, it was hard to explain, so I pulled off my trainer and showed him.

'Much pain?', he asks.

'Much pain,' I wail.

'Ah, I fix,' he said. Twenty minutes, a scalpel, a needle and some Lidocaine later, I was up and walking, almost pain-free. What an amazing guy.

The last few laps are horrible. You imagine that you will fly through them and sail over the finish line in ecstasy. The reality is that time seems to stop and almost go backwards. I also get anxious as the end gets closer. I'm exhausted and dread the attention that comes with finishing something like this. It's not like I don't appreciate the cheers, well-done's and the hugs. I really do. But it overwhelms me and I wish it over as soon as possible.

The last lap is finally here. It dawns on me that I'm about to finish a Double Deca. Only 13 men and 5 women have finished this monster of a race. And nobody in the UK has ever even attempted one.

I'm wearing my 'Slow as Fuck, Hard as Nails' Brutal Triathlon T-shirt, which I saved for the last day. As I pull it on, I question the 'hard as nails' bit, as there have been an awful lot of tears, but the 'slow as fuck' part seems about right.

I run the whole of the last lap. It doesn't seem real that I will never be on this course again. I try and take in everything, to absorb it all. I also say goodbye to the fat squirrels. I turn at the end of the lap and run back to the finish line, emotion building in my chest. I can see the end, I can see the small group of people preparing for me to cross the line. They hold the finish banner across the path and wait for me.

I run into the banner and stretch my arms along it, mainly because I don't know what else to do with them. Everyone hugs me. Laura calls out to be careful as I have lost so much weight that I might break, as Shanda picks me up and spins me around. Georgetta gives me a massive cuddle and tells me that she's so proud of me. Laura hands me a huge bunch of flowers and I get another hug. I'm given a bottle of champagne that I'm expected to do the obligatory popping of the cork and spraying over everyone. I've been dreading this part as I hate champagne with a passion, and considering my history with alcohol, I'm reluctant to have it as part of my finish. But being the reserved Brit that I am, I take the bottle and awkwardly go through the motions.

'Drink it!' someone says.

'I don't drink,' I say. I always feel good when I say that out loud.

———

And then it's all over. Shanda is keen for us to get back to the hotel so I can shower and we can all hit the mall for some dress shopping. While we have been on the run course, all she wanted to do was go and buy some black dresses for the awards ceremony. And now I've stopped, I realise that she is *deadly* serious. I hobble to my tent, grab

## DOUBLE DECA DIARIES

some essentials and then I'm scooped up and put into the back of Marcus's car and before I know it, we are whizzing back to the hotel. I'm given a couple of hours to rest, wash and eat. I'm a little overwhelmed. I close the door of the bathroom and switch on the shower. Taking off my clothes, I look at myself in the mirror and I'm completely stunned. I have lost a ridiculous amount of weight and I look horrible. I am all skin and bones and it's not a good look. After having a shower and a bath, I lie on the bed, wrapped in fluffy, white hotel towels. My food arrives and I'm surrounded with McDonalds and doughnuts. I eat it all and fall asleep immediately. About 30 minutes later, I'm awake again and for a moment I'm totally confused. 'Where's my tent and why am I in a towel?', I wonder, before waking up properly and realising that I've actually, finally finished the Double Deca.

Shanda tells me it's time to hit the mall. I groan. Even in normal life, shopping is not my thing. When I need stuff, I get it online. Even food. I hate big, busy shops. I hate people shopping and getting in my way. I hate it all. But a promise is a promise and also, Shanda is not someone you can say no to.

Driving across León, I take a moment to savour something pretty special. I'm sitting in a car with amazing people from all over the world: Canada, America, Mexico and Germany. And me, from the UK. We are all laughing and messing about. The sun is out and the music is loud. I feel blessed to be surrounded by these people and having this experience.

The dress shopping is painful. I would rather go back to the run course and do some more laps. I have to keep sitting down because the pain in my feet is so bad. After about three hours, the dresses

## DOUBLE DECA DIARIES

and shoes are bought and I can finally go back to the hotel. And the bed. More McDonalds follows and then I'm out for ten hours of blissful, uninterrupted sleep.

The next day is the awards ceremony, which is more about the food than the medals. We all pile our plates high with more food than we can actually eat because our stomachs have shrunk so much. After certificates, photos and obviously, the medals have been awarded, it's time for me to go.

I get a lift from the race director's brother and after a fast and hot drive, we arrive at the airport. He lifts my gear out of the back, wishes me well and he is gone. I'm still wearing a black flowery dress, which I feel really self-conscious in. I attempt to wrestle my huge Bergen pack onto my back and to force my badly-behaved bike box into the airport. Once I'm in the waiting area, I escape to the toilets and change into trackies and a T-shirt. Feeling more like myself, I return to my kit, pull out a book and prepare to kill a lot of time.

A couple of flights later and I'm so relieved to get off the plane. I haven't been able to get out of my seat due to the two people next to me, who slept for the entire flight and I was too polite to wake them up. Sitting still after completing a Double Deca is horrendously painful, my joints screaming at me to move, and my ankles have swollen so much that I actually wondered if they may explode at some point.

My bike box takes ages to make it through to the luggage collection area and I sit on the floor, because standing just takes up too much energy. Once I have all of my bags, I load myself up and prepare

## DOUBLE DECA DIARIES

myself to make the long journey (maybe a mile) to where my van has been parked for the last month.

As I push through into Gatwick arrivals lounge, I see someone I know. And then someone else who looks familiar. I realise, with a jolt, that some of my lovely friends – Matthew, Kathi and Claire and Graham – have come to meet me. They have a 'Welcome Home' sign and a big 'Well Done' balloon.

I'm stunned and tears spring to my eyes. I never expected it and I've never had anyone do it before either. We make our way to the coffee shop to sit and drink lattes.

And then I tell them all about how I somehow managed to finish a Double Deca.

## LIFE LESSON
# FUCK IT

The other day I was with a good friend, and he turned and said to me that they thought I had absolutely no chance of finishing the Double Deca. In fact, they went on to say (while I stared, mouth hanging open in mock surprise) that they thought I was crazy to even go to Mexico, and that I wouldn't even make it through the swim.

This made me smile. And then laugh. Really laugh…

Why? Because I had thought the exact same thing in the weeks leading up to the race. And before I boarded the plane. And the day before I started the race and then the hour before sat by the pool, waiting nervously to start…

In the lead-up to the Double Deca, my life had taken a few twists and turns. A couple of personal problems, some financial issues and something I hadn't dealt with from earlier in the year all demanded my reluctant attention. And if I'm honest, I fell into a bit of a dark place. I wasn't functioning very well and it was all I could do to just get through each day. I had even stopped making to-do lists (one of my favourite things). Yes. Things were that bad.

My training had become sporadic, my eating was chaotic and all I wanted to do was sleep. And apart from a few close friends, I shut off from everyone. These were all the classic signs of depression. And with the amount that was going on at that point, it was hardly surprising. But what was surprising was that I knew going to Mexico was the very best thing I could do. Although, perhaps not from a financial point of view…

So, ignoring all sensible advice, I decided I would go. But instead of piling the pressure on myself, worrying about not finishing and experiencing the embarrassment of yet another dreaded DNF,

I reframed the event as an adventure. I decided that if I didn't finish, I would go on a cycling mini-break around parts of Mexico (and probably get murdered) or something equally as exciting/impulsive/dangerous.*

The point I'm trying to make is that sometimes life is a complete bastard, and all your well-made plans and (maybe slightly unrealistic) dreams get blown into the sea. Like a marquee on the coast path during a Brutal event.

But that is not the time to stop or give up. That, in my opinion, is exactly the time to do it all anyway. Throw caution to the (45mph) winds and say 'Fuck it'. What do you have to lose? Stand up and be brave. You might not feel it, but nobody knows that. And, to be honest, nobody really cares. Not as much as you think they do, at any rate.

As another good friend said to me after my (very long) swim, 'everyone has got problems'. And it's true. And some of those problems are a lot worse than yours. (He didn't say that bit, but I reckon he thought it). That's not to say that you don't deserve to feel crappy, but it is good sometimes to lift your head up and look around.

The last thing I try to remember when going through tough times is that this will pass. And that nothing stays the same. Not even if you want it to. So ride the storm. Or better still, ride your bike for 2,240 miles.

Actually, don't do that. It really hurts.

---

*The above is obviously not the best advice for anyone taking on a Double Deca. Train hard, eat well and don't go mental in the month leading up to the race would be a much better plan.*

# ACKNOWLEDGEMENTS

Writing this book has been a very long, and at times, difficult journey. It has also been written from memory, which like me, isn't perfect.

It would be impossible to list all the people who have helped me over the years, and I would only forget someone if I tried (see above). But I want to thank my wonderful family, friends, and the Brutal crew for making Brutal Events a reality; it couldn't have happened without you. Also, to everyone who ever had the unfortunate job of crewing me, thank you for everything you did.

Huge thanks to my close friends for being there when it mattered. You know who you are.

Thank you to Giles Elliott for being a fantastic editor and Mark Beaumont for his help in getting this book published.

Finally, thank you to Kathi Harman for her outstanding photography. Also, to Katrin Meier and Babs Boardwell for their images too.

## ALSO AVAILABLE BY CLAIRE SMITH

After losing a beloved friend, ultra-endurance athlete Claire Smith decided to take on the longest run of her life:

John o' Groats to Land's End.

If that wasn't hard enough, Claire chose to make the whole journey self-supported. She would transport her own equipment, purchase food and supplies en route, and sleep out at night. All in the middle of a global pandemic.

This book documents the challenges, laughs, tears, punctures, broken wheels and blistered feet along the way. Complete with photos, maps, routes and mileage, it provides a full record of this epic adventure.

**AVAILABLE FROM AMAZON NOW**

Printed in Great Britain
by Amazon